4|1|16

AMERICAN SLAVERY

Recent Titles in Historical Explorations of Literature

The Harlem Renaissance: A Historical Exploration of Literature
Lynn Domina

AMERICAN SLAVERY

A Historical Exploration of Literature

Robert Felgar

HISTORICAL EXPLORATIONS OF LITERATURE

GREENWOOD

AN IMPRINT OF ABC-CLIO, LLC
Santa Barbara, California • Denver, Colorado • Oxford, England

Library of Congress Cataloging-in-Publication Data

American slavery : a historical exploration of literature / Robert Felgar.
     pages cm. — (Historical explorations of literature)
     Includes index.
     ISBN 978-1-61069-647-0 (hard copy : alk. paper) — ISBN 978-1-61069-648-7 (ebook)   1. American literature— 19th century—History and criticism.   2. Slavery in literature. 3. Douglass, Frederick, 1818–1895. Narrative of the life of Frederick Douglass, an American slave.   4. Stowe, Harriet Beecher, 1811–1896. Uncle Tom's cabin.   5. Jacobs, Harriet A. (Harriet Ann), 1813–1897. Incidents in the life of a slave girl.   6. Twain, Mark, 1835–1910. Adventures of Huckleberry Finn.   7. Slavery—United States— History—19th century—Sources.   I. Felgar, Robert, 1944–
     PS217.S55A45   2015
     810.9'3552—dc23   2014025757
ISBN: 978-1-61069-647-0
EISBN: 978-1-61069-648-7

19   18   17   16   15   1   2   3   4   5

This book is also available on the World Wide Web as an eBook. Visit www.abc-clio.com for details.

Greenwood
An Imprint of ABC-CLIO, LLC

ABC-CLIO, LLC
130 Cremona Drive, P.O. Box 1911
Santa Barbara, California 93116-1911

This book is printed on acid-free paper ∞
Manufactured in the United States of America

To Sophie

In Appreciation:
Many and deep thanks to
Susan Hurst, English Department Secretary at
Jacksonville State University,
for her unflagging typing, her infectious sense of humor,
and her tolerance for the author's foibles.

Contents

I

Introduction

The United States originated in a contradiction that cannot be resolved: a country supposedly based on freedom was also based on slavery. This contradiction led to the Civil War and the Civil Rights Movement, both of which lessened but did not eliminate it. In the nineteenth century, four works of American literature in particular registered the tremors caused by the conflict between freedom and slavery: Frederick Douglass's *Narrative of the Life of Frederick Douglass* (1845), Harriet Beecher Stowe's *Uncle Tom's Cabin* (1852), Harriet Jacobs's *Incidents in the Life of a Slave Girl* (1861), and Mark Twain's *Adventures of Huckleberry Finn* (1884). All four reveal the disaster produced by basing a society on a monumental contradiction; all four are implicit and explicit demands that the country must eliminate slavery if it is to be based on freedom.

The most highly regarded slave narrative in American literature, Douglass's autobiography uses the life of its hero as a platform from which to attack the institution of slavery so as to help end it. Douglass knew all too well what he faced, because he knew slavery, slaveowners, and slavebreakers intimately, and he later realized the "peculiar institution" was

not going to wither away but would have to be destroyed by military violence (one of his sons fought in the Union Army). The documents reproduced here contextualize Douglass's achievement to illustrate, and thus
bring to life, a vague concept to many nineteenth-century white Americans, the overseer. For instance, the excerpt from Douglass's third version of his life story, *The Life and Times of Frederick Douglass,* makes
it all too clear that Mr. Covey, the sadistic overseer Douglass depicts so
memorably in his 1845 *Narrative,* was far from the worst. The Frederick
Law Olmsted selection from his *The Cotton Kingdom* will help today's
students understand that the brutal treatment of Douglass's aunt in the
Narrative was typical of the way black women were treated rather than
an exception. The two letters reproduced from *The Farmers' Register* will
help contemporary readers grasp how little overseers understood about
the slaves they abused, the point being that if they had understood them,
the overseers would have had to face the fact that slaves were every bit as
human as their overseers were.

In addition to understanding the topic of overseers, contemporary students of Douglass's *Narrative* will also benefit considerably from a knowledge of nineteenth-century American schoolbooks. As Douglass himself
mentions, he was profoundly influenced by *The Columbian Orator,* a popular collection of writings used in American schools in the nineteenth
century. Today's students will hear the echoes of "Dialogue between a
Master and a Slave" and "Oration on the Manumission of Slaves" in Douglass's autobiography; they will also come to understand why Douglass
was attracted to Arthur O'Connor's "Speech on Catholic Emancipation,"
a speech that suggests parallels between Ireland's Catholics and America's
slaves.

The next section of *American Slavery* examines how *Uncle Tom's Cabin*
(1852) views slave auctions and the Underground Railroad. The excerpt
from Solomon Northup's *Twelve Years a Slave* will help students understand harrowing aspects of these appalling transactions that Stowe does
not engage. The selection from Henry Bibb's *Narrative of the Life and
Adventures of Henry Bibb* adds details to Stowe's concept of slave auctions, thereby helping contemporary readers get a stronger grasp of slave
auctions than Stowe's novel alone provides. The third excerpt in this selection, taken from *Narrative of Sojourner Truth,* may surprise students by its
depiction of a rare act of mercy in the otherwise utterly sordid business of
selling human beings: Truth's parents were sold together instead of sold
separately, as so often happened.

This chapter also explores the Underground Railroad, which some students have heard of, however little they know about it. All three of the excerpts about it contextualize this strategy for getting slaves safely into free states, resulting in a deeper understanding of Stowe's version of the URR, as it is sometimes called. Today's readers of *Uncle Tom's Cabin* will find the story of Henry Box Brown, from William Still's *The Underground Railroad,* particularly interesting and revealing: Henry Box Brown mailed himself out of slavery by climbing into a box that was mailed to sympathizers of his desire to escape from slavery; this ingenious strategy may encourage contemporary readers to doubt the accuracy of many of Stowe's portraits of black people as simpleminded.

The third focus of this volume is Harriet Jacobs's *Incidents in the Life of a Slave Girl,* which is contextualized by documents that illuminate Nat Turner's Rebellion, nineteenth-century views of slavery, and the Fugitive Slave Law (1850), all topics that figure prominently in the novel. Jacobs devotes most of Chapter XII to Turner's Rebellion. Her novel will mean much more to students who are knowledgeable about that insurrection and its widespread implications, particularly for the preposterous notion that slaves were contented. The excerpt from Thomas R. Gray's pamphlet, *The Confessions of Nat Turner,* will help today's students understand why there was so much fear in Edenton, North Carolina, the setting for *Incidents,* after the rebellion Turner led. The two letters reprinted here try to downplay the insurrection in an attempt to reassure white readers that they can safely retain their sense of complacency about slaves, but just twenty-six years after the publication of these letters, thousands of African Americans volunteered to serve in the Union Army. Thomas Wentworth Higginson's article on the rebellion, appearing thirty years later, is much more truthful than Gray's: students will come to see that the people in Edenton were right to be frightened, because Turner and his men were fighting for their freedom.

Knowledge of why the Fugitive Slave Law of 1850 is so important comes as a revelation to contemporary students, but that knowledge is crucial for understanding and appreciating *Incidents.* It was a draconian measure, designed to force everyone, in the South or the North, to report runaway slaves. But it so infuriated Northerners, many of whom had thought little about slavery before 1850, that a law that would supposedly protect the interests of slaveowners ended up making a civil war to end slavery more likely.

Reproduced here, in addition to a copy of the law itself, are excerpts from Ralph Waldo Emerson's speech on it as well as from Frederick

Douglass's. Emerson's condemnation of the law will help today's students understand why Jacobs was so frightened of the law: she could have been another Shadrach Minkins, whom Emerson is so upset about in his speech, and been returned to her owner, Dr. Flint. Douglass's fiery condemnation of the Fugitive Slave Law will help contemporary students understand why it was totally unacceptable to many whites in the North, where Jacobs and her two children eventually end up.

The section on nineteenth-century views of American slavery is designed to help students grasp different attitudes toward slavery during Jacobs's lifetime. Today's students find John C. Calhoun's defense of slavery absolutely appalling; it was published when Jacobs was twenty-four years old, and Calhoun is beyond doubt convinced slavery is justified, just as Dr. Flint is in *Incidents,* proving how hard it is to change the mind of people who do not understand they do not understand. On the other hand, the excerpts from Angela E. Grimké and Lydia Maria Child reveal two women who well understand the horror of chattel slavery. As Abraham Lincoln put it later, if a person does not understand that slavery is wrong, then nothing is wrong for that person. That view strikes a resonant chord with contemporary American students.

The final chapter examines *Adventures of Huckleberry Finn* as a historical exploration of American slavery. Concentrating on abolition, and then on slavery and Christianity, the chapter provides students with documents that will bring Twain's best-known novel to life in ways that are not available to students who may not be knowledgeable about American history. For example, when William Lloyd Garrison, the most famous but not the most effective white abolitionist, told his listeners in a speech he delivered in 1831 (*Huckleberry Finn* is set in 1835 or 1845) that he recanted his support of gradual abolition of slavery, by saying, "tell the mother to gradually extricate her babe from the fire into which it has fallen," our students will deeply understand how abominable slavery was: it is like being turned into ashes. The excerpt from Henry Highland Garnet's "An Address to the Slaves of the United States" will be especially stirring to adolescent males in that Garnet appeals to the manhood of his listeners.

The last section on *Huckleberry Finn* explores the topic of slavery and Christianity through excerpts from James Henley Thornwell's "A Southern Christian View of Slavery" (1861) and through Richard Furman's "Exposition of the Views of the Baptists Relative to the Coloured [*sic*] Population of the United States" (1822). Today's students will need to understand that Thornwell, like the Phelpses in *Huckleberry Finn,* refused to acknowledge any contradiction between institutionalized

Christianity and their behavior, or is there? If the latter is what Twain is suggesting, then in Twain's view institutionalized Christianity is not Christianity. Furman's exposition will also help contextualize for today's students the Phelpses' complacency about slavery and their "kind" treatment of Jim.

II

Chronology

1808   Congress prohibits African slave trade; ignored much of the time, the internal slave trade continued until 1865.

1811   75 slaves killed in insurrection in Louisiana.

1815   Underground Railroad established by Levi Coffin.

1816   Richard Allen establishes AME (African Methodist Episcopal) Church.

       American Colonization Society established to transport free blacks to Africa.

1819   "A Fireball in the Night." This is what Thomas Jefferson called the "Missouri Compromise."

1820   Missouri Compromise: no slavery allowed north, 36 degrees, 30 minutes latitude.

       Missouri admitted as a slave state.

1821   Early antislavery newspaper, *The Genius of Universal Emancipation,* published by Benjamin Lundy.

1822   Liberia founded by ACS.

Denmark Vesey leads slave revolt in Charleston, South Carolina.

1827   First (or one of first) black newspapers published, *Freedom's Journal.*

1829   David Walker's *Appeal:* extremely outspoken demand that slavery be abolished.

1830   First National Negro Convention (Philadelphia).

1831   William Lloyd Garrison begins publication of *The Liberator;* it demands immediate emancipation of the slaves.

Nat Turner's Rebellion: this slave revolt will figure prominently in *Incidents in the Life of a Slave Girl.*

1833   American Anti-Slavery Society founded.

1835   Boston nearly lynches William Lloyd Garrison.

1836   Gag rule adopted in House of Representatives: all anti-slavery petitions tabled.

1837   Rev Elijah P. Lovejoy killed by mob in Alton, Illinois. He becomes a martyr to abolitionists.

1839   *Amistad* revolt: 53 slaves take over Spanish slave ship.

1841   *Creole* affair: Slaves on the *Creole* rebel and sail to Bahamas.

1844   Gag rule lifted.

1845   Baptist Church split over slavery.

1846   Thoreau refuses to pay poll tax to protest slavery and Mexican War.

1848   Free Soil party formed; it opposes the expansion of slavery into western parts of the United States that are not yet states.

1850   Congress adopts the Compromise of 1850: California admitted as a free state but slavery allowed in other former Mexican territories. Bans sale of slaves in Washington, DC; requires that fugitive slaves be returned to their masters.

1851   Shadrach Minkins, a runaway slave, rescued from court custody by a crowd in Boston.

1852   *Uncle Tom's Cabin* published.

1854   William Lloyd Garrison burns Constitution in public, describing it as "a covenant with death and an agreement with hell."

1855   Death penalty passed for helping a fugitive slave in Kansas; Douglass nominated by Liberty Party to be secretary of state in New York State.

1856	John Brown and six other men kill five supporters of slavery.
1857	In the *Dred Scott* decision the Supreme Court rules that neither the Bill of Rights nor the Constitution applies to black Americans and that the Missouri Compromise of 1850 is not constitutional.
1859	John Brown's Raid on Harpers Ferry, Virginia; Brown, a friend of Douglass, is hanged.
1860	Lincoln elected president; South Carolina secedes from the United States.
1861–1865	Civil War; Douglass urges Lincoln to allow black men to fight for the Union, which the president finally agrees to in 1863; one of Douglass's own sons, Lewis, serves.
1863	Emancipation Proclamation.
1865	April 14: Lincoln assassinated.
	December 18: Slavery abolished by Thirteenth Amendment.
	December 24: Ku Klux Klan founded.
1866	Civil Rights Act grants citizenship to anyone born in United States.
1867	Federal troops occupy the South to impose martial law during Reconstruction.
1870	Fifteenth Amendment grants right to vote, but African American voters in the South and women everywhere remain disenfranchised.
1877	Reconstruction ends.
1896	*Plessy v. Ferguson*: U.S. Supreme Court approves segregation as long as facilities are "separate but equal."

Narrative of the Life of Frederick Douglass, an American Slave, Written by Himself (1845)

HISTORICAL BACKGROUND

Narrative of the Life of Frederick Douglass reflects key aspects of nineteenth-century American history, particularly slavery. When Douglass's *Narrative* was published in 1845, slavery had been entrenched for well over two hundred years. Slavery was the foundation of society in the South and the major form of wealth for the masters of large plantations. In other words, it was not going to be abolished voluntarily because it was the basis of the social and economic power of the planter aristocracy, which was determined to hold on to its slavery-based privileges, regardless of the cost. Slaves, however capable and impressive they might be, and Douglass was one of the most capable and impressive Americans who ever lived, remained commodities that could be bought and sold at the will of their owners. They could not vote, be legally married, live where they wanted to, run for political office, learn to read and write (in most Southern states), or serve on juries. Given what was at stake, it is clear that war was the only way legal slavery could have ended. It was also clear that the only way to maintain the system of slavery was through the use of violence, because no

Douglass was an imposing and dignified figure, as this portrait indicates, as opposed to many Southern representations of black men as debased and ridiculous. (National Park Service, Frederick Douglass National Historic Site)

one would submit to such a system unless coerced.

Nineteenth-century American history can be seen as a fight between those who wanted to uphold the system of slavery and those who wanted to abolish it. Much of the fight used legal and political weapons. In 1808 Congress prohibited the African slave trade, but the law was often flouted, and, in any case, the internal slave trade continued until the end of the Civil War in 1865. In 1820 a compromise regarding the spreading of slavery outside the South, known as the Missouri Compromise, prohibited slavery in the United States north of 36 degrees longitude, and Missouri was admitted as a slave state. The House of Representatives, a few years later, passed a gag rule that required all antislavery petitions to be tabled (it was lifted in 1844). The year after Douglass's *Narrative* was published in 1845, Henry David Thoreau, the author of *Walden* and *Civil Disobedience,* defied the poll tax to protest slavery. In 1850 Congress passed another compromise, one that required that fugitive slaves be returned to their owners; violations of this law could include substantial fines and imprisonment. Seven years later, the Supreme Court ruled, in the *Dred Scott* (an African American slave) decision, that neither the Constitution nor the Bill of Rights applied to African Americans and that the Missouri Compromise was not constitutional. The election of Abraham Lincoln to the presidency in 1860 meant the end of slavery, because one of Lincoln's goals was the preservation of the Union (South Carolina seceded from the Union in the same year); the other was to end slavery, since it was the basis of Southern society; and he needed the approximately 186,000 African American troops (including one of Douglass's sons), many from the South, to defeat the Confederacy. In other words, to preserve the Union, Lincoln had to end slavery.

Legal and political strategies regarding slavery continued during and after the Civil War (1861–1865). Lincoln delivered the Emancipation

Proclamation on January 1, 1863, which declared slavery illegal in states rebelling against the Union. Toward the end of 1865, the Thirteenth Amendment was passed by Congress: it abolished slavery in the United States. The next year, the Civil Rights Act granted citizenship to everyone born in the United States, and in 1896, the year after Douglass died, the Supreme Court, in *Plessy vs. Ferguson*, approved segregation as long as facilities were separate but equal, an impossible distinction in reality, but one that had legal standing until the 1960s.

Such a contentious legal and political battle also included other methods, some violent and some nonviolent, of overturning or supporting slavery, which is the central fact of nineteenth-century American history. A few years before Douglass was born in 1818, 75 slaves were killed in Louisiana during a slave revolt. In 1815, Levi Coffin, whose work appears in this volume (in IV. *Uncle Tom's Cabin* (1852)), established the Underground Railroad, a system for enabling slaves, including Douglass, to escape from the South to the North or Canada. One of the most famous slave insurrections occurred in Charleston, South Carolina, in 1822, under the leadership of Denmark Vesey. In 1829, David Walker, a free black clothes dealer in Boston, encouraged African Americans in his appeal to end slavery by any means necessary, and he made his case in a very aggressive manner. Two years later, when Douglass was thirteen, two key events occurred: Nat Turner led the most famous slave insurrection in American history; it erupted in Virginia and terrified whites. In the same year, William Lloyd Garrison, the most famous of all the white abolitionists (people who wanted to abolish slavery), began publishing *The Liberator.* In it, he demanded the immediate emancipation of the slaves; he also provided the preface to Douglass's *Narrative;* he wanted the North to secede, which could have been a disaster for African Americans in the South.

When Douglass was entering young manhood, the American Anti-Slavery Society was founded (1833). Douglass became a frequent speaker and prominent member of this key group, which did so much to abolish slavery. In 1852 the novel that President Lincoln supposedly said caused the Civil War, *Uncle Tom's Cabin,* was published. Like Harriet Jacobs's *Incidents in the Life of a Slave Girl* (1861), it appealed to the hearts of Northern mothers, who then appealed to their husbands to end slavery. In 1859, John Brown, who was a friend of Douglass, made his famous raid on Harpers Ferry in Virginia, for which he was hanged. In other words, nineteenth-century American history can be seen as the inexorable move toward the destruction of slavery; Douglass's 1845 *Narrative* is a key document in this history.

ABOUT FREDERICK DOUGLASS

Frederick Douglass (1818–1895) died not knowing the year of his birth. The consensus now is that it was 1818, but Douglass's ignorance of his birth date made it all too clear to him that even though he became one of the outstanding Americans of the nineteenth century, many whites in the South regarded the date of birth of a black boy as of no consequence, simply because of skin color. He was never sure of who his white father was, either, although it may have been his first master, Aaron Anthony; his mother was a slave named Harriet Bailey, whom he knew only as a child. Two events stand out in his youth: his learning of how to read and write and his confrontation with Mr. Covey, a slave breaker and overseer. When Douglass went to live with the Anthony family, Mrs. Anthony started teaching him the alphabet and how to spell simple words, but her husband stopped this, claiming that it was dangerous and illegal to teach a slave to read. While it was true in many slave states that it was illegal to teach slaves to read and write, it was not true in Maryland. The key point about literacy and Douglass is that he realized it equaled freedom and also of course opened the door for him to become one of the most

Douglass retained his charismatic appearance into old age; he delivered powerful speeches on human rights until the end of his life. (Library of Congress)

important and prominent writers in American history. The other signal event in his childhood was his physical confrontation with Mr. Covey: this fight taught Douglass about self-respect and self-redemption. By challenging Mr. Covey's brutality, Douglass provided an example to other black men of resisting oppression by white men, a strategy he emphasized when he encouraged President Lincoln to allow the drafting of black men during the Civil War.

In 1838, he, like hundreds of thousands of the slaves before him, escaped from slavery, although he was subject to arrest in the North until some of his English friends, while he was on a speaking tour in England, paid for him. Douglass's fight with Mr. Covey and escape from slavery served as models for other black men enslaved in the South, but not so much so for black women, who often had a major complication to contend with, children. Following his escape, Douglass became one of the key figures in the abolition movement, along with William Lloyd Garrison and Wendell Phillips, but Douglass had to be careful about those two white men not being threatened by his superior intellectual abilities. Douglass was also a magnificent public speaker with a charismatic presence, traits that served the cause of abolition particularly well. One of his most powerful speeches was entitled "What to the Slave Is the Fourth of July?" delivered on July 5, 1852, to make the point that that holiday did not apply to slaves. He delivered hundreds of abolitionist speeches throughout New England and the Midwest, and eventually in England. And although he was unaware of John Brown's plans to lead a raid on Harpers Ferry, he did support that ultimate abolitionist with money and a house of refuge. After the raid, Douglass went to Canada because anyone associated with Brown was considered dangerous.

After publishing the first version of his autobiography in 1845, he rewrote it two more times, but the 1845 version remains the most powerful. He also edited newspapers, delivered perhaps thousands of speeches, and wrote numerous letters. He gave his support to women's rights but insisted the right of black men to vote had to take precedence over women's right to vote. In other words, he was a tireless promoter of abolition and civil rights, and he also urged President Lincoln to use black soldiers in combat on the Union side, which may have been decisive in determining its outcome. Toward the end of his life, he accepted several federal government positions, including minister to Haiti.

His personal life revolved around women and children. His first wife was a black woman named Anna Douglass, who is mentioned briefly toward the end of the 1845 *Narrative*. The couple had five children, and one of the sons served in the Union Army. His second wife, Helen Pitts, a white woman quite a bit younger than Douglass, was the daughter of one of Douglass's abolitionist friends. It is quite clear that Douglass was also good friends with two other women, Ottilie Assing and Julia Griffiths; the former, whom Douglass met in Germany, committed suicide, possibly because she believed he was going to marry her, but he did not.

He has received numerous honors, and his legacy is almost beyond measure. The honors include such examples as a 1965 postage stamp named after him;

Douglass liked to point out that his first wife was the color of his mother, his second the color of his father; Helen Pitts was an abolitionist and devoted to Douglass's legacy. (National Park Service, Frederick Douglass National Historic Site)

a statue of him in Central Park; the Frederick Douglass—Susan B. Anthony Memorial Bridge in the city of Rochester, New York; and a magnificent statue of him at the county courthouse in Easton, Maryland (when Douglass praised that area of Maryland, some people were shocked because he had been a slave there, but Douglass pointed out it was the system of slavery he despised, not that area of Maryland).

Perhaps the cornerstone of his legacy is that, along with Lincoln, he was essential to the movement to abolish slavery in the United States; Douglass pushed the cautious Civil War president to act sooner than he would have without such pressure from Douglass. Lincoln was a politician, Douglass an agitator. As a charismatic and eloquent public speaker, he also left a permanent mark on history: his famous "What to the Slave Is the 4th of July" speech will live forever, but he delivered numerous other speeches, such as "The Hypocrisy of American Slavery" (1852), that are well worth reading today. As a symbol of determination and leadership, Douglass leaves a solid legacy also: Paul Laurence Dunbar's poem "Douglass" proclaims that Douglass was irreplaceable; his death in 1895 marked the end of an era. In the field of letters Douglass occupies a permanent position: *Narrative of the Life of Frederick Douglass, An American Slave* (1845) remains one of the most eloquent and impassioned pleas for the destruction of slavery ever written. The descriptive phrase in the title is itself decisive: how can a person be an American and a slave at the same time? Along with Lincoln, Douglass leaves one of the largest and most important legacies in American history.

He was at the center of nineteenth-century American history, especially in the realm of civil rights and the abolition of slavery. Very few other Americans equal or surpass him in importance.

HISTORICAL EXPLORATIONS

Overseers

Overseers were employed on large plantations to supervise the work of slaves. Their employers expected them to maximize profit without working slaves to death, although this sometimes happened. Because overseers were looked down on by plantation owners and slaves, they were in an impossible position; it is no wonder the turnover rate was high. They tended to be brutal white men who were willing to inflict horrible punishment on slaves who resisted their orders; whipping and flogging were frequently used to punish slaves, as Douglass and his Aunt Hester found out. The system of slavery required violence from overseers to maintain its existence.

In Douglass's *Narrative,* the overseer, Mr. Edward Covey, was also a slaveowner. He owned several slaves and also got to use other slaveholders' slaves for free for a year, in return for breaking their spirits. Not only cruel and brutal, he was also sly and shrewd. Douglass notes particularly Covey's strategy of leaving slaves for a while and then quietly sneaking back so they would think he was everywhere, like a deity. He also rested in the afternoon so as to be fresh later in the day to push his men to keep working. Eventually, Covey pushed the fifteen-year-old Douglass too far, which resulted in a fight between the two that lasted almost two hours. Covey even asked two other slaves to help him tie up Douglass, but this plan failed when Douglass kicked one of them, and the other refused to help. Douglass then let it be known that the next white man who wanted to whip him would be whipping a corpse, because he would have to kill Douglass first. Never punished for defeating Covey, Douglass mused that it was because Covey did not want his reputation as a slavebreaker and overseer to be tarnished; possibly his victory went unpunished because someone intervened on his behalf. In any case, the victory over Covey brought Douglass's sagging spirits back to life and made him a new man. It also provided a powerful and resonant symbol of resisting a system that was designed to put out the spark of determination and hope.

The same incident also suggested the horrific price paid by whites to maintain their "superiority" over blacks. This is a burden too heavy for any white person to carry, but Covey is not aware of that and is, as a result, a victim of the same system trying to control Douglass. Covey's cruelty and brutality undermine his assumptions that slavery is right and that he therefore has the right to dominate Douglass. Douglass's humanity is obvious throughout his autobiography, but Covey, like most white people in the United States in the nineteenth century, has unconsciously internalized the notion of black "inferiority"; regardless of the counterevidence Douglass personifies, Covey clings to a lie because of his own social position.

Introduction to Frederick Douglass, *The Life and Times of Frederick Douglass* (1892)

The Life and Times of Frederick Douglass is Douglass's third rendering of his autobiography. Not as successful as the first two versions, it nevertheless does contain a fuller exploration of overseers than the first one, including an analysis of an overseer who, remarkably enough, makes even Mr. Covey seem restrained: Austin Gore. Gore seems to have had no scruples whatsoever when it came to the slaves he supervised; nor did he face any consequences for his depraved treatment of slaves, even including the murder of poor Denby. Gore apparently found utter brutality an exhilarating experience. Because slaves were not allowed to testify against white people and because slaves were the only witnesses of Gore's murder of Denby, there could be no trial. Even when a warrant was issued in a case similar to Gore's, Douglass points out that it was never served. Murdering slaves went unpunished.

From Frederick Douglass, *The Life and Times of Frederick Douglass* (1892)

The comparatively moderate rule of Mr. Hopkins as overseer on Col. Lloyd's plantation was succeeded by that of another whose name was Austin Gore. I hardly know how to bring this fitly before the reader, for under him there was more suffering from violence and bloodshed than had, according to the older slaves, ever been experienced before at that place. He was an overseer, and possessed the peculiar characteristics of his class, yet to call him merely an overseer would not give one a fair conception of the man. I speak of overseers as a class, for they were such. They were as distinct from the slave-holding gentry of the South as are the fish-women of Paris, and the coal-heavers of London, distinct from other grades of society. They constituted a separate fraternity at the South. They were arranged and classified by that great law of attraction which determines the sphere and affinities of men; which ordains that men whose malign and brutal propensities preponderate over their moral and intellectual endowments shall naturally fall into those employments which promise the largest gratification to those predominating instincts or propensities. The office of overseer took this raw material of vulgarity and brutality, and stamped it as a distinct class in Southern life. But in this class, as in all classes, there were sometimes persons of marked individuality, yet with a general resemblance to the mass. Mr. Gore was one of those to whom a general characterization would do no manner of justice. He was an overseer, but he was something more. With the malign and tyrannical qualities of an overseer he combined something of the lawful master. He had the artfulness and mean ambition of his class, without its disgusting swagger and noisy bravado. There was an easy air of independence about him; a calm self-possession; at the same time a sternness of glance which might well daunt less timid hearts than those of poor slaves, accustomed from childhood to cower before a driver's lash. He was one of those overseers who could torture the slightest word or look into "impudence," and he had the nerve not only to resent but to punish promptly and severely. There could be no answering back. Guilty or not guilty, to be accused was to be sure of a flogging. His very presence was fearful, and I shunned him as I would have shunned a rattlesnake. His piercing black eyes and sharp, shrill voice ever awakened sensations of dread. Other overseers, how brutal soever they might be, would sometimes seek to gain favour with the slaves, by indulging in a little pleasantry; but Gore never said a funny thing, or perpetrated a joke. He was always cold, distant, and unapproachable— the *overseer* on Col. Edward Lloyd's plantation—and needed no higher pleasure than the performance of the duties of his office. When he used the lash, it was from a sense of duty, without fear of consequences. There was a stern will, an iron-like reality about him, which would easily have made him chief of a band of pirates, had his environments been favourable to such a sphere. Among many other deeds of shocking cruelty committed by him was the murder of a young coloured man named Bill Denby. He was a powerful fellow, full of animal spirits, and one of the most valuable of Col. Lloyd's slaves. In some way—I know not what—he offended this Mr. Austin Gore, and in accordance with the usual custom the latter undertook to flog him. He had given him but few stripes when Denby broke away from him, plunged into the creek, and standing there with the water up to his neck refused to come out; whereupon, for this refusal, Gore *shot him dead;* It is said that Gore gave Denby three calls to come out, telling him if he did not obey the last call he should shoot him. When the last call was given Denby still stood his ground, and Gore, without further parley, or without making any further effort to induce obedience, raised his gun deliberately to his face, took deadly aim at his standing victim, and with one click of the gun the mangled body sank out of sight, and only his warm red blood marked the place where he had stood.

This fiendish murder produced, as it could not help doing, a tremendous sensation. The slaves were panic-stricken, and howled with alarm. The atrocity roused my old master, and he spoke out in reprobation of it. Both he and Colonel Lloyd arraigned Gore for his cruelty; but he, calm and collected, as though nothing unusual had happened, declared that Denby had become unmanageable; that he set a dangerous example to the other slaves, and that unless some such prompt measure was resorted to, there would be an end to all rule and order on the plantation. That convenient covert for all manner of villainy and outrage, that cowardly alarm-cry, that the slaves would "take the place," was pleaded, just as it had been in thousands of similar cases. Gore's defence was evidently considered satisfactory, for he was continued in his office, without being subjected to a judicial

Note the extreme understatement in the phrase a "Graduate from the Peculiar Institution," as if slavery was a quaint oddity Douglass was fleeing from. (Library of Congress)

investigation. The murder was committed in the presence of slaves only, and they, being slaves, could neither institute a suit nor testify against the murderer. Mr. Gore lived in St. Michaels, Talbot Co., Maryland, and I have no reason to doubt, from what I know to have been the moral sentiment of the place, that he was as highly esteemed and as much respected as though his guilty soul had not been stained with innocent blood.

I speak advisedly when I say that killing a slave, or any colored person, in Talbot Co., Maryland, was not treated as a crime, either by the courts or the community. Mr. Thomas Lanman, ship carpenter of St. Michael's, killed two slaves, one of whom he butchered with a hatchet, by knocking his brains out. He used to boast of having committed the awful and bloody deed. I have heard him do so laughingly, declaring himself a benefactor of his country, and that "when others would do as much as he had done, they would be rid of the d—d niggers."

Another notorious fact which I may state was the murder of a young girl between fifteen and sixteen years of age, by her mistress, Mrs. Giles Hicks, who lived but a short distance from Colonel Lloyd's. This wicked woman, in the paroxysm of her wrath, not content with killing her victim, literally mangled her face, and broke her breast-bone. Wild and infuriated as she was, she took the precaution to cause the burial of the girl; but, the facts of the case getting abroad, the remains were disinterred, and a coroner's jury assembled, who, after due deliberation, decided that "the girl had come to her death from severe beating." The offence for which this girl was thus hurried out of the world was this, she had been set that night, and several preceding nights, to mind Mrs. Hicks' baby, and having fallen into a sound sleep, the crying of the baby did not wake her, as it did its mother. The tardiness of the girl excited Mrs. Hicks, who, after calling her many times, seized a piece of fire-wood from the fire-place, and pounded in her skull and breast-bone till death ensued. I will not say that this murder most foul produced no sensation. It *did* produce a sensation. A warrant was issued for the arrest of Mrs. Hicks, but incredible to tell, for some reason or other, that warrant was never served, and she not only escaped condign punishment, but also the pain and mortification of being arraigned before a court of justice.

Source: Douglass, Frederick. *The Life and Times of Frederick Douglass.* Boston: DeWolfe and Fiske Co., 1892, pp. 75–81.

Introduction to Frederick Law Olmsted,
The Cotton Kingdom (1861)

Best known for designing Central Park in New York City, Olmsted also made notable contributions in many other areas of nineteenth-century American life. He supported the Union cause by helping administer the U.S. Sanitary Commission; he also designed the campus of Stanford University in Palo Alto, California, as well as numerous public parks throughout the United States. He traveled throughout the South in the 1850s, which resulted in *The Cotton Kingdom* (1861), a condensed version of three volumes based on his travels in the South. The consensus of opinion is that his descriptions of slavery and plantation life are quite accurate and objective. In the following excerpt, the overseer on a plantation in Mississippi has absolutely no qualms whatsoever about flogging a young black woman, regardless of the amount of pain he inflicts on her. In fact, his only reaction is amused irritation that she avoided work for a day and lied to him regarding her absence. The power of this scene is largely generated by the discrepancy between Olmsted's repressed horror at what he witnesses and the indifference of the overseer and the young gentleman who accompanies him to the intense suffering of the young woman. Olmsted suggests this callous disregard of the feelings of slaves underwrites the system of slavery itself.

From Frederick Law Olmsted, *The Cotton Kingdom* (1861)

I happened to see the severest corporeal punishment of a Negro that I witnessed at the South while visiting this estate. . . . The manner of the overseer, who inflicted the punishment, and his subsequent conversation with me about it, indicated that it was by no means unusual in severity.

I had accidently encountered him, and he was showing me his plantation. In going from one side of it to the other, we had twice crossed a deep gully, at the bottom of which was a thick covert of brushwood. We were crossing it a third time, and had nearly passed through the brush, when the overseer suddenly stopped his horse exclaiming, "What's that? Hallo! Who are you, there?"

It was a girl lying at full length on the ground at the bottom of the gully, evidently intending to hide herself from us in the bushes.

"Who are you, there?"

"Sam's Sall, sir."

"What are you skulking there for?"

The girl half rose, but gave no answer.

"Have you been here all day?"

"No, sir."

"How did you get here?"

The girl made no reply.

"Where have you been all day?"

The answer was unintelligible.

After some further questioning, she said her father accidentally locked her in, when he went out in the morning.

"How did you manage to get out?"

"Pushed a plank off, sir, and crawled out."

The overseer was silent for a moment, looking at the girl, and then said, "That won't do; come out here." The girl arose at once, and walked towards him. She was about eighteen years of age. A bunch of keys hung at her waist, which the overseer espied, and he said, "Your father locked you in; but you have got the keys." After a little hesitation, she replied that these were the keys of some other locks; her father had the door-key.

Whether her story was true or false, could have been ascertained in two minutes by riding on to the gang with which her father was at work, but the overseer had made up his mind.

"That won't do," said he; "get down." The girl knelt on the ground; he got off his horse, and holding him with his left hand, struck her thirty or forty blows across the shoulder with his tough, flexible, "raw-hide" whip (a terrible instrument for the purpose). They were well laid on, at arm's length, but with no appearance of angry excitement on the part of the overseer. At every stroke the girl winced and exclaimed, "Yes, sir!" or "Ah, sir!" or "Please, sir!" not groaning or screaming. At length he stopped and said, "Now tell me the truth." The girl repeated the same story. "You have not got enough yet," said he; "pull up your clothes-lie down."

The girl without any hesitation, without a word or look of remonstrance or entreaty, drew closely all her garments under her shoulders, and lay down upon the ground with her face toward the overseer, who continued to flog her with the raw-hide, across her naked loins and thighs, with as much strength as before. She now shrunk away from him, not rising, but writhing, groveling, and screaming, "Oh, don't, sir! Oh, please stop, master! Please, sir! Please, sir! Oh, that's enough, master! Oh, Lord! Oh, master, master! Oh, God, master, do stop! Oh, God, master! Oh, God, master!"

A young gentleman of fifteen was with us; he had ridden in front, and now turning on his horse, looked back with an expression only of impatience at the delay. It was the first time I had ever seen a woman flogged. I had seen a man cudgeled and beaten, in the heat of passion, before, but never flogged with a hundredth part of the severity used in this case.

I glanced again at the perfectly passionless but rather grim business-like face of the overseer, and again at the young gentleman, who had turned away; if not indifferent he had evidently not the faintest sympathy with my emotion. Only my horse chafed. I gave him rein and spur and we plunged into the bushes and scrambled fiercely up the steep acclivity. The screaming yells and the whip strokes had ceased when I reached the top of the bank. Choking, sobbing, spasmodic groans only were heard. I rode on to where the road, coming diagonally up the ravine, ran out upon the cotton-field. My young companion met me there, and immediately afterward the overseer. He laughed as he joined us, and said: "She meant to cheat me out of a day's work, and she has done it, too."

Source: Olmsted, Frederick Law. *The Cotton Kingdom.* London: Sampson Low, 1861, volume 2, pp. 204–206.

Introduction to Two Letters from *The Farmers' Register*

The Farmers' Register was a nineteenth-century agricultural periodical published to help farmers, including slaveowners, with their concerns and problems. The following two letters were written by unnamed Virginia cotton planters in 1837. The first writer manages his slaves without using an overseer and seems to think this method is preferable to employing overseers because it allows him to understand his slaves better than masters who rely on overseers do. But if he really understood them, he would not criticize them for hypocrisy when they "act the fool's part," because he would realize they are merely doing what enslaved whites would have done in the same circumstances. "It greatly impairs the happiness of a [N]egro, to be allowed to cultivate an insubordinate temper." Happy slaves are obedient slaves, he argues, overlooking his own distaste for hypocrisy.

The second writer acknowledges that on small farms, the owner may do well enough without an overseer, but on farms of 800 acres or more, overseers are a near necessity. He argues that slaves who are used to an overseer will be unable to resist temptation if they are not kept under one, because they do not know the difference between right and wrong, a point that if applied to the letter writer would mean he too would need to be kept under an overseer who would teach him that slavery is wrong. If masters treat their slaves well, they will be "the happiest laboring class in the world," a sentiment at odds with the reality of slave insurrections, black abolitionists like Douglass, runaway slaves, and the Civil War. In other words, both letter writers project fantasy on to the slave world rather than face the reality of slavery.

From Two Letters from *The Farmers' Register*

It might be inferred, from the manner in which many masters (who have been raised, too, in the midst of a slave population) treat their slaves, that they were as ignorant of the character, feelings, and sympathies of the negro, as they are of those of a Hottentot or Laplander. The most common error is underrating the capacity of the slave. I have spent much time with this population, in the capacity of a master, and managed them without the intervention of overseers; and must confess that my opinion of their sagacity is greatly raised by this intercourse. I have found them apt to learn, very tractable, and remarkable for patience and evenness of temper. They are very grateful for good treatment, if proper discipline and authority is kept up over them. They soon ascertain the character of those in authority over them, their peculiarities of temperament and disposition, and frequently, under the cloak of great stupidity, make dupes of the master and overseer. The most general defect in the character of the negro is hypocrisy; and this hypocrisy frequently makes him pretend to more ignorance than he possesses; and if his master treats him as a fool, he will be sure to act the fool's part. This is a very convenient trait, as it frequently serves as an apology for awkwardness and neglect of duty. The most important part of management of slaves, is always to keep them under proper subjection. They must obey at all times, and under all circumstances, cheerfully and with alacrity. It greatly impairs the happiness of a negro, to be allowed to cultivate an insubordinate temper. Unconditional submission is the only footing upon which slavery should be placed. It is precisely similar to the attitude of a minor to his parent, or a soldier to his general. But, it is not intended by this remark to justify harsh and reproachful language on all occasions, from the master. His authority should be exercised in a firm, but mild manner. . . . I never saw any degree of courtesy shown to a negro, (that was kept under good subjection,) but was returned with usury. Cuffee [a generalized slave name] is hard to outdo in politeness.

The most important subject to attend to in the management of negroes, is to give them a sufficiency of food. I have heard many comparisons made between negro slavery and the operative classes of old countries, to prove that too much meat was given them. But it is no argument to a humane master, to starve and half clothe his slaves, because the poor Irish are naked, and get meat only once a week. I am clearly of opinion that a half starved hireling in Russia, Germany or Great Britain, exhibits to his employer the most degrading attitude that one portion of the species ever stood towards the other, and I do not believe that any lesson can be learned from them, either beneficial to the Virginia slave or his master. But I think it probable that the poverty of the diet of the German and Irish labourer, is much alleviated by a great variety of succulent vegetables; such as the potatoe [sic], beet, turnip, &c., and mostly by the common use of milk and butter. But corn meal bread, with little or no meat, and no vegetable diet, is extremely hard fare. I believe that there are extremely few masters who starve their slaves to actual suffering; in fact, I am unacquainted with any such. But, I have no doubt that the slow motion, and thin expression of countenance, of many slaves, are owing to a want of a sufficiency of nourishing food. The great susceptibility of many families of negroes to scrofula, is to be attributed to hard and scanty living. There is, however, a great change for the better, in the article of diet to negroes, within the last ten or fifteen years. . . .

A negro slave is so constituted that he is dependent in a great measure for happiness on his food. And nothing has a greater tendency to inspire cheerfulness and industry, than to look forward to the prospect of a good meal. It must, too, be a source of pleasing [contemplation] to the master, to afford the additional happiness which such luxuries never fail to yield. I am very certain, from an attentive observation to this subject, that a negro deprived of meat diet, is not able to endure the labor that those can perform who are liberally supplied with it; and that the master who gives his field hands half a pound of meat per day, and two quarts of meal, (or something short of this when an allowance of vegetables is made,) is better compensated by slave labor, than those who give the ordinary quantity. Their food should be cooked for them twice a day, and carried out to the field. It is a general custom in this part of the state, to have their food cooked but once a day, and to require each negro to cook for himself at night, and carry with him his food for the morning's meal in the field; but his love of indulgence, or fatigue, frequently induces him to fall to sleep as soon as he reaches his cabin, and if he is unfortunate enough not to wake at midnight and cook his morning's meal, (which indeed is a frequent habit with them,) he is compelled to fast until his dinner hour the next day.

The next most important matter to be attended to, is the slaves' lodging . . . [H]ewed log cabins with white oak sills, 16 feet by 18, make very comfortable houses. The roof should be framed. The old fashioned cabins, with log roofs, and slabs not nailed, but merely confined by logs, almost invariably leak, and keep the cabin floor always wet; which, I have no doubt is one origin of the catarrhal affections which terminate in what is called "negro consumption." But these cabins are going fast out of use. It is highly important that dirt-floors should be raised a foot higher than the surrounding surface of the earth, and well rammed [compacted], to keep them dry. The hewed log cabins with hewed sills, will out last three sets of cabin roofed houses.

Source: The Farmers' Register (A Monthly Publication Devoted to the Improvement of the Practice, and Support of the Interests of Agriculture) 5 (May 1, 1837): 32–33.

Some of the contributors to your periodical are advocating a system of farming, so far as it refers to our slaves, without the aid of overseers—substituting a scheme of pecuniary rewards according to merit, and withholding them for want of it. On small farms, when the owner is an active energetic man, he may manage his concerns well enough without aid; but on farms of 800 acres, or more, I think he will find a difficult task to manage his negroes unless assisted by an overseer.

When negroes are accustomed to an overseer, and you dispense with services of one, they *must* be exposed to a great deal of temptation, far more than they can resist. And education has not taught them the difference between right and wrong; at any rate, their ideas on the subject must be confused. What they learn of the moral code, is gathered from observation, and the example of others, their superiors. How can any person, who, has no overseer, be all at hours with his negroes, when he is delivering his grain for example. Let him turn his back, and a cunning fellow will help himself to a bushel of corn or wheat, and he will never be informed upon by his fellow laborers, though ever so honest; for an informer, in their eyes, is held in greater detestation that the most notorious thief.

I admit that many overseers are vain, weak tyrants, "dressed in a little brief authority [Shakespeare, *Measure for Measure*]," but probably a larger proportion of farmers of Virginia are indifferent cultivators of the soil. I regard an overseer as an indispensable agent, whose first qualities should be honesty and firmness, united with forbearance and good temper. Sobriety is a *sine qua non*. A written agreement should be drawn up between the employer and the employed, to be signed by both, setting forth the terms, and mentioning the most important requisitions, which will occur to every one. An overseer's wages should always be paid in money; for if you give him a part of the crops, your land will be worked to death, and never have a dozen loads of manure spread upon it. In addition to this, your views and his will frequently come into collision.

Your overseer should be treated with marked respect; for if you treat him contemptuously or familiarly, your authority and his are injured. He should not be allowed to strike a negro with his fist or a stick, nor ever to punish with severity; for it is not the severity, but certainty of punishment that wins implicit obedience.

The subject before me turns my thoughts to the food, houses, and clothing of the negro. The master sho[u]ld ever bear in mind, that he is the guardian and protector of his slaves, who if well treated and used, are the happiest laboring class in the world. . . .

Liberally and plentifully fed, warmly clad and housed, your negroes work harder and more willingly, will be more healthy, and their moral character be improved, for they will not be urged by a hungry longing for meat, to steal their masters' hogs, sheep, and poultry, or to make predatory excursions upon his neighbors. Your negroes will breed much faster when well clothed, fed and housed; which fact, offers an inducement to those slave owners, whose hearts do not overflow with feelings of humanity.

The character of the negro is much underrated. It is like the plastic clay, which, may be moulded into agreeable or disagreeable figures, according to the skill of the moulder. The man who storms at, and curses his negroes, and who tells them they are a parcel of infernal rascals, not to be trusted, will surely make them just what he calls them; and so far from loving such a master, they will hate him. Now, if you be not suspicious, and induce them to think, by slight trusts, that they are not unworthy of some confidence, you will make them honest, useful, and affectionate creatures.

Source: The Farmers' Register (A Monthly Publication Devoted to the Improvement of the Practice, and Support of the Interests of Agriculture) 5 (September 1837): 301–302.

Discussion Questions

1. How does Mr. Covey, the overseer in the 1845 *Narrative,* compare to the overseers in the documents?
2. What sort of white men were attracted to the position of overseer, and why?
3. What makes Austin Gore, the overseer in *The Life and Times of Frederick Douglass,* crueler than Mr. Covey?
4. Does Douglass's polished prose style lessen the impact of his depiction of Mr. Covey and Mr. Gore? Why or why not?

5. Given that both slaves and many whites regarded overseers as the bottom of society, who do you think they took out their resulting frustrations on and why?

6. What kind of temperament did the position of overseer require according to the historical documents in this section?

7. Do you know anyone who could meet these requirements?

8. Account for the absolute ruthlessness of some overseers, such as the one mentioned in *The Cotton Kingdom:* what would have happened to the system of slavery if he had had a heart?

9. There were some black overseers in the Old South. Why did they have a particularly difficult time managing slaves?

10. Why did overseers believe that they understood slaves? Why did slaves want to encourage this falsehood?

11. Why did the Nazis think they understood the Jews they were incinerating in their concentration camps during World War II?

12. Explain why the overseers depicted by Douglass and the other writers in this section had to be so heartless if slavery was to survive.

13. Can you see yourself or anyone else being an overseer if you were desperate for a job but could find no other position?

14. How do you think slaveowners and their overseers lived with the two contradictory notions that slaves were basically docile and content but also required the use of brute force?

Suggested Readings

Andrews, William A. 1991. *Critical Essays on Frederick Douglass.* Torndike, Maine: G.K. Hall.

Andrews, William L. 1986. *To Tell a Free Story.* Urbana: University of Illinois Press.

Colaiaco, James. 2006. *Frederick Douglass and the Fourth of July.* New York: Palgrave Macmillan.

Dickson, Preston J. 1985. *Young Frederick Douglass.* Baltimore: Johns Hopkins University Press.

Douglass, Frederick. 1990. *The Heroic Slave, in Three Classic African-American Novels,* ed. William L. Andrews. New York: Signet.

Ernest, John. 1995. *Resistance and Reformation in Nineteenth-Century American Literature.* Jackson: University Press of Mississippi.

Felgar, Robert. "The Rediscovery of Frederick Douglass." *The Mississippi Quarterly* 35 (1982): 427–438.

Levine, Robert S. 1997. *Martin Delany, Frederick Douglass, and the Politics of Representative Identity.* Chapel Hill: University of North Carolina Press.

McFeeley, William S. 1991. *Frederick Douglass.* New York: Norton.

Oxford Frederick Douglass Reader, ed. William L Andrews. 1996. New York: Oxford University Press.

Quarles, Benjamin. 1968. *Frederick Douglass.* Englewood Cliffs, NJ: Prentice Hall.

Sale, Maggie M. 1997. *The Slumbering Volcano: American Slave Ship Revolts and the Production of Rebellious Masculinity.* Durham, NC: Duke University Press Books.

Wilson, Jeremiah Moses. 2004. *Creative Conflict in African American Thought: Frederick Douglass, Alexander Crummell, Booker T. Washington, W.E.B. Du Bois, and Marcus Garvey.* Cambridge: Cambridge University Press.

Zafar, Rafia. 1997. *We Wear the Mask.* New York: Columbia University Press.

HISTORICAL EXPLORATIONS

Nineteenth-Century American Schoolbooks

The Columbian Orator (1797), edited by Caleb Bingham (1757–1817), a notable editor of nineteenth-century readers, was a powerful force in Douglass's intellectual development, as he acknowledges in Chapter VII of *Narrative of the Life of Frederick Douglass.* Readers such as this one and *McGuffey's Reader* were read by thousands of American schoolboys in the nineteenth century; they played a role in American history that probably no contemporary student reader enjoys, because they helped shape the political views of people like Douglass and William Lloyd Garrison. The subtitle gives an idea of how wide-ranging Bingham's book was: *Containing a Variety of Original and Selected Pieces; Together with Rules; Calculated to Improve Youth and Others in the Ornamental and Useful Act of Eloquence.* As someone who became perhaps the premier public speaker in nineteenth-century United States Douglass may also have been influenced by this book's emphasis on oratory as a means of historical change. Its Table of Contents lists such important speeches as George Washington's First Speech to Congress in 1789, his address to the people of the United States in 1796, and a speech by the Roman consul and orator Cicero against a traitor named Catiline. At the age of twelve, when Douglass got his copy, he may have been inspired to see himself as entering history at a comparable level of achievement.

**Introduction to *The Columbian Orator,*
"Dialogue between a Master and Slave" (1797)**

The logic in this dialogue from *The Columbian Orator* is similar to the logic Douglass used in his own attacks on slavery when he was an adult, for example, in his speech, "What to the Slave Is the Fourth of July?" (delivered on July 5, 1852, to suggest the absurdity of July 4 applying to slaves). In the speech, Douglass asks, who does not know slavery is wrong for them? The slave in the dialogue asks similar devastating questions, such as how can the master make up for depriving the former of his freedom? As Douglass said in his *Narrative,*

> Every opportunity I got, I used to read this book [*The Columbian Orator*]. Among much of the interesting matter, I found in it a dialogue between a master and his slave. The slave was represented as having run away from his master three times. The dialogue represented the conversation which took place between them, when the slave was retaken the third time. In this dialogue, the whole argument in behalf of slavery was brought forward by the master, all of which was disposed of by the slave. The slave was made to say some very smart as well as impressive things in reply to his master—things which had the desired though unexpected effect; for the conversation resulted in the voluntary emancipation of the slave on the part of the master. (Chapter VII)

From *The Columbian Orator,* "Dialogue between a Master and Slave" (1797)

Master. Now, villain! What have you to say for this second attempt to run away? Is there any punishment that you do not deserve?

Slave. I well know that nothing I can say will avail. I submit to my fate.

Master.	But are you not a base fellow, a hardened and ungrateful rascal?
Slave.	I am a slave. That is answer enough.
Master.	I am not content with that answer. I thought I discerned in you some tokens of a mind superior to your condition. I treated you accordingly. You have been comfortably fed and lodged, not overworked, and attended with the most humane care when you were sick. And is this the return?
Slave.	Since you condescend to talk with me, as man to man, I will reply. What have you done, what can you do for me, that will compensate for the liberty which you have taken away?
Master.	I did not take it away. You were a slave when I fairly purchased you.
Slave.	Did I give my consent to the purchase?
Master.	You had no consent to give. You had already lost the right of disposing of yourself.
Slave.	I had lost the power, but how the right? I was treacherously kidnapped in my own country, when following an honest occupation. I was put in chains, sold to one of your countrymen, carried by force on board his ship, brought hither, and exposed to sale like a beast in the market, where you bought me. What step in all this progress of violence and injustice can give a *right?* Was it in the villain who stole me, in the slave-merchant who tempted him to do so, or in you who encouraged the slave-merchant to bring his cargo of human cattle to cultivate your lands?
Master.	It is in the order of Providence that one man should become subservient to another. It ever has been so, and ever will be. I found the custom, and did not make it.
Slave.	You cannot but be sensible, that the robber who puts a pistol to your breast may make just the same plea. Providence gives him a power over your life and property; it gave my enemies a power over my liberty. But it has also given me legs to escape with; and what should prevent me from using them? Nay, what should restrain me from retaliating the wrongs I have suffered, if a favourable occasion should offer?

Master. Gratitude! I repeat, gratitude! Have I not endeavored ever since I possessed you to alleviate your misfortunes by kind treatment; and does that confer no obligation? Consider how much worse your condition might have been under another master.

Slave. You have done nothing for me more than for your working cattle. Are they not well fed and tended? Do you work them harder than your slaves? Is not the rule of treating both designed only for your own advantage? You treat both your men and beast slaves better than some of your neighbours, because you are more prudent and wealthy than they.

Master. You might add, more humane too.

Slave. Humane! Does it deserve that appellation to keep your fellowmen in forced subjection, deprived of all exercise of their free will, liable to all the injuries that your own caprice, or the brutality of your overseers, may heap on them, and devoted, soul and body, only to your pleasure and emolument? Can gratitude take place between creatures in such a state, and the tyrant who holds them in it? Look at these limbs; are they not those of a man? Think that I have the spirit of a man too.

Master. But it was my intention not only to make your life tolerably comfortable at present, but to provide for you in your old age.

Slave. Alas! Is a life like mine, torn from country, friends, and all I held dear, and compelled to toil under the burning sun for a master, worth thinking about for old age? No; the sooner it ends, the sooner I shall obtain that relief for which my soul pants.

Master. Is it impossible, then, to hold you by any ties but those of constraint and severity?

Slave. It is impossible to make one, who has felt the value of freedom, acquiesce in being a slave.

Master. Suppose I were to restore you to your liberty, would you reckon that a favour?

Slave. The greatest; for although it would only be undoing a wrong, I know too well how few among mankind are capable of sacrificing interest to justice, not to prize the exertion when it is made.

Master. I do it, then; be free.

Slave. Now I am indeed your servant, though not your slave. And as the first return I can make for your kindness. I will tell you freely the condition in which you live. You are surrounded with implacable foes, who long for a safe opportunity to revenge upon you and the other planters all the miseries they have endured. The more generous their natures, the more indignant they feel against that cruel injustice which has dragged them hither, and doomed them to perpetual servitude. You can rely on no kindness on your part to soften the obduracy of their resentment. You have reduced them to the state of brute beasts; and if they have not the stupidity of beasts of burden, they must have the ferocity of beasts of prey. Superior force alone can give you security. As soon as that fails, you are at the mercy of the merciless. Such is the social bond between master and slave!

Source: Bingham, Caleb, Ed. *The Columbian Orator.* Boston, 1832, pp. 240–242.

Introduction to Extract from "A Discourse Delivered before the New York Society for Promoting the Manumission of Slaves," April 12, 1797, by Rev. Samuel Miller

The selection in *The Columbian Orator* from "Oration on the Manumission of Slaves," delivered by Rev. Samuel Miller (1769–1850) on April 12, 1797, is so historically useful that a larger extract is reprinted here than Caleb Bingham provided in his reader. The Reverend Miller was a Presbyterian minister who taught church history at Princeton Theological Seminary for a number of years. He was an adamant supporter of the manumission (emancipation) of slaves, as his speech indicates. Miller uses many arguments that Douglass uses in his 1845 *Narrative,* as did other abolitionists. For example, he makes quick work of using Christian ideas to support slavery, a point that Douglass was always particularly incensed about in the 1845 *Narrative* as well as elsewhere. As enlightened as Miller is, though, he does share the widespread assumption that Africans are not civilized. In this assumption, he is similar to later white abolitionists like William Lloyd Garrison and Wendell Phillips, who did not regard Douglass and other black abolitionists their intellectual equals, a particularly galling irritant to Douglass.

From "A Discourse Delivered before the New York Society for Promoting the Manumission of Slaves," April 12, 1797, by Rev. Samuel Miller

That, in the close of the eighteenth century, it should be esteemed proper and necessary, in any civilized country, to institute discourse to oppose the slavery and commerce of the human species, is a wonderful fact in the annals of society! But that this country should be America, is a solecism only to be accounted for by the general inconsistency of the human character. But, after all the surprise that Patriotism can feel, and all the indignation that Morality can suggest on this subject, the humiliating tale must be told—that in this free country—in this country, the plains of which are still stained with blood shed in the cause of liberty,—in this country, from which has been proclaimed to distant lands, as the basis of our political existence, the noble principle, that "ALL MEN ARE BORN FREE AND EQUAL,"—in this country there are slaves!—men are bought and sold! Strange, indeed! That the bosom which glows at the name of liberty in general, and the arm which has been so vigorously exerted in vindication of human rights, should yet be found leagued on the side of oppression, and opposing their avowed principles!

Much, indeed, has been done by many benevolent individuals and societies, to abolish this disgraceful practice, and to improve the condition of those unhappy people, whom the ignorance or the avarice of our ancestors has bequeathed to us as slaves. Still, however, notwithstanding all the labours and eloquence which have been directed against it, the evil continues, still laws and practices exist, which loudly call for reform, still more than half a million of our fellow creatures in the United States are deprived of that which, next to life, is the dearest birth-right of man.

Abolitionists **William Lloyd Garrison** and **Wendell Phillips**, to the left and right in this image, provided Douglass with prefatory material for his 1845 *Narrative,* which added credibility to the black writer's story in the eyes of white readers at the time. **George Thompson,** in the middle, was a strong English supporter of abolition. (Universal History Archive/UIG via Getty Images)

To deliver the plain dictates of humanity, justice, religion, and good policy, on this subject, is the design of the present discourse. In doing this, it will not be expected that any thing new should be offered. It is not a new subject; and every point of view in which it can be considered has been long since rendered familiar by the ingenious and the humane. All that is left for me is, to bring to your remembrance principles which, however well known, cannot be too often repeated; and to exhibit some of the most obvious arguments against an evil which, though generally acknowledged, is still practically persisted in.

And here I shall pass over in silence the unnumbered cruelties, and the violations of every natural and social tie, which mark the African trade, and which attend the injured captives in dragging them from their native shores, and from all the attachments of life. I shall not call you to contemplate the miseries and hardships which follow them into servitude, and render their life a cup of unmingled bitterness. Unwilling to wound your feelings, or my own, by the melancholy recital, over these scenes I would willingly draw a veil; and confine myself to principles and views of the subject more immediately applicable to ourselves.

That enslaving, or continuing to hold in slavery, those who have forfeited their liberty by no crime, is contrary to the dictates both of justice and humanity, I trust few who hear me will be disposed to deny. However the judgment of some may be biased by the supposed peculiarity of certain cases, I presume that, with regard to the abstract principle, there can be but one opinion among enlightened and candid minds. What is the end of all social connection but the advancement of human happiness? And what can be a more plain and indisputable principle of republican government, than that all the right which society possess over individuals, or one man over another, must be founded either upon contract, express or implied, or upon forfeiture by crime? But, are the Africans and their descendants enslaved upon either of these principles? Have they voluntarily surrendered their liberty to their whiter brethren? Or have they forfeited their natural right to it by the violation of any law? Neither of these is pretended by the most zealous advocates for slavery. By what ties, then, are they held in servitude? By the ties of force and injustice only; by ties which are equally opposed to the reason of things, and to the fundamental principles of all legitimate association.

In the present age and country, none, I presume, will rest a defence of slavery on the ground of superior force; the right of captivity; or any similar principle, which the ignorance and the ferocity of ancient times admitted as a justifiable tenure of property. It is to be hoped the time is passed, never more to return; when men would recognize maxims as subversive of morality as they are of social happiness. Can the laws and rights of war be properly drawn into precedent for the imitation of sober and regular government? Can we sanction the detestable idea, that liberty is only an advantage gained by strength, and not a right derived from nature's God? Such sentiments become the abodes of demons, rather than societies of civilized men.

Pride, indeed, may contend, that these unhappy subjects of our oppression are an *inferior race of beings;* and are therefore assigned by the strictest justice to a depressed and servile station in society. But in what does this inferiority consist? In a difference of *complexion* and *figure?* Let the narrow and illiberal mind, who can advance such an argument, recollect whither it will carry him. In traversing the various regions of the earth, from the Equator to the Pole, we find an infinite diversity of shades in the complexion of men, from the darkest to the fairest hues. If, then, the proper station of the African is that of servitude and depression, we must also contend, that every Portuguese and Spaniard is, though in a less degree, inferior to us, and should be subject to a measure of the same degradation. Nay, if the tints of colour be considered the test of human dignity, we may justly assume a haughty superiority over our southern brethren of this continent, and devise their subjugation. In short, upon this principle, where shall liberty end? Or where shall slavery begin? At what grade is it that the ties of blood are to cease? And how many shades must we descend still lower in the scale, before mercy is to vanish with them?

But, perhaps, it will be suggested, that the Africans and their descendants are inferior to their whiter brethren in *intellectual capacity,* if not in complexion and figure. This is strongly asserted, but upon what ground? Because we do not see men who labour under every disadvantage, and who have every opening faculty blasted and destroyed by their depressed condition, signalize themselves as philosophers? Because we do not find men who are almost entirely cut off from every source of mental improvement, rising to literary honours? To suppose the Africans of an inferior radical character, because they have not thus distinguished themselves, is just as rational as to suppose every private citizen of an inferior species, who has not raised himself to the condition of royalty. But, the truth is, many of the negroes discover great ingenuity, notwithstanding their circumstances are so depressed, and so unfavourable to all cultivation. They become excellent mechanics and practical musicians, and, indeed, learn every thing their masters take the pains to teach them. And how far they might improve in this respect, were the same advantages conferred on them that freemen enjoy, is impossible for us to decide until the experiment be made.

Aristotle long ago said—"Men of little genius, and great bodily strength, are by nature destined to serve, and those of a better capacity to command. The natives of Greece, and of some other countries, being naturally superior in genius, have a natural right to empire; and the rest of mankind, being naturally stupid, are destined to labour and slavery" (*De Republica*). What would this great philosopher have thought of his own reasoning, had he lived till the present day? On the one hand, he would have seen his countrymen, of whose genius he boasts so much, lose with their liberty all mental character; while, on the other, he would have seen many nations, whom he consigned to everlasting stupidity, shew themselves equal in intellectual power to the most exalted of human kind.

Again—Avarice may clamorously contend, that the *laws of property* justify slavery; and that every one has an undoubted right to whatever has been obtained by *fair purchase* or *regular descent.* To this demand the answer is plain. The right which every man has to his personal liberty is paramount to all the laws of property. The right which every one has to *himself* infinitely transcends all other human tenures. Of consequence, the latter can never be set in opposition to the former. I do not mean, at present, to decide the question, whether the possessors of slaves, when called upon by public authority to manumit them, should be indemnified for the loss they sustain. This is a separate question, and must be decided by a different tribunal from that before which I bring the general subject. All I contend for at present is, that no claims of property can ever justly interfere with, or be suffered to impede the operation of that noble and eternal principle, that "all men are endowed by their Creator with certain unalienable rights—and that among these are life, liberty, and the pursuit of happiness."

These principles and remarks would doubtless appear self-evident to all, were the case of the unhappy Africans for a moment made our own. Were it made a question; whether justice permitted the sable race of Guinea to carry us away captive from our own country, and from all its tender attachments, to their own land; and there enslave us and our posterity for ever;—were it made a question, I say, whether all this would be consistent with justice and humanity, one universal and clamorous with justice and humanity, one universal and clamorous negative would show how abhorrent the principle is from our minds, when not blinded by prejudice. Tell us, ye who were lately pining in ALGERINE BONDAGE! Tell us whether all the wretched sophistry of pride, or of avarice, could ever reconcile you to the chains of barbarians, or convince you that man had a right to oppress and injure man? Tell us what were your feelings, when you heard the pityless tyrant, who had taken or bought you, plead either of these rights for your detention; and justify himself by the specious pretences of capture or of purchase, in riveting your chains?

Let none say, that, notwithstanding all these reasonings, the slaves are *happier* in a state of servitude, than they would be if set at liberty, especially when they are treated with lenity, and provided for in a comfortable manner. That there are different degrees of wretchedness among them, in different circumstances, no one can doubt: and when they fall into the hands of the humane and kind, their depression is less—far less miserable, than when the torture of whips, the pains of hunger and nakedness, and the unreasonable impositions of hard talk-masters, are added servitude. On this account, I am happy in being able to say, that the lot of slaves among us is, in general, much more tolerable than that of those in some other parts even of our own country. But still they are both in bondage. However favoured the situation of either, they are both deprived of that blessing, in possession of which the barren rock has its joys, and without which Eden itself would be a gloomy scene. After all the sordid pleas of those who would measure out enjoyment for them, they are forced to submit to an evil which, "however disguised, is a bitter draught, and ever will be so till Nature herself shall change."

But higher laws than those of common justice and humanity may be urged against slavery. I mean THE LAWS OF GOD, revealed in the scriptures of truth. This divine system, in which we profess to believe and to glory, teaches us, that *God has made of one blood all nations of men that dwell on the face of the whole earth.* It teaches us, that, of whatever kindred or people, we are all children of the same common Father; dependent on the same mighty power; and candidates for the same glorious immortality. It teaches us, that we should do to all men whatever we, in like circumstances, would that they should do unto us. It teaches us, in a word, that love to man, and a constant pursuit of human happiness, is the sum of all social duty.—Principles these, which wage eternal war both with political and domestic slavery—Principles which forbid every species of domination, excepting that which is founded on consent, or which the welfare of society requires.

There have not been wanting, indeed, men as ignorant as they were impious, who have appealed to the sacred scriptures for a defence of slavery. They have dared to seek for a justification of injuries and oppression in a volume, which teaches nothing but *peace on earth, and good will towards men.* As a specimen of their reasoning—Some have contended, "that the Africans are the posterity of HAM, one of the sons of NOAH; that, as it was declared by divine inspiration, that his descendants should be servants to their brethren, so reducing them to a state of slavery is only accomplishing the will of heaven."—But this plea can never be maintained, either upon the ground of *fact,* or of *sober principle.* The curse pronounced upon HAM was evidently a limited one, and extended only to a part of his posterity. It was only said, that the descendants of CANAAN, one of the four sons of HAM, should serve the posterity of SHEM and JAPHET. This curse, then, had nothing to do with the Africa nations, who have been so much abused by the civilized world; but was partly fulfilled, when the descendants of CANAAN in PALESTINE became *hewers of wood and drawers of water* to the ISRAELITES, who were the descendents of SHEM: and afterwards was completely accomplished, when the CARTHAGINIANS and TYRIANS were subdued by SCIPIO and ALEXANDER.

But, admitting the curse pronounced upon HAM to have all the meaning and extension which the advocates for slavery contend; yet we are to remember it *was prophetical* in its nature; and though infinite Wisdom designed to fulfil it, still is plain, the agents in bringing about the fulfillment cannot be considered the less criminal on this account. It was prophesied, that the SAVIOUR OF THE WORLD should be crucified, long before that important event took place; and yet, I presume, none ever supposed that this consideration exculpated his murderers. The truth is, if our being made instruments of accomplishing the designs of heaven takes away guilt, there is no such thing as crime in the world; the most execrable cruelty that ever disgraced mankind must be pronounced right; and the work of carnage and death, in every age, must receive the benediction of the wise and the good!

The practice of the JEWS, the chosen people of God, has also been supposed, by some, to furnish a precedent which we might lawfully follow. That the children of Israel had the permission of God to purchase bondmen and bondwomen of the heathen nations which were round about them, and even to retain some of their own people in servitude, for a limited time, is readily granted. But this permission appears to have been particularly designed for that people, and was not extended to the rest of mankind. It stands on the same ground with many other things, which they were permitted to do, on account of their separation from the rest of the world, and on account of the comparatively servile nature of their dispensation; but in which it would be extremely criminal for us to imitate them. As well might the midnight murderer plead, as an apology for his crime, that God's chosen people were once ordered to destroy the guilty heathen who inhabited the promised land. Besides, if this permission, given to the children of Israel, on a special occasion, and for wise purposes, be considered as extending to all succeeding times and people, where shall its operation begin? And where shall it end? If this principle be admitted, then every nation on earth is at liberty to purchase and enslave the citizens of every other. If this be the case, we have a right to make merchandize of our white brethren in Europe, if any can be found so base as to seize and sell them to us; and they, on the other hand, have a like privilege to institute a trade in the flesh of AMERI-CAN FREEMEN!—Will any say, that this is a forced conclusion? No—though justice, humanity, and religion all rise up against it, it naturally flows from the principle above stated, and is quite as tenable in every point of view.

But farther—the writings of the Apostles, it seems, have been thought by some to furnish a warrant for slavery. In one of the Epistles we find these words—*Let as many servants as are under the yoke, count their masters worthy of all honour, that the name of God and his doctrine be not blasphemed. And let them who have believing masters not despise them, because they are brethren, but rather do them service.* (I Timothy, 6) Now, even taking for granted what, perhaps, may reasonably be called in question, that the persons referred to in this passage were slaves *for life,* and under *involuntary* servitude—still it furnishes no such argument as many imagine. It must be remembered, that the great Author of our religion did not think proper directly to interfere with the political arrangements, and the civil laws, which were established when his Gospel was first preached among men. He always rather inculcated submission, and patience under the most oppressive injuries. This doctrine the Apostle applies, in the present instance, to a particular class of persons, to whom he thought the admonition necessary;

and all that he intends to inculcate on such is, that, during the continuance of their servitude, (the origin, nature, or duration of which
does not appear) they should faithfully perform their duty to their
masters, and patiently submit to their lot. But, does this precept
justify those who hold their fellow creatures in illegal and forcible
subjection? By no means—No more than the precepts, *Resist not
evil;* and *If any man smite thee on thy right cheek, turn to him the
other also,* justify the evil and the abuse which they forbid us to
resist—No more than the precept, *Let every man be subject to the
powers that be,* can be construed into a justification of the cruelty
and despotism which, in those days, and ever since, rulers have
exercised over their subjects.

But, though it be granted that Christ and his Apostles, for the
reason which has been just assigned, did not in so many words
prohibit the practice of slavery; it is evident they taught principles
and doctrines utterly abhorrent from such a practice. And they who
imbibe the true spirit of their religion, will not hesitate a moment
to pronounce, that invading the liberty and diminishing the happiness of a fellow creature, are directly opposite to the benign genius
of Christianity. Hence it is a remarkable and well known fact, that,
after the introduction of this religion into the ROMAN EMPIRE,
every successive law that was made relating to slaves, was more
and more in their favour, abating the rigours of servitude, until, at
last, all the subjects of the empire were declared equally free. Nay,
a celebrated historian has not scrupled to account for the degree
of liberty which is at present enjoyed, throughout most parts of
Europe, by the mild and benevolent influence of a system, the uniform tendency of which is, to *let the oppressed go free, and to
break every yoke.*

But in vain is a large proportion of mankind addressed on the
principles of morality and religion. These they will seldom regard, as
long as they suppose *interest* and *policy* to deliver different precepts.
For the sake of such, therefore, I add, with the utmost confidence,
that slavery is not more opposed to justice, humanity, and religion,
than it is to the interest of individuals, and to the true policy and happiness of that society in which it is suffered to exist.

Slavery will always be found, in proportion to the extent and
severity with which it prevails, to injure the morals of a people.

That it tends to produce, on the one hand, haughtiness, a spirit of domination, cruelty, and lewdness, among the whites, appears probable, upon the slightest consideration of the subject, and is abundantly proved by experience. And, on the other hand, that it has an equal tendency, to produce and cherish almost every species of vice, among the slaves themselves, none, I presume, will hesitate to admit. Should any have a remaining doubt whether this be the case, let them compare the state of morals in those parts of our own country, in which slavery is either unknown, or exists in the most lenient form, with that which is exhibited in those states in which slaves are more numerous and more degraded. That there is a sensible difference between the moral aspect of the one and the other, no one will controvert. That the comparison furnishes a result unfavourable to the latter, the most decided partiality for them can neither conceal nor deny. And that this difference of national and moral character depends, to say the least, in some degree, on the state of slavery in each respectively, I believe the most accurate and candid observers have readily granted.

In this State, as well as in most others in the union, the testimony of a slave cannot be admitted in judicial process, excepting in a few cases. What is the ground of this law? The answer is obvious,— "slavery debases the mind, and corrupts the moral character." The unhappy victims of oppression, feeling themselves precluded by violence, from enjoying the benefits of society, neglect the social virtues. Finding their own rights habitually invaded, they soon learn to disregard the rights of others. Living perpetually under the frowns of power, they are insensibly taught the arts of deception, treachery, and fraud, until every moral feeling is blunted or destroyed. Hence slaves, in all ages and countries, have generally exhibited the most odious moral depravity. And nations which, for refinement, virtue, and happiness, were once the glory of the world, under the iron rod of despotism; we now behold sunk into the lowest state of debasement.

Nor has slavery a more mischievous effect on the morals of society, than it has on national industry, population, and general improvement. Men not only become lazy and idle when they can make others the servile instruments of their will, but labour will soon be esteemed disreputable and degrading, when it is chiefly performed by slaves. And whatever diminished industry, discourages population, and sows the seeds of social weakness and disorder. Besides, slaves, in general, do less work, and waste and destroy much more than free labourers. Feeling no interest in the property of their owners, they will seldom perform more labour, or exercise more care, than will be merely sufficient to save them from punishment. Of course, agriculture, carried on by such *uninterested machines, must necessarily languish;* lands must become comparatively unproductive; and every species of national prosperity must be impeded, or decline. Those who are acquainted with history, or who take notice of what is daily exhibited in our own country, will be at no loss for facts to exemplify and confirm what is here advanced.

In this part of the United States, indeed, the pernicious effects of slavery are displayed in a comparatively moderate degree. But even in our own State they are distinctly perceptible. Even here we should be a happier and a wealthier people, were every labourer a freeman, and, of consequence, the product of every man's labour his own property.—Would to God, however, there were not some of our SISTER REPUBLICS, whose situation is more perilous, and whose prospects are more gloomy! Our southern Brethren, deaf to the dictates of policy, to say nothing of higher considerations, have unhappily suffered the evil in question to take such deep root among them, and to spread its baneful influence so far and wide, that, if it do not prove the ruin, it will probably prove, at least, the long and awful scourge of their land.—"I tremble," says one Thomas Jefferson who cannot be suspected of undue partiality for the depressed Africans, "I tremble for my country when I remember that God is just—that his justice cannot sleep for ever—and that an exchange of circumstances is among probable events. The Almighty has no attribute which can take side with us in such a conflict."

I have hitherto confined myself to the consideration of slavery as it exists among ourselves, and of that unjust domination which is exercised over the Africans and their descendants, who are already in our country.—It is with a regret and indignation which I am unable to express, that I call your attention, before concluding, to the conduct of some among us, who, instead of diminishing, strive to increase the evil in question. While the friends of humanity, in Europe and

America, are weeping over their injured fellow creatures, and directing their ingenuity and their labours to the removal of so disgraceful a monument of cruelty and avarice, there are not wanting men, who claim the title, and enjoy the privileges of American citizens, who still employ themselves in the odious traffic of human flesh. Yes, in direct opposition to public sentiment, and a law of the land, there are ships fitted out, every year, in the ports of the United States, to transport the inhabitants of Africa, from their native shores, and consign them to all the torments of West India oppression,—Fellow citizens! Is Justice asleep? Is Humanity discouraged and silent, on account of the many injuries she has sustained? Were not this the case, methinks the pursuit of the beasts of the forest would be forgotten; and such monsters of wickedness would, in their stead, be hunted from the abodes of men.

Oh Africa! Unhappy, ill-fated region! How long shall thy savage inhabitants have reason to utter complaints, and to imprecate the vengeance of heaven against civilization and Christianity? Is it not enough that nature's God has consigned thee to arid plains, to noxious vapours, to devouring beasts of prey, and to all the scorching influences of the torrid zone? Must rapine and violence, captivity and slavery, be superadded to thy torments; and be inflicted too by men, who wear the garb of justice and humanity; who boast the principles of a sublime morality; and who hypocritically adopt the accents of the benevolent religion of Jesus? Oh Africa! Thou loud proclaimer of the rapacity, the treachery, and cruelty of civilized man! Thou everlasting monument of European and American disgrace! "Remember not against us our offences, nor the offences of our forefathers;" be tender in the great day of enquiry; and shew a Christian world thou canst suffer and forgive!

Such then, is the nature and magnitude of an evil existing among us, and for the diminution and final extinction of which, the society which I now address was instituted:—an evil which reason, justice, and the religion of Christ, and found policy, with one voice condemn:—and evil, therefore, against which, whether we consider ourselves as men, as Christians, or as patriots, we are bound to unite all our force, and to discourage by all just and equitable means. Commanded by such high authority, and solicited by so many interesting considerations, I persuade myself, that my fellow citizens will neither consider it an object unworthy of their attention, nor be deterred by all the clamours of prejudice and of avarice, from contributing their influence and their exertions to its speedy and everlasting abolition.

Many have been the proposals of benevolent men to remedy this grand evil, and to ameliorate the condition of the injured negroes. But, while I revere the very mistakes of those who have shewn themselves friends to human happiness, yet the most of these proposals appear to me incumbered with insuperable difficulties, and, in some points of view, to involve greater mischief than the original disorder designed to be cured. Immediately to emancipate *seven hundred thousand* slaves, and send them forth into society, with all the ignorance, habits, and vices of their degraded education about them, would probably produce effects more unhappy than any one is able to calculate or conceive. Nor does the plan appear much more plausible, which some have proposed, to collect, and send them back to the country, from whence they or their fathers have been violently dragged; or to form them into a colony, in some retired part of our own territory. I shall not pronounce either of these impracticable; because one of them has been attempted by an European nation, and not altogether without success. I shall not say, that such a removal would be less happy for the subjects of it, than their present condition; because, in particular instances, it might prove otherwise. But, in my view, the difficulties and objections attending such a plan, especially on a large scale, are far greater and more numerous than many sanguine speculators have seemed to suppose.

Perhaps no method can be devised, to deliver our country from the evil in question, more safe, more promising, and more easy of execution, than one which has been partially adopted in some of the states, and hitherto with all the success that could have been expected. This plan is, to frame laws, which will bring about emancipation in gradual manner; which will, at the same time, provide for the intellectual and moral cultivation of slaves, that they may be prepared to exercise the rights, and discharge the duties of citizens, when liberty shall be given them; and which, having thus fitted them for the station, will confer upon them, in due time, the privileges and dignity of other freemen. By the operation of such a plan, it is easy to see that slavery, at no great distance of time, would be banished from the United States; the mischiefs attending an universal and immediate emancipation would be, in a great measure, if not entirely, prevented; and beings, who are now gnawing the vitals, and wasting the strength of the body politic, might be converted into wholesome and useful members of it. Say not that they are unfit for the rank of citizens, and can never be made honest and industrious members of the community. Say not that their ignorance and brutality must operate as everlasting bars against their being elevated to this station. All just reasoning abjures the flimsy pretext. Make them freemen; and they will soon be found to have the manners, the character, and the virtues of freemen.

In two of our sister States, the important work of which I am speaking is already, in a great measure, achieved. In Massachusetts and New Hampshire there is not a single slave! In both they were all emancipated in a single day; and no inconvenience resulted from an event so honourable to humanity. Noble example! Happy triumph of truth and justice over a mistaken and sordid policy! When shall a similar wisdom pervade the union, and rescue our national character from disgrace? When shall this topstone be laid upon our republican fabric, which, until then, must exhibit a most defective and inconsistent appearance?

In the pursuit of this laudable and important object, you, my fellow citizens of the society whom I now address, need no exhortations of mine to inspire you with zeal—no hints from me to direct your exertions. Your labours have been so indefatigable and successful, that I have only to repeat the injunction of holy writ,—*Be not weary in well doing.* To tell this audience, that you have no wish to oppose the laws of your country, nor to invade the rights of private property—To say, that you have no desire to excite a spirit of discontent and insolence among those whom the public will, however mistaken, has devoted to slavery—To say, that your only objects, as a Society, are, to rescue those who are *unlawfully* held in bondage; to promote, by all just means, such a gradual manumission, as shall be consistent with the public good; and to cultivate a spirit of sobriety, honesty, and good behavior among the negroes of every description—To say that these are your only objects, would be condescending to obviate prejudices, and to repel calumnies, which, as I am persuaded they have no just ground, are entitled to but little attention;—prejudices and calumnies, to which the tenor of your proceedings, if examined, will furnish an abundant and honourable answer.

But, amidst all the opposition which you are called to encounter, in pursuing the objects of your association, you have grounds of encouragement and support of the most substantial kind. The good effects of your benevolent exertions are already great and extensive. You cannot look back, without the highest pleasure, on the hundreds, unlawfully held in servitude, whose chains you have broken, and whom you have elevated, in some measure, to the rank of men. You cannot contemplate, without satisfaction, the perceptible and happy influence which your proceedings have had in impressing the rude minds of the Africans, in general, among us; in giving them some ideas of the importance of their moral conduct; and in leading many of them to sober and industrious pursuits.—And above all, it must reward your past labours, and animate your future exertions, to behold a seminary for the education of the descendants of Africans, grown up under your fostering care, to a respectability which promises extensive usefulness, and which demands the gratitude and support of every good citizen.

Go on, then, my Friends and Colleagues, with unabating zeal. You are engaged in the cause of human happiness, and, therefore, in the cause of God. Be not discouraged by the magnitude of the evil which you have associated to encounter; nor by the difficulties which occur in your way. The sentiments of the wise and the good, and the fundamental principles of our government, must have a powerful operation, and they are both on your side.

The time, I trust, is not far distant, when there shall be no slavery to lament—no oppression to oppose in the United States:—when the emancipating spirit of our Constitution shall go forth in "the greatness of her strength," breaking in pieces every chain, and trampling down every unjust effort of power:—when she shall proclaim, even to the stranger and the sojourner, the moment he sets his foot upon American earth, that the ground on which he treads is sacred to Liberty; and that the air which he breathes, nourishes freemen only:—when every being, who bears the name of man, whatever complexion an equatorial Sun may have burnt upon him, and with whatever solemn injustice his rights may have been infringed, shall enjoy the privileges, and be raised to the dignity which belong to the human character.

> *Source:* Miller, Samuel, Rev. "A Discourse Delivered before the
> New York Society for Promoting the Manumission of Slaves,"
> April 12, 1797. New York: T. and J. Swords, 1797, pp. 9–23.

Introduction to "Part of Mr. O'Connor's Speech in the Irish House of Commons, in Favor of the Bill for Emancipating the Roman Catholics, 1795," from *The Columbian Orator*

In *Narrative of the Life of Frederick Douglass,* Douglass mistakenly ascribes this oration to Richard Brinsley Sheridan, the Irish playwright most famous for writing *The School for Scandal* and *The Rivals,* but it was actually delivered by Arthur O'Connor (1763–1852), a famous Irish politician who wanted Irish independence from England. As Douglass says in Chapter VII,

> In the same book, I met with one of Sheridan's mighty speeches on and in behalf of Catholic Emancipation. These [O'Connor's speech and the dialogue between a master and a slave] were choice documents to me. I read them over and over again with unabated interest. They gave tongue to interesting thoughts of my own soul, which had frequently flashed through my mind, and died away for want of utterance. . . . What I got from Sheridan was a bold denunciation of slavery, and a powerful vindication of human rights. The reading of these documents enabled me to utter my thoughts, and to meet the arguments brought forward to sustain slavery; but while they relieved me of one difficulty, they brought another even more painful than the one of which I was relieved. The more I read, the more I was led to abhor and detest my enslavers.

Catholic Emancipation meant reducing some of the restrictions placed on English Catholics, such as denying the pope's authority and denying the literal meaning of Communion. Douglass no doubt saw the parallels between Irish Catholics and African American slaves. The British minister O'Connor castigates William Pitt, who strongly opposed Catholic Emancipation. The war O'Connor condemns is the war against Napoleon, a war that cost the British much blood and treasure. The references to the American Revolution may have suggested to Douglass the need for a second revolution, this one to end slavery.

From "Part of Mr. O'Connor's Speech in the Irish House of Commons, in Favor of the Bill for Emancipating the Roman Catholics, 1795," *The Columbian Orator*

If I were to judge from the dead silence with which my speech has been received, I should suspect that what I have said was not very palatable to some men in this House. But I have not risked connexions, endeared to me by every tie of blood and friendship, to support one set of men I preference to another. I have hazarded too much, by the part I have taken, to allow the breath of calumny to taint the objects I have had in view. Immutable principles, on which the happiness and liberty of my countrymen depend, convey to my mind the only substantial boon for which great sacrifices should be made.

And I here avow myself the zealous and earnest advocate for the most unqualified emancipation of my catholic countrymen; in the hope and conviction, that the monopoly of the rights and liberties of my country, which has hitherto effectually withstood the efforts of a part of the people, must yield to the unanimous will, to the decided interest, and to the general effort of a whole united people. It is from this conviction, and it is for that transcendently important object, that, while the noble Lord and the Right Honorable Secretary, are offering to risk their lives and fortunes in support of a system that militates against the liberty of my countrymen, I will risk every thing dear to me on earth.

It is for this great object I have, I fear, more that risked connexions dearer to me than life itself. But he must be a spiritless man, and this a spiritless nation, not to resent the baseness of a British Minister [William Pitt], who has raised our hopes in order to seduce a rival to share with him the disgrace of this accursed political crusade, and blast them afterwards, that he may degrade a competitor to the station of a dependent. And, that he may destroy friendship which his nature never knew, he has sported with the feelings of a whole nation. Raising the cup with one hand to the parched lip of expectancy, he has dashed it to the earth with the other, in all the wantonness of insult, and with all the aggravation of contempt.

Does he imagine, that the people of this country, after he has tantalized them with the cheering hope of present alleviation, and of future prosperity, will tamely bear to be forced to a re-endurance of their former sufferings, and to a re-appointment of their former spoilers? Does he, from confidence of long success in debauching the human mind, exact from you, calling yourselves the representatives of the people of Ireland, to reject a bill, which has received the unanimous consent of your constituents? Or does he mean to puzzle the versatile disposition of this House, on which he has made so many successful experiments already, by distracting you between obedience to his imperious mandates, and obedience to the will of the people you should represent?

Or does he flatter himself, that he shall now succeed, because he has succeeded in betraying his own country, into exchanging that peace, by which she might have retrieved her shattered finances, for a war, in which he has squandered twenty times a greater treasure, in the course of two years, than with all his famed economy, he had been able to save, in the course of ten? For a war in which the prime youth of the world have been offered up, victims to his ambition and his schemes, as boundless and presumptuous, as ill-concerted and ill-combined for a war in which the plains of every nation in Europe have been crimsoned with oceans of blood; for a war in which his country has reaped nothing but disgrace, and which must ultimately prove her ruin?

Does he flatter himself, that he shall be enabled, Satan like, to end his political career by involving the whole empire in a civil war, from which nothing can accrue, but a doleful and barren conquest to the victor? I trust the people of England are too wise and too just to attempt to force measures upon us which they would themselves reject with disdain. I trust they have not themselves so soon forgotten the lesson they so recently learned from America, which should serve as a lasting example to nations, against employing force to subdue the spirit of a people, determined to be free!

But if they should be so weak, or so wicked, as to suffer themselves to be seduced by a man, to whose soul, duplicity and finesse are as congenial, as ingenuousness and fair dealing is a stranger, to become the instruments of supporting a few odious public characters in power and rapacity, against the interest and against the sense of a whole people; if we are to be dragooned into measures against our will, by a nation that would lose her last life, and expend her last guinea, in resenting a similar insult, if offered to herself, I trust she will find in the people of this country a spirit in no wise inferior to her own.

You are at this moment at the most awful period of your lives. The Minister of England has committed you with your country; and on this night your adoption or rejection of this bill, must determine, in the eyes of the Irish nation, which you represent, the Minister of England, or the people of Ireland! And, although you are convinced, you do not represent the people of Ireland; although you are convinced, every man of you, that you are self-created, it does not alter the nature of the contest; it is still a contest between the Minister of England and the people of Ireland; and the weakness of your title should only make you the more circumspect in the exercise of your power.

Fortunately, the views of the British Minister have been detected; fortunately, the people of this country see him in his true colours. Like the desperate gamester, who has lost his all, in the wildest schemes of aggrandizement, he looks round for some dupe to supply him with the further means of future projects; and in the crafty subtleness of his soul, he fondly imagines, he has found that easy dupe in the credulity of the Irish nation. After he has exhausted his own country in a crusade against that phantom, political opinion, he flatters himself he shall be enabled to resuscitate her at the expense of yours.

As you value the peace and happiness of your country; as you value the rights and liberties of the soil that has given you birth; and if you are not lost to every sense of feeling for your own consequence and importance as men, I call on you this night to make your stand. I call on you to rally round the independence of your country, whose existence has been so artfully assailed. Believe me, the British Minister will leave you in the lurch, when he sees that the people of this nation are too much in earnest to be tricked out of their rights, or the independence of their country.

What a display of legislation have we had on this night? Artificers who neither know the foundation on which they work, the instruments they ought to use, nor the materials required! Is it on the narrow basis of monopoly and exclusion you would erect a temple to the growing liberty of your country? If you will legislate; know, that on the broad basis of immutable justice only, you can raise a lasting, beauteous temple to the liberty of your island; whose ample base shall lodge, and whose roof shall shelter her united family from the rankling inclemency of rejection and exclusion. Know, that reason is that silken thread by which the lawgiver leads his people; and above all, know, that in the knowledge of the temper of the public mind, consists the skill and the wisdom of the legislator.

Do not imagine that the minds of your countrymen have been stationary, while that of all Europe has been rapidly progressive; for you must be blind not to perceive, that the whole European mind has undergone a revolution, neither confined to this nor to that country; but as general as the great causes which have given it birth, and still continue to feed its growth. In vain do these men, who subsist but on the abuses of the government under which they live, flatter themselves, that what we have seen these last six years is but the fever of the moment, which will pass away as soon as the patient has been let blood enough.

As well may they attempt to alter the course of nature, without altering her laws. If they would effect a counter revolution in the European mind, they must destroy commerce and its effects; they must abolish every trace of the mariner's compass; they must consign every book to the flames; they must obliterate every vestige of the invention of the press; they must destroy the conduit of intelligence, by destroying the institution of the post office. Then, and not till then, they and their abuses may live on, in all the security which ignorance, superstition, and want of concert in the people can bestow.

But while I would overwhelm with despair those men who have been nursed in the lap of venality and prostitution; who have been educated in contempt and ridicule of a love for their country; and who have grown grey in scoffing at every thing like public spirit, let me congratulate every true friend to mankind, that that commerce, which has begotten so much independence, will continue to beget more; and let me congratulate every friend to the human species, that the press, which has sent such a mass of information into the world will continue, with accelerated rapidity, to pour forth its treasures so beneficial to mankind.

It is to these great causes we are indebted, that the combination of priests and despots, which so long tyrannized over the civil and political liberty of Europe, has been dissolved. It is to these great causes we are indebted, that no priest, be his religion what it may, dares preach the doctrine which inculcates the necessity of sacrificing every right and every blessing this world can afford, as the only mean of obtaining eternal happiness in the life to come.

This was the doctrine by which the despotism of Europe was so long supported; this was the doctrine by which the political popery of Europe was supported; but the doctrine and the despotism may now sleep in the same grave, until the trumpet of ignorance, superstition, and bigotry, shall sound their resurrection.

Source: O'Connor, Arthur. "Part of Mr. O'Connor's Speech in the Irish House of Commons, in Favor of the Bill for Emancipating the Roman Catholics, 1795." *The Columbian Orator,* ed. Caleb Bingham. Boston, 1832, pp. 243–247.

Discussion Questions

1. Why do you think readers are no longer popular in America, although they commanded a large readership in nineteenth-century America?
2. Why was *The Columbian Orator* of central importance in Douglass's life?
3. Why would Douglass have been particularly attracted to the use of logic in "Dialogue between a Master and a Slave"? How devastating is his own use of logic when he attacks slavery?
4. Why would most slaveowners refuse to free their slaves even in the face of irrefutable arguments against slavery, like the ones in "Dialogue between a Master and a Slave"?
5. Do you know of similar situations today in regard to homophobia, racism, or Islamophobia?
6. Research some of Douglass's other writings to see how he himself uses the question and answer format found in "Dialogue between a Master and a Slave."
7. Account for the fact that some whites, such as Rev. Samuel Miller, understood that slavery is wrong, but still retained racist fantasies that black people are inferior to white people.

8. The Reverend Miller throws out the argument justifying slavery based on Ham's seeing his father naked in the Old Testament, without relying on modern-day anthropology, which has suggested that the ancient Jews believed incest between a father and a son was the worst sin imaginable, thus the excessive punishment for Ham seeing Noah naked. Which rejection of the Ham/Noah incident do you find most compelling, Miller's or anthropology's? Why?

9. Is Miller right that because Christ did not condemn slavery, slavery is necessarily acceptable? Why or why not?

10. Do you agree with Miller that slavery does general damage to a society's moral values? Why or why not?

11. Douglass unknowingly helped build ships in his 1845 *Narrative* that would be used in the slave trade; what does Miller say about making a living by selling human beings?

12. Why was Douglass probably so attracted to Arthur O'Connor's speech on Roman Catholic rights in Great Britain? Do you think religious persecution can be as bad as slavery? Why or why not?

13. In what other ways was eighteenth-century Great Britain like nineteenth-century America, besides the persecution of Catholics?

Suggested Readings

Bruce, Jr., Dickson D. 2001. *The Origins of African American Literature, 1680–1865.* Charlottesville: University of Virginia Press.

Butterfield, Stephen. 1974. *Black Autobiography in America.* Amherst: University of Massachusetts Press.

Diedrich, Maria. 1999. *Love across the Color Lines: Ottilie Assing and Frederick Douglass.* New York: Hill and Wang.

Douglass, Frederick. 1979. *Frederick Douglass Papers,* ed. John W. Blassingame. New Haven, CT: Yale University Press.

Frederick Douglass: New Literary and Historical Essays, ed. Eric Sundquist. 1990. Cambridge: Cambridge University Press.

Martin, Jr., Waldo E. 1984. *The Mind of Frederick Douglass.* Chapel Hill: University of North Carolina Press.

Sundquist, Eric. 1993. *To Wake the Nations: Race in the Making of American Literature.* Cambridge, MA: Belknap Press of Harvard University Press.

Wallace, Maurice D. 2002. *Constructing the Black Masculine: Identity and Ideality in African American Men's Literature and Culture, 1775–1995.* Durham, NC: Duke University Press Books.

Areas for Research

A particularly interesting area for research in *Narrative of the Life of Frederick Douglass* is to ask what changes Douglass made in the factual history behind it and also how it compares to the other two versions of his life story. In the *Narrative,* for example, Douglass does not mention that Captain Thomas Auld promised Douglass he would set him free when he turned 25, but he later acknowledges that. In the *Narrative* he also refuses to name the slave, Sandy Jenkins, who betrayed Douglass and his friends in the former's first attempt at escape, but he does name him in *The Life and Times of Frederick Douglass* (1892).

Also worth investigating is the place of *Narrative of the Life of Frederick Douglass* in nineteenth-century American history and literature. There were a number of other slave narratives published before and after 1845, when it appeared, but they were not usually translated or as popular as the *Narrative.* Research into this area could explain the keys to Douglass's success and why Harriet Jacobs's *Incidents in the Life of a Slave Girl* (1861) passed quickly into oblivion upon first publication but is now one of the most often taught works in American colleges.

Closely related to that area of research is Douglass's particular role in the cause of abolition. He urged President Lincoln to allow black soldiers to fight for the Union, and one of his sons eventually did serve, but why did Lincoln and many other Northern whites initially resist Douglass's pleas to enlist black troops in the Union cause? And why were they not paid what their white counterparts were or allowed to be promoted to the highest ranks? In other words, why did racism persist even as legal slavery was being destroyed?

A troubling but revealing area of research would be the contention that Douglass, as he grew older and much more prosperous, forgot his roots sometimes, as in putting distance between himself and some other former slaves. And concerns have been raised about his robust ego, which some of his contemporaries found offputting. Also of concern to some observers of Douglass then and now is the charge of adultery. He was close friends with Julia Griffiths and Ottilie Assing; although the charge of infidelity with the former may well be untrue, it is apparently not with the latter, who committed suicide, perhaps as a result of Douglass's remarrying someone else after his first wife died. A question for the contemporary reader is whether or not it is legitimate to view Douglass's life and work with his liaison with Assing in mind. Assuming there is truth to the suggestion that Douglass had some less than admirable traits, does that detract from his historical stature?

WHY WE READ *NARRATIVE OF THE LIFE OF FREDERICK DOUGLASS* TODAY

Narrative of the Life of Frederick Douglass is still read because, among other reasons, it is a key document in nineteenth-century American history. It makes an overwhelming case for the absolute necessity of destroying the worst social evil in American history: the institution of slavery. It asks how a society that claims to be based on liberty and equality can hold anyone in bondage because of skin color. It demonstrates the utter humanity of its hero at every turn and the rejection of that humanity because of a social system based on the ownership of human beings by the wealthy few. It demonstrates the hopelessly indefensible foundation of a system based on a few people owning many people. This is what nineteenth-century American history is largely about, with reverberations that are still being felt.

It is also still being read because it presents a powerful image of what an American can do, even against what appear to be hopeless odds. However unlikely it is that this concept can be realized in actual cases, it does fit Frederick Douglass, which gives hope to others faced with insurmountable obstacles. Douglass's *Narrative* occupies the center of that thinking in American history that determination and courage will prevail. He is like Emerson's representative men, a typical example of what determination can do.

It is still read, too, because it is the most highly regarded of all the slave narratives by many scholars. Not only are its literary qualities admired—its mastery of the conventions of this genre—but also its popular appeal to readers' appreciation of suspense, excitement, and the defeat of evil by good. Douglass shrewdly appeals to a broad popular audience as well as to influential Northern whites and blacks who could use it to support abolition. In writing the *Narrative,* Douglass wanted and received the support of men like Wendell Phillips and William Lloyd Garrison, as well that of a large popular audience. He needed backing from both sectors to bring about the destruction of slavery.

Uncle Tom's Cabin (1852)

HISTORICAL BACKGROUND

Like *Narrative of the Life of Frederick Douglass, Uncle Tom's Cabin, or, Life Among the Lowly* (1852) is deeply anchored in nineteenth-century American history, particularly that century's increasing concern with slavery, but Harriet Beecher Stowe's novel is more attuned to the effects of slavery on an entire black family than Douglass's autobiography is. Stowe also hoped that slavery could be ended without violence, but feelings ran too high for that possibility to be realized. Slavery was extremely well entrenched and far too important to the social and economic position of white owners to expect them to voluntarily free their slaves. Like most white abolitionists, though, Stowe did not believe in social equality for black people nor did she doubt the racial superiority of whites.

Three years before Stowe was born in 1811, Congress did abolish the African slave trade, but this law was often broken, and the internal slave trade persisted until 1865, thirteen years after *Uncle Tom's Cabin* was published in book form. The Missouri Compromise of 1820 made slavery illegal north of 36 degrees longitude, and Missouri was admitted as a slave

UNCLE TOM'S CABIN;

OR,

LIFE AMONG THE LOWLY.

BY

HARRIET BEECHER STOWE.

VOL. I.

Actually, Uncle Tom no more owned this cabin than he did himself. (Library of Congress)

state. A few years later, the House of Representatives passed a gag rule that required all antislavery petitions to be tabled (that rule was lifted in 1844). The year after that, the famous author of *Walden* and *Civil Disobedience,* Henry David Thoreau, refused to pay a poll tax to protest against slavery. The event that outraged abolitionists the most was the Fugitive Slave Act (1850), a law Stowe was incensed about; it required the return of fugitive slaves at the cost of fines and imprisonment of those who disobeyed. Five years after the appearance of *Uncle Tom's Cabin* (1852), the Supreme Court ruled, in one of its most infamous decisions, that neither the Constitution nor the Bill of Rights applied to black people; it is usually referred to as the *Dred Scott* decision. The Court also ruled in 1857 that the Missouri Compromise was unconstitutional. With the election of Abraham Lincoln to the presidency, and the outbreak of the Civil War the next year, slavery was doomed, and *Uncle Tom's Cabin* greatly influenced Northern opinion against slavery. Lincoln realized that to preserve the Union he would have to destroy slavery, because it was the foundation of the South's way of life; he also needed the support of thousands of black men, many of them former slaves, to defeat the South's armies.

On January 1, 1863, Lincoln delivered the Emancipation Proclamation, which said that slavery was illegal in Confederate States. The Thirteenth Amendment was passed by Congress toward the end of 1865: it abolished slavery in the country as a whole. In the following year, the Civil Rights Act gave citizenship to anyone born in the United States, and thirty years after that, in *Plessy vs. Ferguson,* the Supreme Court approved segregation as long as facilities were separate but equal, a false distinction but one that had legal standing until the 1960s.

Such a contentious legal and political battle also included other methods, some violent and some nonviolent, of overturning or supporting slavery, which is the central fact of nineteenth-century American history. For instance, a few years after Stowe was born in 1822, seventy-five slaves were killed in Louisiana during a slave revolt. In 1815, Levi Coffin, whose work appears in this chapter, established the Underground Railroad, a system for enabling slaves like Eliza and her son Harry in *Uncle Tom's Cabin,* to escape from the South to the North or Canada. One of the most famous insurrections occurred in Charleston, South Carolina, in 1822, under the leadership of Denmark Vesey. In 1829, a free black clothes dealer in Boston, David Walker, encouraged African Americans in his appeal to end slavery by any means necessary, a case he made in a very aggressive manner. Two years later, when Stowe was twenty, two key events occurred: Nat Turner led the most famous slave insurrection in American history; it erupted in Virginia and terrified whites. In the same year, William Lloyd Garrison, the most famous of all the white abolitionists (people who wanted to abolish slavery), began publishing *The Liberator.* In it, he demanded the immediate emancipation of the slaves; he wanted the North to secede, which could have been a disaster for African Americans in the South.

When Stowe was entering young womanhood, the American Anti-Slavery Society was founded. She became an active member of this group, which did so much to abolish slavery. In 1852, she published the novel that Lincoln supposedly said caused the Civil War, *Uncle Tom's Cabin.* Like Harriet Jacobs's *Incidents in the Life of a Slave Girl* (1861), it appealed to the

A powerful rendition of one of the scenes found in Levi Coffin's *Reminiscences.* He was one of the most important figures in the Underground Railroad. (Bettmann/ Corbis)

hearts of Northern mothers, who then urged their husbands to end slavery. In 1859, John Brown made his famous raid on Harpers Ferry in Virginia, for which he was hanged.

In other words, nineteenth-century American history can be seen as the inexorable move toward the destruction of slavery; Stowe's 1852 *Uncle Tom's Cabin* is a key document in this history.

ABOUT HARRIET BEECHER STOWE

Harriet Beecher Stowe's background seems to have been almost tailor-made to shape her into the author of *Uncle Tom's Cabin,* particularly the deaths of her mother and one of her own children, which made her sensitive to the plights of black mothers, and also her reading of fugitive slave narratives, which deeply informed her most famous novel. Born into a large family in Litchfield, Connecticut, she was exposed to and strongly influenced by her father, Lyman Beecher, and his deeply held Protestant views, especially his condemnation of slavery. *Uncle Tom's Cabin* shows numerous examples of her use of the principles of Christianity to attack slavery; Tom himself is particularly devout, always turning the other cheek, to the point that he lies in the background of the modern-day notion of an Uncle Tom. Stowe shrewdly appeals to the religious views of her American readers because she knew they would identify with those views and come to agree with her about slavery being an abomination.

When Stowe was in her early twenties, the family moved to Cincinnati, where she saw fugitive slaves and became aware of how contentious an issue slavery was when some of the students at a seminary her father headed left because of his weak support for abolition. In Cincinnati, she married Calvin Stowe and had many children by him, including Samuel, who died before he was a year old. This event has a direct bearing on the writing of *Uncle Tom's Cabin* because in a letter dated

Harriett Beecher Stowe is the woman President Lincoln supposedly said caused the Civil War by writing *Uncle Tom's Cabin*. (Library of Congress)

December 16, 1852, Stowe wrote to Eliza Cabot Follen, an abolitionist, that the death of Samuel enabled her to identify with slave mothers who had lost their children. Much of the appeal of her most famous novel is to the hearts of Northern white mothers who would experience the triumph of gender over race because of their maternal feelings for children. Although few white mothers in the nineteenth century would have seen Eliza, a slave mother in *Uncle Tom's Cabin,* as their social equal, they would have acknowledged she should not be separated from her child.

Stowe moved back to New England the year before the Fugitive Slave Act was passed in 1850, as Calvin Stowe joined the faculty at Bowdoin College in Maine. This law infuriated Stowe and many others because it forced Northerners to acknowledge that they were directly involved with slavery in that they were required, under stiff penalties of fines and imprisonment, to return runaway slaves to their owners. It is quite possible that had the Fugitive Slave Act not been passed, Stowe would not have written *Uncle Tom's Cabin.* Next to the Bible, Stowe's most famous novel was the best-selling book in nineteenth-century America; about three hundred thousand copies were sold in 1852 alone. In much of the twentieth century, it became widely regarded as sentimental and therefore condemned as of low literary quality because modernism was so dominant; it prized irony, narrative complexity, and indirection, but Stowe was trying to end slavery, not meet the strictures of twentieth-century literary critics. Today, *Uncle Tom's Cabin* tends to be recognized for what Stowe was trying to do rather than condemned because of modernism's censure, although many contemporary readers are leery of its racial and sexual politics: Stowe depicts African Americans as childlike and inferior to whites; Uncle Tom himself is represented as beyond saintly and completely asexual.

After 1852, she published *Key to Uncle Tom's Cabin.* In it she specifically mentions as an influence Josiah Henson's *Life of Josiah Henson,* a selection from which appears in this chapter. She also wrote another antislavery novel, *Dred: A Tale of the Great Swamp* (1856); it, too, sold well but was not nearly as influential as *Uncle Tom's Cabin.* She also turned to local color fiction, joining Sarah Orne Jewett and Mary E. Wilkins Freeman in exploring life in a particular region of America. Her personal life was marked by the death of her husband in 1886 and the fact that of her seven children, only three survived her. Childbirth put a tremendous strain on her health, and it is remarkable that she made time and gathered her energies together to do so much writing. She also had to worry about money constantly until the royalties from *Uncle Tom's Cabin* began to pour in.

HISTORICAL EXPLORATIONS

Slave Auctions

Stowe devotes two chapters of *Uncle Tom's Cabin* to one of the most rep-rehensible and cruelest parts of slavery, the slave auction. In Chapter XII, she depicts the selling of a ten-and-a-half-month old baby and its mother's subsequent suicide by drowning, in Chapter XXX the selling of a slave mother, Susan and her daughter Emmeline, the latter to Simon Legree, and the selling of Tom himself, also to Simon Legree, an utterly brutalized slave owner. Both chapters concur with the historical record that black families were frequently subjected to division without the slightest regard for the feelings of parents and children. The slave trader in Chapter XII, Mr. Haley, reassures Lucy, the mother of the infant who is sold away from her, that she will soon recover from her loss; he regards her as no more than a dog or a horse.

Whether the auction was based on the highest bid or grab and go (a buyer would pay a certain fee and then grab whatever African he chose to), the slaves were treated like chattel. They were poked, prodded, made to open their mouths so their teeth could be inspected, forced to caper or jump to determine how spry they were, made to flex their muscles, and sometimes greased to conceal wounds or so they would look health-ier. Black women were examined for their sexual potential. If Africans had just arrived on slave ships (which might have names like "Mercy" or "Charity"), they were often surrounded by slaves who spoke different languages but who were equally disoriented, not knowing what was going to happen to them. They experienced all this after surviving the hor-rors of the Middle Passage across the Atlantic from West Africa. Sharks sometimes followed slave ships because dead Africans were tossed over-board. Survivors were kept chained together below decks in unspeakable conditions.

And yet the whites at slave auctions regarded the slaves as their inferiors, not realizing that buying and selling them refuted their sense of superiority. Although there were insurrections aboard slave ships (e.g., the *Amistad* revolt and Herman Melville's treatment of another one in his tale *Benito Cereno*), for the most part the Afri-cans were kept under control because the whites had weapons, and the Africans were at their mercy. Newly arrived Africans did not speak

English, did not know who to trust, where safe haven might lie, and what was safe to eat. The whites misinterpreted all this as evidence of their superiority, not understanding that the Africans were reacting to their enslavement the same way the whites would have, had the situation been reversed.

Stowe's strategy in *Uncle Tom's Cabin* (a title indicating not ownership but only occupancy, because Tom did not own anything, including himself) was to emphasize the feelings of black people subjected to slavery in general and auctions in particular in Chapters XII and XXX. Her thinking was that white mothers would empathize with Lucy, who was so distraught at the selling of her baby that she drowned herself, that they would urge the abolition of slavery. The separation of families was beyond cruelty, as Stowe could well understand, because she was herself a mother. She realized it was ignorance about slavery and lack of moral empathy and imagination on the part of Northern whites that permitted slavery in the South to survive. She hoped to wake up white readers to the overwhelming cruelty of slavery in general and slave auctions in particular. Such an awakening led to the abolition of the "peculiar institution," as slavery in the South was often referred to.

Introduction to Solomon Northup, *Twelve Years a Slave* (1853)

Published the year after *Uncle Tom's Cabin, Twelve Years a Slave* (1853) is credited to Solomon Northup (1808–) but was probably written by a white writer named David Wilson. Stowe mentions Northup in the *Key to Uncle Tom's Cabin,* her attempt to verify the historical truth of her most famous novel. Northup was born free but was kidnapped by two con artists who promised him better employment. His case was well known in the nineteenth-century because of the outrage over a free black man being returned to slavery for twelve years. After Northup regained his freedom, he was active in the abolitionist cause and then slipped into obscurity; it is still not known when he died. His or David Wilson's version of a slave auction is particularly harrowing. Northup and his fellow slaves are described as if they are animals for sale, each with different advantages; the idea that they are human beings occurs to none of the whites, and Eliza recalls Stowe's Lucy in her intense love for her children, from whom she is permanently separated during the auction, even though one buyer agrees to purchase Emily, Eliza's daughter, along with Eliza.

From Solomon Northup, *Twelve Years a Slave* (1853)

Chapter VI

Freeman's industry—cleanliness and clothes—exercising in the show room—the dance—Bob, the fiddler—arrival of customers—slaves examined—the old gentleman of New Orleans—sale of David, Caroline and Lethe—parting of Randall and Eliza—small pox—the hospital—recovery and return to freeman's slave pen—the purchaser of Eliza, Harry and Platt—Eliza's agony on parting from little Emily.

The very amiable, pious-hearted Mr. Theophilus Freeman, partner or consignee of James H. Burch, and keeper of the slave pen in New-Orleans, was out among his animals early in the morning. With an occasional kick of the older men and women, and many a sharp crack of the whip about the ears of the younger slaves, it was not long before they were all astir, and wide awake. Mr. Theophilus Freeman bustled about in a very industrious manner, getting his property ready for the sales-room, intending, no doubt, to do that day a rousing business.

In the first place we were required to wash thoroughly, and those with beards, to shave. We were then furnished with a new suit each, cheap, but clean. The men had hat, coat, shirt, pants and shoes; the women frocks of calico, and handkerchiefs to bind about their heads. We were now conducted into a large room in the front part of the building to which the yard was attached, in order to be properly trained, before the admission of customers. The men were arranged on one side of the room, the women on the other. The tallest was placed at the head of the row, then the next tallest, and so on in the order of their respective heights. Emily was at the foot of the line of women. Freeman charged us to remember our places; exhorted us to appear smart and lively,—sometimes threatening, and again, holding out various inducements. During the day he exercised us in the art of "looking smart," and of moving to our places with exact precision.

After being fed, in the afternoon, we were again paraded and made to dance. Bob, a colored boy, who had some time belonged to Freeman, played on the violin. Standing near him, I made bold to inquire if he could play the "Virginia Reel." He answered he could not, and asked me if I could play. Replying in the affirmative, he handed me the violin. I struck up a tune, and finished it. Freeman ordered me to continue playing, and seemed well pleased, telling Bob that I far excelled him—a remark that seemed to grieve my musical companion very much.

Next day many customers called to examine Freeman's "new lot." The latter gentleman was very loquacious, dwelling at much length upon our several good points and qualities. He would make us hold up our heads, walk briskly back and forth, while customers would feel of our hands and arms and bodies, turn us about, ask us what we could do, make us open our mouths and show our teeth, precisely as a jockey examines a horse which he is about to barter for or purchase. Sometimes a man or woman was taken back to the small house in the yard, stripped, and inspected more minutely. Scars upon a slave's back were considered evidence of a rebellious or unruly spirit, and hurt his sale.

One old gentleman, who said he wanted a coachman, appeared to take a fancy to me. From his conversation with Burch, I learned he was a resident in the city. I very much desired that he would buy me, because I conceived it would not be difficult to make my escape from New Orleans on some northern vessel. Freeman asked him fifteen hundred dollars for me. The old gentleman insisted it was too much, as times were very hard. Freeman, however, declared that I was sound and healthy, of a good constitution, and intelligent. He made it a point to enlarge upon my musical attainments. The old gentleman argued quite adroitly that there was nothing extraordinary about the nigger, and finally, to my regret, went out, saying he would call again. During the day, however, a number of sales were made. David and Caroline were purchased together by a Natchez planter. They left us, grinning broadly, and in the most happy state of mind, caused by the fact of their not being separated. Lethe was sold to a planter of Baton Rouge, her eyes flashing with anger as she was led away.

The same man also purchased Randall. The little fellow was made to jump, and run across the floor, and perform many other feats, exhibiting his activity and condition. All the time the trade was going on, Eliza was crying aloud, and wringing her hands. She besought the man not to buy him, unless he also bought herself and

Emily. She promised, in that case, to be the most faithful slave that ever lived. The man answered that he could not afford it, and then Eliza burst into a paroxysm of grief, weeping plaintively. Freeman turned round to her, savagely, with his whip in his uplifted hand, ordering her to stop her noise, or he would flog her. He would not have such work—such snivelling; and unless she ceased that minute, he would take her to the yard and give her a hundred lashes. Yes, he would take the nonsense out of her pretty quick—if he didn't, might he be d—d. Eliza shrunk before him, and tried to wipe away her tears, but it was all in vain. She wanted to be with her children, she said, the little time she had to live. All the frowns and threats of Freeman, could not wholly silence the afflicted mother. She kept on begging and beseeching them, most piteously not to separate the three. Over and over again she told them how she loved her boy. A great many times she repeated her former promises—how very faithful and obedient she would be; how hard she would labor day and night, to the last moment of her life, if he would only buy them all together. But it was of no avail; the man could not afford it. The bargain was agreed upon, and Randall must go alone. Then Eliza ran to him; embraced him passionately; kissed him again and again; told him to remember her—all the while her tears falling in the boy's face like rain.

Freeman damned her, calling her a blubbering, bawling wench, and ordered her to go to her place, and behave herself; and be somebody. He swore he wouldn't stand such stuff but a little longer. He would soon give her something to cry about, if she was not mighty careful, and *that* she might depend upon.

The planter from Baton Rouge, with his new purchases, was ready to depart.

"Don't cry, mama. I will be a good boy. Don't cry," said Randall, looking back, as they passed out of the door.

What has become of the lad, God knows. It was a mournful scene indeed. I would have cried myself if I had dared.

That night, nearly all who came in on the brig *Orleans,* were taken ill. They complained of violent pain in the head and back. Little Emily—a thing unusual with her—cried constantly. In the morning, a physician was called in, but was unable to determine the nature of our complaint. While examining me, and asking questions touching my symptoms, I gave it as my opinion that it was an attack of smallpox—mentioning the fact of Robert's death as the reason of my belief. It might be so indeed, he thought, and he would send for the head physician of the hospital. Shortly, the head physician came—a small, light-haired man, whom they called Dr. Carr. He pronounced it small-pox, whereupon there was much alarm throughout the yard. Soon after Dr. Carr left, Eliza, Emmy, Harry and myself were put into a hack and driven to the hospital, a large white marble building, standing on the outskirts of the city. Harry and I were placed in a room in one of the upper stories. I became very sick. For three days I was entirely blind. While lying in this state one day, Bob came in, saying to Dr. Carr that Freeman had sent him over to inquire how we were getting on. Tell him, said the doctor, that Platt is very bad, but that if he survives until nine o'clock, he may recover.

I expected to die. Though there was little in the prospect before me worth living for, the near approach of death appalled me. I thought I could have been resigned to yield up my life in the bosom of my family, but to expire in the midst of strangers, under such circumstances, was a bitter reflection.

There were a great number in the hospital, of both sexes, and of all ages. In the rear of the building coffins were manufactured. When one died, the bell tolled—a signal to the undertaker to come and bear away the body to the potter's field. Many times, each day and night, the tolling bell sent forth its melancholy voice, announcing another death. But my time had not yet come. The crisis having passed, I began to revive, and at the end of two weeks and two days, returned with Harry to the pen, bearing upon my face the effects of the malady, which to this day continues to disfigure it. Eliza and Emily were also brought back next day in a hack, and again were we paraded in the sales-room, for the inspection and examination of purchasers. I still indulged the hope that the old gentleman in search of a coachman would call again, as he had promised, and purchase me. In that event I felt an abiding confidence that I would soon regain my liberty. Customer after customer entered, but the old gentleman never made his appearance.

At length, one day, while we were in the yard, Freeman came out and ordered us to our places, in the great room. A gentleman was waiting for us as we entered, and inasmuch as he will be often mentioned in the progress of this narrative, a description of his personal appearance, and my estimation of his character, at first sight, may not be out of place.

He was a man above the ordinary height, somewhat bent and stooping forward. He was a good-looking man, and appeared to have reached about the middle age of life. There was nothing repulsive in his presence; but on the other hand, there was something cheerful and attractive in his face, and in his tone of voice. The finer elements were all kindly mingled in his breast, as any one could see. He moved about among us, asking many questions, as to what we could do, and what labor we had been accustomed to; if we thought we would like to live with him, and would be good boys if he would buy us, and other interrogatories of like character.

After some further inspection, and conversation touching prices, he finally offered Freeman one thousand dollars for me, nine hundred for Harry, and seven hundred for Eliza. Whether the small-pox had depreciated our value, or from what cause Freeman had concluded to fall five hundred dollars from the price I was before held at, I cannot say. At any rate, after a little shrewd reflection, he announced his acceptance of the offer.

As soon as Eliza heard it, she was in an agony again. By this time she had become haggard and hollow-eyed with sickness and with sorrow. It would be a relief if I could consistently pass over in silence the scene that now ensued. It recalls memories more mournful and affecting than any language can portray. I have seen mothers kissing for the last time the faces of their dead offspring; I have seen them looking down into the grave, as the earth fell with a dull sound upon their coffins, hiding them from their eyes forever; but never have I seen such an exhibition of intense, unmeasured, and unbounded grief, as when Eliza was parted from her child. She broke from her place in the line of women, and rushing down where Emily was standing, caught her in her arms. The child, sensible of some impending danger, instinctively fastened her hands around her mother's neck, and nestled her little head upon her bosom. Freeman sternly ordered her to be quiet, but she did not heed him. He caught her by the arm and pulled her rudely, but she only clung the closer to the child. Then, with a volley of great oaths, he struck her such a heartless blow, that she staggered backward, and was like to fall. Oh! how piteously then did she beseech and beg and pray that they might not be separated. Why could they not be purchased together? Why not let her have one of her dear children? "Mercy, mercy, master!" she cried, falling on her knees. "Please, master, buy Emily. I can never work any if she is taken from me: I will die."

Freeman interfered again, but, disregarding him, she still plead most earnestly, telling how Randall had been taken from her—how she would never see him again, and now it was too bad—oh, God! it was too bad, too cruel, to take her away from Emily—her pride—her only darling, that could not live, it was so young, without its mother!

Finally, after much more of supplication, the purchaser of Eliza stepped forward, evidently affected, and said to Freeman he would buy Emily, and asked him what her price was.

"What is her price? Buy her?" was the responsive interrogatory of Theophilus Freeman. And instantly answering his own inquiry, he added, "I won't sell her. She's not for sale."

The man remarked he was not in need of one so young—that it would be of no profit to him, but since the mother was so fond of her, rather than see them separated, he would pay a reasonable price. But to this humane proposal Freeman was entirely deaf. He would not sell her then on any account whatever. There were heaps and piles of money to be made of her, he said, when she was a few years older. There were men enough in New Orleans who would give five thousand dollars for such an extra, handsome, fancy piece as Emily would be, rather than not get her. No, no, he would not sell her then. She was a beauty—a picture—a doll—one of the regular bloods—none of your thick-lipped, bullet-headed, cotton-picking niggers—if she was might he be d—d.

When Eliza heard Freeman's determination not to part with Emily, she became absolutely frantic.

"I will not go without her. They shall not take her from me," she fairly shrieked, her shrieks commingling with the loud and angry voice of Freeman, commanding her to be silent.

Meantime Harry and myself had been to the yard and returned with our blankets, and were at the front door ready to leave. Our purchaser stood near us, gazing at Eliza with an expression indicative of regret at having bought her at the expense of so much sorrow. We waited some time, when, finally, Freeman, out of patience, tore

Emily from her mother by main force, the two clinging to each other with all their might.

"Don't leave me, mama—don't leave me," screamed the child, as its mother was pushed harshly forward; "Don't leave me—come back, mama," she still cried, stretching forth her little arms imploringly. But she cried in vain. Out of the door and into the street we were quickly hurried. Still we could hear her calling to her mother, "Come back—don't leave me—come back, mama," until her infant voice grew faint and still more faint, and gradually died away as distance intervened, and finally was wholly lost.

Eliza never after saw or heard of Emily or Randall. Day nor night, however, were they ever absent from her memory. In the cotton field, in the cabin, always and everywhere, she was talking of them—often to them, as if they were actually present. Only when absorbed in that illusion, or asleep, did she ever have a moment's comfort afterwards.

She was no common slave, as has been said. To a large share of natural intelligence which she possessed, was added a general knowledge and information on most subjects. She had enjoyed opportunities such as are afforded to very few of her oppressed class. She had been lifted up into the regions of a higher life. Freedom—freedom for herself and for her offspring, for many years had been her cloud by day, her pillar of fire by night. In her pilgrimage through the wilderness of bondage, with eyes fixed upon that hope-inspiring beacon, she had at length ascended to "the top of Pisgah," and beheld "the land of promise." In an unexpected moment she was utterly overwhelmed with disappointment and despair. The glorious vision of liberty faded from her sight as they led her away into captivity. Now "she weepeth sore in the night, and tears are on her cheeks: all her friends have dealt treacherously with her: they have become her enemies."

Source: Northup, Solomon. *Twelve Years a Slave.* New York: Miller, Orton and Mulligan, 1855, pp. 78–88.

Introduction to Henry Bibb, *Narrative of the Life and Adventures of Henry Bibb, an American Slave* (1849)

Henry Bibb (1815–1854) was apparently the son of a white man named James Bibb, who was a state senator from Kentucky; his mother was a slave. Henry Bibb escaped from slavery numerous times and was recaptured numerous times, but he eventually escaped to Canada, where he launched the first African American newspaper, *Voice of the Fugitive.* Bibb was also very active in the cause of abolition, giving many speeches against slavery. His autobiography is notable for his passing as a slave trader himself (Bibb could sometimes pass as white). He had to be careful about revealing his intelligence to whites because they would be leery that he would escape, and they were right. Bibb was unusual in his support for establishing a black colony in Canada, because most black abolitionists argued that former slaves should stay in the United States rather than start life over in Canada or the African country of Liberia.

From Henry Bibb, *Narrative of the Life and Adventures of Henry Bibb, an American Slave* (1849)

Chapter IX

Our arrival and examination at Vicksburg.—An account of slave sales.—Cruel punishment with the paddle.—Attempts to sell myself by Garrison's direction.—Amusing interview with a slave buyer.— Deacon Whitfield's examination.—He purchases the family.— Character of the Deacon.

When we arrived at the city of Vicksburg, he [Garrison, Bibb's owner] intended to sell a portion of his slaves there, and stopped for three weeks trying to sell. But he met with very poor success.

We had there to pass through an examination, or inspection by a city officer, whose business it was to inspect slave property that was brought to that Market for sale. He examined our backs to see if we had been much scarred by the lash. He examined our limbs, to see whether we were inferior.

As it is hard to tell the ages of slaves, they look in their mouths at their teeth, and prick up the skin on the back of their hands, and if the person is very far advanced in life, when the skin is pricked up, the pucker will stand up so many seconds on the back of the hand.

But the most rigorous examinations of slaves by those slave inspectors, is on the mental capacity. If they are found to be very intelligent, this is pronounced the most objectionable of all other qualities connected with the life of a slave. In fact, it undermines the whole fabric of his chattelhood; it prepares for what slave-holders are pleased to pronounce the unpardonable sin when committed by a slave. It lays the foundation for running away, and going to Canada. They also see in it a love for freedom, patriotism, insurrection, bloodshed, and exterminating war against American slavery.

Hence they are very careful to inquire whether a slave who is for sale can read or write. This question has been asked me often by slave traders, and cotton planters, while I was there for market. After conversing with me, they have sworn by their Maker, that they would not have me among their negroes; and that they saw the devil in my eye; I would run away, &c.

I have frequently been asked also, if I had ever answer run away; but Garrison would generally answer this question for me in the negative. He could have sold my little family without any trouble, for the sum of one thousand dollars. But for fear he might not get me off at so great an advantage, as the people did not like my appearance, he could do better by selling us all together. They all wanted my wife, while but very few wanted me. He asked twenty-five hundred dollars, but was not able to get us off at that price.

He tried to speculate on my Christian character. He tried to make it appear that I was so pious and honest that I would not run away for ill treatment; which was a gross mistake, for I never had religion enough to keep me from running away from slavery in my life.

But we were taken from Vicksburgh, to the city of New Orleans, where we were to be sold at any rate. We were taken to a trader's yard or a slave prison on the corner of St. Joseph street. This was a common resort for slave traders, and planters who wanted to buy slaves; and all classes of slaves were kept there for sale, to be sold in private or public—young or old, males or females, children or parents, husbands or wives.

Every day at 10 o'clock they were exposed for sale. They had to be in trim for showing themselves to the public for sale. Every one's head had to be combed, and their faces washed, and those who were inclined to look dark and rough, were compelled to wash in greasy dish water, to look slick and lively.

When spectators would come in the yard, the slaves were ordered out to form a line. They were made to stand up straight, and look as sprightly as they could; and when they were asked a question, they had to answer it as promptly as they could, and try to induce the spectators to buy them. If they failed to do this, they were severely paddled after the spectators were gone. The object for using the paddle in the place of a lash was, to conceal the marks which would be made by the flogging. And the object for flogging under such circumstances, is to make the slaves anxious to be sold.

The paddle is made of a piece of hickory timber, about one inch thick, three inches in width, and about eighteen inches in length. The part [that] is applied to the flesh is bored full of quarter inch auger holes, and every time this is applied to the flesh of the victim, the blood gushes through the holes of the paddle, or a blister makes its appearance. The persons who are thus flogged, are always stripped naked, and their hands tied together. They are then bent over double, their knees are forced between their elbows, and a stick is put through between the elbows and the bend of the legs in order to hold the victim in that position, while the paddle is applied to those parts of the body which would not be so likely to be seen by those who wanted to buy slaves.

I was kept in this prison for several months, and no one would buy me for fear I would run away. One day while I was in this prison, Garrison got mad with my wife, and took her off in one of the rooms, with his paddle in hand, swearing that he would paddle her; and I could afford her no protection at all, while the strong arm of the law, public opinion and custom, were all against me. I have often heard Garrison say, that he had rather paddle a female, than eat when he was hungry—that it was music for him to hear them scream, and to see their blood run.

After the lapse of several months, he found that he could not dispose of my person to a good advantage, while he kept me in that prison confined among the other slaves. I do not speak with vanity when I say the contrast was so great between myself and ordinary slaves, from the fact that I had enjoyed superior advantages, to which I have already referred. They have their slaves classed off and numbered.

Garrison came to me one day and informed me that I might go out through the city and find myself a master. I was to go to the Hotels, boarding houses, &c.—tell them that my wife was a good cook, wash-woman, &c.,—and that I was a good dining room servant, carriage driver, or porter—and in this way I might find some gentleman who would buy us both; and that this was the only hope of our being sold together.

But before starting me out, he dressed me up in a suit of his old clothes, so as to make me look respectable, and I was so much better dressed than usual that I felt quite gay. He would not allow my wife to go out with me however, for fear we might get away. I was out every day for several weeks, three or four hours in each day, trying to find a new master, but without success.

Many of the old French inhabitants have taken slaves for their wives, in this city, and their own children for their servants. Such commonly are called Creoles. They are better treated than other slaves, and I resembled this class in appearance so much that the French did not want me. Many of them set their mulatto children free, and make slaveholders of them.

At length one day I heard that there was a gentleman in the city from the State of Tennessee, to buy slaves. He had brought down two rafts of lumber for market, and I thought if I could get him to buy me with my family, and take us to Tennessee, from there, I would stand a better opportunity to run away again and get to Canada, than I would from the extreme South.

So I brushed up myself and walked down to the river's bank, where the man was pointed out to me, standing on board of his raft, I approached him, and after passing the usual compliments I said:

"Sir, I understand that you wish to purchase a lot of servants and I have called to know if it is so."

He smiled and appeared to be much pleased at my visit on such laudable business, supposing me to be a slave trader. He commenced rubbing his hands together, and replied by saying: "Yes sir, I am glad to see you. It is a part of my business here to buy slaves, and if I could get you to take my lumber in part pay I should like to buy four or five of your slaves at any rate. What kind of slaves have you, sir?"

After I found that he took me to be a slave trader I knew that it would be of no use for me to tell him that I was myself a slave looking for a master, for he would have doubtless brought up the same objection that others had brought up,—that I was too white; and that they were afraid that I could read and write; and would never serve as a slave, but run away. My reply to the question respecting the quality of my slaves was, that I did not think his lumber would suit me—that I must have the cash for my negroes, and turned on my heel and left him!

I returned to the prison and informed my wife of the fact that I had been taken to be a slaveholder. She thought that in addition to my light complexion, my being dressed up in Garrison's old slave trading clothes might have caused the man to think that I was a slave trader, and she was afraid that we should yet be separated if I should not succeed in finding somebody to buy us.

Every day to us was a day of trouble, and every night brought new and fearful apprehensions that the golden link which binds together husband and wife might be broken by the heartless tyrant before the light of another day.

Deep has been the anguish of my soul when looking over my little family during the silent hours of the night, knowing the great danger of our being sold off at auction the next day and parted forever. That this might not come to pass, many have been the tears and prayers which I have offered up to the God of Israel that we might be preserved.

While waiting here to be disposed of, I heard of one Francis Whitfield, a cotton planter, who wanted to buy slaves. He was represented to be a very pious soul, being a deacon of a Baptist church. As the regulations, as well as public opinion generally, were against slaves meeting for religious worship, I thought it would give me a better opportunity to attend to my religious duties should I fall into the hands of this deacon.

So I called on him and tried to show to the best advantage, for the purpose of inducing him to buy me and my family. When I approached him, I felt much pleased at his external appearance— I addressed him in the following words as well as I can remember:

"Sir, I understand you are desirous of purchasing slaves?"

With a very pleasant smile, he replied, "Yes, I do want to buy some, are you for sale?"

"Yes sir, with my wife and one child."

Garrison had given me a note to show wherever I went, that I was for sale, speaking of my wife and child, giving us a very good character of course—and I handed him the note.

After reading it over he remarked, "I have a few questions to ask you, and if you will tell me the truth like a good boy, perhaps I may buy you with your family. In the first place, my boy, you are a little too near white. I want you to tell me now whether you can read or write?"

My reply was in the negative.

"Now I want you to tell we [*sic*] whether you have run away? Don't tell me no stories now, like a good fellow, and perhaps I may buy you."

But as I was not under oath to tell him the whole truth, I only gave him a part of it, by telling him that I had run away once.

He appeared to be pleased at that, but cautioned me to tell him the truth, and asked me how long I stayed away, when I ran off?

I told him that I was gone a month.

He assented to this by a bow of his head, and making a long grunt saying, "That's right, tell me the truth like a good boy."

The whole truth was that I had been off in the state of Ohio, and other free states, and even to Canada; besides this I was notorious for running away, from my boyhood.

I never told him that I had been a runaway longer than one month—neither did I tell him that I had not run away more than once in my life; for these questions he never asked me.

I afterwards found him to be one of the basest hypocrites that I ever saw. He looked like a saint—talked like the best of slave holding Christians, and acted at home like the devil.

When he saw my wife and child, he concluded to buy us. He paid for me twelve hundred dollars, and one thousand for my wife and child. He also bought several other slaves at the same time, and took them home with him. His residence was in the parish of Claiborn, fifty miles up from the mouth of Red River.

When we arrived there, we found his slaves poor, ragged, stupid, and half-starved. The food he allowed them per week, was one peck of corn for each grown person, one pound of pork, and sometimes molasses. This was all that they were allowed and if they got more they stole it.

He had one of the most cruel overseers to be found in that section of country. He weighed and measured out to them, their week's allowance of food every Sabbath morning. The overseer's horn was sounded two hours before daylight for them in the morning, in order that they should be ready for work before daylight. They were worked from daylight until after dark, without stopping but one half hour to eat or rest, which was at noon. And at the busy season of the year, they were compelled to work just as hard on the Sabbath, as on any other day.

Source: Bibb, Henry. *Narrative of the Life and Adventures of Henry Bibb.* New York: Author, 1842, pp. 101–111.

Introduction of Sojourner Truth, *Narrative of Sojourner Truth: A Northern Slave* (1850)

Sojourner Truth (1797–1883) is remembered most for her speech, "Ar'n't I a Woman?," delivered in 1851 to the Women's Rights Convention in Akron, Ohio. When a supporter of slavery bet $40 that Truth was a man, she bared a breast to prove him wrong. A tireless speaker for the abolition of slavery, she also supported women's rights, and although illiterate, she produced an autobiography with the help of a white woman named Olive Gilbert. Six feet tall, with a powerful speaking voice, Truth was one of the most impressive public speakers in nineteenth-century America. Her commanding personality and strong religious faith

The opposite of Stowe's humble Uncle Tom, Truth demanded in powerful and outspoken speeches that black women should be treated like human beings. (Library of Congress)

combined to produce one of the most important opponents of slavery during the abolition period. The excerpt from *Narrative of Sojourner Truth* indicates that on occasion there were auctions with an element of humanity: Truth's parents were auctioned off together so that her mother could care for her aged father, who had no market value.

From Sojourner Truth, *Narrative of Sojourner Truth: A Northern Slave* (1850)

The Auction

At length, the never-to-be-forgotten day of the terrible auction arrived, when the "slaves, horses, and other cattle" of Charles Ardinburgh [Truth's former owner], deceased, were to be put under the hammer, and again change masters. Not only Isabella [Truth's first name at birth] and Peter, but their mother, were now destined to the auction block, and would have been struck off with the rest to the highest bidder, but for the following circumstance: A question arose among the heirs, "Who shall be burthened with Bomefree [Truth's father], when we have sent away his faithful Mau-mau Bett [Truth's mother]?" He was becoming weak and infirm; his limbs were painfully rheumatic and distorted–more from exposure and hardship than from old age, though he was several years older than Mau-mau Bett: he was no longer considered of value, but must soon be a burthen and care to some one. After some contention on the point at issue, none being willing to be burthened with him, it was finally agreed, as most expedient for the heirs, that the price of Mau-mau Bett should be sacrificed, and she receive her freedom, on condition that she take care of and support her faithful James,–faithful, not only to her as a husband, but proverbially faithful as a slave to those who would not willingly sacrifice a dollar for his comfort, now that he had commenced his descent into the dark vale of decrepitude and suffering. This important decision was received as joyful news indeed to our ancient couple, who were the objects of it, and who were trying to prepare their hearts for a severe struggle, and one altogether new to them, as they had never before been separated; for, though ignorant, helpless, crushed in spirit, and weighed down with hardship and cruel bereavement, they were still human, and their human hearts beat within them with as true an affection as ever caused a human heart to beat. And their anticipated separation now, in the decline of life, after the last child had been torn from them, must have been truly appalling. Another privilege was granted them–that of remaining occupants of the same dark, humid cellar I have before described: otherwise, they were to support themselves as they best could. And as her mother was still able to do considerable work, and her father a little, they got on for some time very comfortably. The strangers who rented the house were humane people, and very kind to them; they were not rich, and owned no slaves. How long this state of things continued, we are unable to say, as Isabella had not then sufficiently cultivated her organ of time to calculate years, or even weeks or hours. But she thinks her mother must have lived several years after the death of Master Charles. She remembers going to visit her parents some three or four times before the death of her mother, and a good deal of time seemed to her to intervene between each visit.

At length her mother's health began to decline–a fever-sore made its ravages on one of her limbs, and the palsy began to shake her frame; still, she and James tottered about, picking up a little here and there, which, added to the mites contributed by their kind neighbors, sufficed to sustain life, and drive famine from the door.

Source: Truth, Sojourner. *Narrative of Sojourner Truth.* Boston: Author, 1875 (1850), pp. 18–20.

Discussion Questions

1. Why did Solomon Northup emphasize the separation of mothers and their children in his depiction of a slave auction in *Twelve Years a Slave?*
2. What is the effect of Northup's understated, restrained tone in his narration?
3. Contrast Northup's relation of his adventures to the film version (2013): does the film do justice to Northup? Why or why not?
4. How capable a person was Northup? Does he encounter any whites who have his range of knowledge and abilities?
5. How does Bibb's account of a slave auction compare to Northup's?
6. How much difference does it make in Bibb's experience of slavery that he was a "voluntary" black man, that is, that he could pass for white?
7. How does Bibb's version of a slave auction compare to Stowe's in *Uncle Tom's Cabin?* To Northup's?
8. Why would Truth have included a humane aspect of something as cruel as a slave auction? Would that have played into the hands of defenders of slavery?
9. Does gender seem to make much difference in Truth's version of a slave auction if you compare it to Northup's and Bibb's?
10. Does Truth's version carry more weight than Northup's and Bibb's because she is much better known than they are? If so, is that warranted?
11. Which of the three reports of slave auctions is the most moving? Why?
12. How could slave owners and buyers have tolerated such heartless treatment of black people?
13. Do you think the United States should pay reparations to black people today for what happened to their ancestors? Why or why not?

Suggested Readings

Ammons, Elizabeth. 2007. *Harriet Beecher Stowe's* Uncle Tom's Cabin: *A Casebook.* New York: Oxford University Press.

Ashton, Jean. 1977. *Harriet Beecher Stowe: A Reference Guide.* Boston: G. K. Hall Company.

Belasco, Susan. 2009. *Stowe in Her Own Time: A Biographical Chronicle of Her Life, Drawn from Recollections, Interviews, and Memoirs.* Iowa City: University of Iowa Press.

Brown, Gillian. "Getting in the Kitchen with Dinah: Domestic Politics in *Uncle Tom's Cabin." American Quarterly* 36 (1984): 502–523.

Fielder, Leslie. 1981. "New England and the Invention of the South." *American Literature: The New England Heritage,* eds. James Nagel and Richard Astro. New York: Garland Press.

Foster, Charles H. 1954. *The Rungless Ladder: Harriet Beecher Stowe and New England Puritanism.* Durham, NC: Duke University Press.

Grigsby, John. "Jesus, Judas, Job or 'Jes a Happy Ole Nigga': Or, Will the Real 'Uncle Tom' Please Stand Up?" *Publications of the Mississippi Philological Association* 5 (1986): 51–62.

Hedrick, Joan. 1994. *Harriet Beecher Stowe: A Life.* New York: Oxford University Press.

Hildreth, Margaret Holbrook. 1976. *Harriet Beecher Stowe: A Bibliography.* North Haven, CT: Archon Books.

Kirkham, Edwin Bruce. 1977. *The Building of "Uncle Tom's Cabin."* Knoxville: University of Tennessee Press.

Lang, Amy Schrager. "Slavery and Sentimentalism: The Strange Case of Augustine St. Clare." *Women's Studies* 12 (1986): 31–54.

Meers, Sarah. 2005. *Uncle Tom Mania: Slavery, Minstrelsy, and Transatlantic Culture in the 1850s.* Athens: University of Georgia Press.

Stowe, Harriet Beecher. 1856, 2006. *Dred: A Tale of the Great Dismal Swamp.* Chapel Hill: University of North Carolina Press.

Weinstein, Cindy. 2004. *The Cambridge Companion to Harriet Beecher Stowe.* New York: Cambridge University Press.

White, Barbara A. 2003. *The Beecher Sisters.* New Haven, CT: Yale University Press.

Winks, Robin. 1985. "The Making of a Fugitive Slave Narrative: Josiah Henson and Uncle Tom: A Case Study." *The Slave's Narrative,* eds. Charles T. Davis and Henry Louis Gates, Jr. New York: Oxford University Press.

HISTORICAL EXPLORATIONS

Underground Railroad

The Underground Railroad was neither underground nor a railroad; it was rather an aboveground network of escape routes from the Northern-border states, like Ohio, to the Canadian border and states where slavery was illegal by the time of the Civil War. Stowe had talked to runaway slaves when she lived in Ohio and helped some of them escape. "Railroad" was a figure of speech for the system that helped Stowe's Eliza, George, and Harry, as well as thousands of actual slaves, escape. Safe houses, where runaways could hide and sleep, were comparable to train stations, abolitionists to train conductors, and the fugitive slaves themselves to passengers. The "passengers" were often cold, wet, hungry, exhausted, terrified, sick, malnourished, and destitute, so the "conductors" and their assistants would have to meet those needs before anything else could be done; people who helped runaway slaves were often putting their lives and livelihood at stake, especially after the passage of the Fugitive Slave Law in 1850, which mandated that citizens of free states were subject to fines or imprisonment if they helped fugitive slaves escape. The "trains" usually ran at night, but the locomotive did not whistle. The most famous "conductor" was Harriet Tubman (1820–1913), herself a successful fugitive, who helped several hundred runaway slaves; she also served as a Union spy during the Civil War.

Introduction to Levi Coffin, *Reminiscences of Levi Coffin* (1880)

Levi Coffin (1798–1877) was one of the most important figures in the Underground Railroad; in fact, sometimes he is referred to as the president of the Underground Railroad. He risked his life and his businesses to help several thousand slaves escape, often by hiding them in his own houses. He and his wife were devout Quakers who believed slavery was incompatible with Christianity. As the excerpt from Coffin's autobiography indicates, he was fearless in his dedication to ending slavery. He spent a considerable amount of his own money to support the Underground Railroad, which required substantial financial support because of the need for food, clothing, shoes, and medicine for the fugitives. Without Levi Coffin, the Underground Railroad would not have been nearly as successful. Harriet Beecher Stowe knew the Coffins when they were living in Cincinnati, and Eliza's escape in *Uncle Tom's Cabin* may be based on an actual escape of a black mother and her baby that Coffin assisted in.

From Levi Coffin, *Reminiscences of Levi Coffin* (1880)

In the year 1836, I built an oil mill and manufactured linseed oil. Notwithstanding all this multiplicity of business, I was never too busy to engage in Underground Railroad affairs. Soon after we located at Newport, [Indiana], I found that we were on a line of the U. G. R. R. Fugitives often passed through that place, and generally stopped among the colored people. There was in that neighborhood a number of families of free colored people, mostly from North Carolina, who were the descendants of slaves who had been liberated by Friends [Quakers] many years before, and sent to free States at the expense of North Carolina Yearly Meeting. I learned that the fugitive slaves who took refuge with these people were often pursued and captured, the colored people not being very skillful in concealing them, or shrewd in making arrangements to forward them to Canada. I was pained to hear of the capture of these fugitives, and inquired of some of the Friends in our village why they did not take them in and secrete them, when they were pursued, and then aid them on their way to Canada? I found that they were afraid of the penalty of the law. I told them that I read in the Bible when I was a boy that it was right to take in the stranger and administer to those in distress, and that I thought it was always safe to do right. The Bible, in bidding us to feed the hungry and clothe the naked, said nothing about color, and I should try to follow out the teachings of that good book. I was willing to receive and aid as many fugitives as were disposed to come to my house. I knew that my wife's feelings and sympathies regarding this matter were the same as mine, and that she was willing to do her part. It soon became known to the colored people in our neighborhood and others, that our house was a depot where the hunted and harassed fugitive journeying northward, on the Underground Railroad, could find succor and sympathy. It also became known at other depots on the various lines that converged at Newport.

In the winter of 1826–27, fugitives began to come to our house, and as it became more widely known on different routes that the slaves fleeing from bondage would find a welcome and shelter at our house, and be forwarded safely on their journey, the number increased. Friends in the neighborhood, who had formerly stood aloof from the work, fearful of the penalty of the law, were encouraged to engage in it when they saw the fearless manner in which I acted, and the success that attended my efforts. They would contribute to clothe the fugitives, and would aid in forwarding them on their way, but were timid about sheltering them under their roof; so that part of the work devolved on us. Some seemed really glad to see the work go on, if somebody else would do it. Others doubted the propriety of it, and tried to discourage me, and dissuade me from running such risks. They manifested great concern for my safety and pecuniary interests, telling me that such a course of action would injure my business and perhaps ruin me; that I ought to consider the welfare of my family; and warning me that my life was in danger, as there were many threats made against me by the slave-hunters and those who sympathized with them.

After listening quietly to these counselors, I told them that I felt no condemnation for anything that I had ever done for the fugitive slaves. If by doing my duty and endeavoring to fulfill the injunctions of the Bible, I injured my business, then let my business go. As to my safety, my life was in the hands of my Divine Master, and I felt that I had his approval. I had no fear of the danger that seemed to threaten my life or my business. If I was faithful to duty, and honest and industrious, I felt that I would be preserved, and that I could make enough to support my family. At one time there came to see me a good old Friend, who was apparently very deeply concerned for my welfare. He said he was as much opposed to slavery as I was, but thought it very wrong to harbor fugitive slaves. No one there knew of what crimes they were guilty; they might have killed their masters, or committed some other atrocious deed, then those who sheltered them, and aided them in their escape from justice would indirectly be accomplices. He mentioned other objections which he wished me to consider, and then talked for some time, trying to convince me of the errors of my ways. I heard him patiently until he had relieved his mind of the burden upon it, and then asked if he thought the Good Samaritan [in the Bible, he treated everyone as his neighbor] stopped to inquire whether the man who fell among thieves was guilty of any crime before he attempted to help him? I asked him if he were to see a stranger who had fallen into the ditch would he not help him out until satisfied that he had committed no atrocious deed? These, and many other questions which I put to him, he did not seem able to answer satisfactorily. He was so perplexed and confused that I really pitied the good old man, and advised him to go home and read his Bible thoroughly, and pray over it, and I thought his concern about my aiding fugitive slaves would be removed from his mind, and that he would feel like helping me in the work. We parted in good feeling, and he always manifested warm friendship toward me until the end of his days.

Many of my pro-slavery customers left me for a time, my sales were diminished, and for a while my business prospects were discouraging, yet my faith was not shaken, nor my efforts for the slaves lessened. New customers soon came in to fill the places of those who had left me. New settlements were rapidly forming to the north of us, and our own was filling up with emigrants from North Carolina, and other States. My trade increased, and I enlarged my business. I was blessed in all my efforts and succeeded beyond my expectations. The Underground Railroad business increased as time advanced, and it was attended with heavy expenses, which I could not have borne had not my affairs been prosperous. I found it necessary to keep a team and a wagon always at command, to convey the fugitive slaves on their journey. Sometimes, when we had large companies, one or two other teams and wagons were required. These journeys had to be made at night, often through deep mud and bad roads, and along byways that were seldom traveled. Every precaution to evade pursuit had to be used, as the hunters were often on the track, and sometimes ahead of the slaves. We had different routes for sending the fugitives to depots, ten, fifteen, or twenty miles distant, and when we heard of slave-hunters having passed on one road, we forwarded our passengers by another.

In some instances where we learned that the pursuers were ahead of them, we sent a messenger and had the fugitives brought back to my house to remain in concealment until the bloodhounds in human shape had lost the trail and given up the pursuit.

I soon became extensively known to the friends of the slaves, at different points on the Ohio River, where fugitives generally crossed, and to those northward of us on the various routes leading to Canada. Depots were established on the different lines of the Underground Railroad, south and north of Newport, and a perfect understanding was maintained between those who kept them. Three principal lines from the South converged at my house; one from Cincinnati, one from Madison, and one from Jeffersonville, Indiana. The roads were always in running order, the connections were good, the conductors active and zealous, and there was no lack of passengers. Seldom a week passed without our receiving passengers by this mysterious road. We found it necessary to be always prepared to receive such company and properly care for them. We knew not what night or what hour of the night we would be roused from slumber by a gentle rap at the door. That was the signal announcing the arrival of a train of the Underground Railroad, for the locomotive did not whistle, nor make any unnecessary noise. I have often been awakened by this signal, and sprang out of bed in the dark and opened the door. Outside in the cold or rain, there would be a two-horse wagon loaded with fugitives, perhaps the greater part of them women and children. I would invite them, in a low tone, to come in, and they would follow me into the darkened house without a word, for we knew not who might be watching and listening. When they were all safely inside and the door fastened, I would cover the windows, strike a light and build a good fire. By this time my wife would be up and preparing victuals for them, and in a short time the cold and hungry fugitives would be made comfortable. I would accompany the conductor of the train to the stable, and care for the horses, that had, perhaps, been driven twenty-five or thirty miles that night, through the cold and rain. The fugitives would rest on pallets before the fire the rest of the night. Frequently, wagon-loads of passengers from the different lines have met at our house, having no previous knowledge of each other. The companies varied in number, from two or three fugitives to seventeen.

The care of so many necessitated much work and anxiety on our part, but we assumed the burden of our own will and bore it cheerfully. It was never too cold or stormy, or the hour of night too late for my wife to rise from sleep, and provide food and comfortable lodging for the fugitives. Her sympathy for those in distress never tired, and her efforts in their behalf never abated. This work was kept up during the time we lived at Newport, a period of more than twenty years. The number of fugitives varied considerably in different years, but the annual average was more than one hundred. They generally came to us destitute of clothing, and were often barefooted. Clothing must be collected and kept on hand, if possible, and money must be raised to buy shoes, and purchase goods to make garments for women and children. The young ladies in the neighborhood organized a sewing society, and met at our house frequently, to make clothes for the fugitives.

Sometimes when the fugitives came to us destitute, we kept them several days, until they could be provided with comfortable clothes. This depended on the circumstances of danger. If they had come a long distance and had been out several weeks or months—as was sometimes the case—and it was not probable that hunters were on their track, we thought it safe for them to remain with us until fitted for traveling through the thinly settled country to the North. Sometimes fugitives have come to our house in rags, foot-sore and toil-worn, and almost wild, having been out for several months traveling at night, hiding in canebrakes or thickets during the day, often being lost and making little headway at night, particularly in cloudy weather, when the north star could not be seen, sometimes almost perishing for want of food, and afraid of every white person they saw, even after they came into a free State, knowing that slaves were often captured and taken back after crossing the Ohio River.

Such as these we have kept until they were recruited in strength, provided with clothes, and able to travel. When they first came to us they were generally unwilling to tell their stories, or let us know what part of the South they came from. They would not give their names, or the names of their masters, correctly, fearing that they would be betrayed. In several instances fugitives came to our house sick from exhaustion and exposure, and lay several weeks. One case was that of a woman and her two children—little girls. Hearing that her children were to be sold away from her, she determined to take them with her and attempt to reach Canada. She had heard that Canada was a place where all were free, and that by traveling toward the north star she could reach it. She managed to get over the Ohio River with her two little girls, and then commenced her long and toilsome journey northward. Fearing to travel on the road, even at night, lest she should meet somebody, she made her way through the woods and across fields, living on fruits and green corn, when she could procure them, and sometimes suffering severely for lack of food. Thus she wandered on, and at last reached our neighborhood. Seeing a cabin where some colored people lived she made her way to it. The people received her kindly, and at once conducted her to our house. She was so exhausted by the hardships of her long journey, and so weakened by hunger, having denied herself to feed her children, that she soon became quite sick. Her children were very tired, but soon recovered their strength, and were in good health. They had no shoes nor clothing except what they had on, and that was in tatters. Dr. Henry H. Way [local doctor] was called in, and faithfully attended the sick woman, until her health was restored. Then the little party were provided with good clothing and other comforts, and were sent on their way to Canada.

Dr. Way was a warm friend to the fugitive slaves, and a hearty co-worker with me in anti-slavery matters. The number of those who were friendly to the fugitives increased in our neighborhood as time passed on. Many were willing to aid in clothing them and helping them on their way, and a few were willing to aid in secreting them, but the depot seemed to be established at my house.

Notwithstanding the many threats of slave-hunters and the strong prejudices of pro-slavery men, I continued to prosper and gained a business influence in the community. Some of my customers, who had left me several years before on account of my anti-slavery sentiments, began to deal with me again. I had been elected a director in the Richmond branch of the State Bank, and was re-elected annually for six or seven years, by the stockholders, to represent our district. When any one wished accommodation from the bank, much depended on the director from the district where the applicant lived. His word or influence would generally decide the matter. The remembrance of this seemed to hold a check on some of the pro-slavery men of our neighborhood. They wished to retain my friendship, and did not openly oppose my U. G. R. R. work as they might otherwise have done. My business influence no doubt operated in some degree to shield me from the attacks of the slave-hunters. These men often threatened to kill me, and at various times offered a reward for my head. I often received anonymous letters warning me that my store, pork-house, and dwelling would be burned to the ground, and one letter, mailed in Kentucky, informed me that a body of armed men were then on their way to Newport to destroy the town. The letter named the night in which the work would be accomplished, and warned me to flee from the place, for if I should be taken my life would pay for my crimes against Southern slaveholders. I had become so accustomed to threats and warnings, that this made no impression on me—struck no terror to my heart. The most of the inhabitants of our village were Friends, and their principles were those of peace and non-resistance. They were not alarmed at the threat to destroy the town, and on the night appointed retired to their beds as usual and slept peacefully. We placed no sentinels to give warning of danger, and had no extra company at our house to guard our lives. We retired to rest at the usual hour, and were not disturbed during the night. In the morning the buildings were all there—there was no smell of fire, no sign of the terrible destruction threatened. I heard of only one person who was alarmed, and he did not live in town.

The fright of this man created considerable amusement at the time and was not soon forgotten. He was a poor laborer, who lived a mile and a half from Newport, in a cabin which he had built in the woods. About half a mile east of his place, two roads crossed each other, one of them leading to Newport, and near the cross-roads was a large pond of water. This incident occurred in the spring of the year. Having heard that on a certain night the town of Newport was to be destroyed by an army from Kentucky, this man was listening, at the time appointed, for the sound of the approaching army. Soon after dark he was sure he heard martial music near the cross-roads. He hastened to town with all speed, and came into my store, almost out of breath, to give the alarm. We laughed at him, and told him that he heard the noise of frogs in that pond of water, but he would not be convinced. To satisfy him, a young man present said he would mount his horse and go with him to hear the music. He went, and soon returned and informed us that the frogs were making a lively noise in the pond in honor of the return of spring; that was all the music to be heard. The laborer was so chagrined at his ludicrous mistake, that he did not show himself in town for some time.

Slave-hunters often passed through our town and sometimes had hired ruffians with them from Richmond, and other neighboring places. They knew me well, and knew that I harbored slaves and aided them to escape, but they never ventured to search my premises, or molest me in any way.

I had many employees about my place of business, and much company about my house, and it seemed too public a place for fugitives to hide. These slave-hunters knew that if they committed any trespass, or went beyond the letter of the law, I would have them arrested, and they knew also that I had many friends who would stand at my back and aid me in prosecuting them. Thus, my business influence and large acquaintance afforded me protection in my labors for the oppressed fugitives. I expressed my anti-slavery sentiments with boldness on every occasion. I told the sympathizers with slave-hunters that I intended to shelter as many runaway slaves as came to my house, and aid them on their way; and advised them to be careful how they interfered with my work. They might get themselves into difficulty if they undertook to capture slaves from my premises, and become involved in a legal prosecution, for most of the arrests of slaves were unlawful. The law required that a writ should be obtained, and a proof that the slave was their property before they could take him away, and if they proceeded contrary to these requirements, and attempted to enter my house, I would have them arrested as kidnappers. These expressions, uttered frequently, had, I thought, a tendency to intimidate the slave-hunters and their friends, and to prevent them from entering my house to search for slaves.

The pursuit was often very close, and we had to resort to various stratagems in order to elude the pursuers. Sometimes a company of fugitives were scattered, and secreted in the neighborhood until the hunters had given up the chase. At other times their route was changed and they were hurried forward with all speed. It was a continual excitement and anxiety to us, but the work was its own reward.

As I have said before, when we knew of no pursuit, and the fugitives needed to rest or to be clothed, or were sick from exposure and fatigue, we have kept them with us for weeks or months. A case of this kind was that of two young men who were brought to our house during a severe cold spell in the early part of winter. They had been out in the snow and ice, and their feet were so badly frozen that their boots had to be cut off, and they were compelled to lie by for three months, being unable to travel. Dr. Henry H. Way, who was always ready to minister to the fugitives, attended them, and by his skillful treatment their feet were saved, though for some time it was thought that a surgical operation would have to be performed. The two men left us in the spring, and went on to Canada. They seemed loth to part from us, and manifested much gratitude for our kindness and care. The next autumn one of them returned to our house to see us, saying that he felt so much indebted to us that he had come back to work for us to try to repay us, in some measure, for what we had done for him. I told him that we had no charge against him, and could not receive anything for our attention to him while he was sick and helpless; but if he thought he would be safe, I would hire him during the winter at good wages. He accepted this offer and proved to be a faithful servant. He attended night-school and made some progress in learning. He returned to Canada in the spring.

Many of the fugitives came long distances, from Alabama, Mississippi, Louisiana, in fact from all parts of the South. Sometimes the poor hunted creatures had been out so long, living in woods and thickets, that they were almost wild when they came in, and so fearful of being betrayed, that it was some time before their confidence could be gained and the true state of their case learned. Although the number of fugitives that I aided on their way was so large, not one, so far as I ever knew, was captured and taken back to slavery. Providence seemed to favor our efforts for the poor slaves, and to crown them with success.

Source: Coffin, Levi. *Reminiscences of Levi Coffin.* Cincinnati: Robert Clarke and Co., 1880 (1876), pp. 107–120.

Introduction to William Still, *The Underground Railroad* (1872)

While Levi Coffin is sometimes referred to as the president of the Underground Railroad, William Still (1821–1902) is sometimes referred to as "the father of the Underground Railroad." He was very active in the abolition movement, and his record of the Underground Railroad is a key source of information about it; fortunately, it was not discovered by proslavery supporters during the active days of the Railroad. Particularly noteworthy is Still's report of the escape of Charles Box Brown, who mailed himself to Philadelphia, in one of the most remarkable strategies used in the Underground Railroad.

From William Still, *The Underground Railroad* (1872)

Henry Box Brown

Arrived by Adams' Express

Although the name of Henry Box Brown has been echoed over the land for a number of years, and the simple facts connected with his marvelous escape from slavery in a box published widely through the medium of anti-slavery papers, nevertheless it is not unreasonable to suppose that very little is generally known in relation to this case.

Briefly, the facts are these, which doubtless have never before been fully published—

Brown was a man of invention as well as a hero. In point of interest, however, his case is no more remarkable than many others. Indeed, neither before nor after escaping did he suffer one-half what many others have experienced.

He was decidedly an unhappy piece of property in the city of Richmond, Va. In the condition of a slave he felt that it would be impossible for him to remain. Full well did he know, however, that it was no holiday task to escape the vigilance of Virginia slave-hunters, or the wrath of an enraged master for committing the unpardonable sin of attempting to escape to a land of liberty. So Brown counted well the cost before venturing upon this hazardous undertaking. Ordinary modes of travel he concluded might prove disastrous to his hopes; he, therefore, hit upon a new invention altogether, which was to have himself boxed up and forwarded to Philadelphia direct by express. The size of the box and how it was to be made to fit him most comfortably, was of his own ordering. Two feet eight inches deep, two feet wide, and three feet long were the exact dimensions of the box, lined with baize. His resources with regard to food and water consisted of the following: One bladder of water and a few small biscuits. His mechanical implement to meet the death-struggle for fresh air, all told, was one large gimlet. Satisfied that it would be far better to peril his life for freedom in this way than to remain under the galling yoke of Slavery, he entered his box, which was safely nailed up and hooped with five hickory hoops, and was then addressed by his next friend, James A. Smith, a shoe dealer, to Wm. H. Johnson, Arch street, Philadelphia, marked, "This side up with care." In this condition he was sent to Adams' Express office in a dray, and thence by overland express to Philadelphia. It was twenty-six hours from the time he left Richmond until his arrival in the City of Brotherly Love. The notice, "This side up, &c.," did not avail with the different expressmen, who hesitated not to handle the box in the usual rough manner common to this class of men. For a while they actually had the box upside down, and had him on his head for miles. A few days before he was expected, certain intimation was conveyed to a member of the Vigilance Committee that a box might be expected by the three o'clock morning train from the South, which might contain a man. One of the most serious walks he ever took—and they had not been a few—to meet and accompany passengers, he took at half past two o'clock that morning to the depot. Not once, but for more than a score of times, he fancied the slave would be dead. He anxiously looked while the freight was being unloaded from the cars, to see if he could recognize a box that might contain a man; one alone had that appearance, and he confessed it really seemed as if there was the scent of death about it. But on inquiry, he soon learned that it was not the one he was looking after, and he was free to say he experienced a marked sense of relief. That same afternoon, however, he received from Richmond a telegram, which read thus, "Your case of goods is shipped and will arrive tomorrow morning."

At this exciting juncture of affairs, Mr. McKim, who had been engineering this important undertaking, deemed it expedient to change the programme slightly in one particular at least to insure greater safety. Instead of having a member of the Committee go again to the depot for the box, which might excite suspicion, it was decided that it would be safest to have the express bring it direct to the Anti-Slavery Office.

But all apprehension of danger did not now disappear, for there was no room to suppose that Adams' Express office had any sympathy with the Abolitionist or the fugitive, consequently for Mr. McKim to appear personally at the express office to give directions with reference to the coming of a box from Richmond which would be directed to Arch street, and yet not intended for that street, but for the Anti-Slavery office at 107 North Fifth street, it needed of course no great discernment to foresee that a step of this kind was wholly impracticable and that a more indirect and covert method would have to be adopted. In this dreadful crisis Mr. McKim, with his usual good judgment and remarkably quick, strategical mind, especially in matters pertaining to the U.G.R.R., hit upon the following plan, namely, to go to his friend, A.E.M. Davis [a member of the Executive Committee of the Pennsylvania Anti-Slavery Society], who was then extensively engaged in mercantile business, and relate the circumstances. Having daily intercourse with said Adams' Express office, and being well acquainted with the firm and some of the drivers, Mr. Davis could, as Mr. McKim thought, talk about "boxes, freight, etc.," from any part of the country without risk. Mr. Davis heard Mr. McKim's plan and instantly approved of it, and was heartily at his service.

Resurrection of Henry Box Brown

"Dan, an Irishman, one of Adams' Express drivers, is just the fellow to go to the depot after the box," said Davis. "He drinks a little too much whiskey sometimes, but he will do anything I ask him to do, promptly and obligingly. I'll trust Dan, for I believe he is the very man." The difficulty which Mr. McKim had been so anxious to overcome was thus pretty well settled. It was agreed that Dan should go after the box next morning before daylight and bring it to the Anti-Slavery office direct, and to make it all the more agreeable for Dan to get up out of his warm bed and go on this errand before day, it was decided that he should have a five dollar gold piece for himself. Thus these preliminaries having been satisfactorily arranged, it only remained for Mr. Davis to see Dan and give him instructions accordingly, etc.

Next morning, according to arrangement, the box was at the Anti-Slavery office in due time. The witnesses present to behold the resurrection were J.M. McKim, Professor C.D. Cleveland, Lewis Thompson, and the writer.

Mr. McKim was deeply interested; but having been long identified with the Anti-Slavery cause as one of its oldest and ablest advocates in the darkest days of slavery and mobs, and always found by the side of the fugitive to counsel and succor, he was on this occasion perfectly composed.

Professor Cleveland, however, was greatly moved. His zeal and earnestness in the cause of freedom, especially in rendering aid to passengers, knew no limit. Ordinarily he could not too often visit these travelers, shake them too warmly by the hand, or impart to them too freely of his substance to aid them on their journey. But now his emotion was overpowering.

Mr. Thompson, of the firm of Merrihew & Thompson—about the only printers in the city who for many years dared to print such incendiary documents as anti-slavery papers and pamphlets—one of the truest friends of the slave, was composed and prepared to witness the scene. All was quiet. The door had been safely locked. The proceedings commenced. Mr. McKim rapped quietly on the lid of the box and called out, "All right!" Instantly came the answer from within, "All right, sir!"

The witnesses will never forget that moment. Saw and hatchet quickly had the five hickory hoops cut and the lid off, and the marvellous resurrection of Brown ensued. Rising up in his box, he reached out his hand, saying, "How do you do, gentlemen?" The little assemblage hardly knew what to think or do at the moment. He was about as wet as if he had come up out of the Delaware. Very soon he remarked that, before leaving Richmond he had selected for his arrival-hymn (if he lived) the Psalm beginning with these words: "I waited patiently for the Lord, and He heard my prayer." And most touchingly did he sing the psalm, much to his own relief, as well as to the delight of his small audience.

He was then christened Henry Box Brown, and soon afterwards was sent to the hospitable residence of James Mott [he and his wife Lucretia were Quaker abolitionists] and A.E.M. Davis, on Ninth street, where, it is needless to say, he met a most cordial reception from Mrs. Lucretia Mott and her household. Clothing and creature comforts were furnished in abundance, and delight and joy filled all hearts in that stronghold of philanthropy.

As he had been so long doubled up in the box he needed to promenade considerably in the fresh air, so James Mott put one of his broad-brim hats on his head and tendered him the hospitalities of his yard as well as his house, and while Brown promenaded the yard flushed with victory, great was the joy of his friends.

After his visit at Mr. Mott's, he spent two days with the writer, and then took his departure for Boston, evidently feeling quite conscious of the wonderful feat he had performed, and at the same time it may be safely said that those who witnessed this strange resurrection were not only elated at his success, but were made to sympathize more deeply than ever before with the slave. Also the noble-hearted Smith who boxed him up was made to rejoice over Brown's victory, and was thereby encouraged to render similar service to two other young bondmen, who appealed to him for deliverance. But, unfortunately, in this attempt the undertaking proved a failure. Two boxes containing the young men alluded to above, after having been duly expressed and some distance on the road, were, through the agency of the telegraph, betrayed, and the heroic young fugitives were captured in their boxes and dragged back to hopeless bondage.

Source: Still, William. *The Underground Railroad.* Philadelphia: Porter and Coates, 1872, pp. 49–53.

Introduction to Josiah Henson, *The Life of Josiah Henson* (1849)

Josiah Henson (1789–1883) may have been the prototype of George Harris in *Uncle Tom's Cabin.* When Henson updated his autobiography for the second time in 1876, it was entitled *Uncle Tom's Story of His Life* and had a preface by Stowe. But Stowe's *The Key to "Uncle Tom's Cabin"* (1853), in which she cites Henson as a source of her novel, was published after the novel, which has caused some readers to doubt her claim. In any event, Henson was a remarkable black abolitionist, who escaped from bondage with his wife and children and made his way to Canada, where they remained after legal slavery was abolished in the United States. It was in Canada where Henson became active in the Underground Railroad and also established a settlement for the slaves who escaped from slavery.

From Josiah Henson, *The Life of Josiah Henson* (1849)

At length the eventful night came. I went up to the house to ask leave to take Tom [Henson's son] home with me, that he might have his clothes mended. No objection was made, and I bade Master Amos "good night" for the last time. It was about the middle of September, and by nine o'clock in the evening all was ready. It was a dark, moonless night, and we got into the little skiff in which I had induced a fellow-slave to take us across the river. It was an agitating and solemn moment. The good fellow who was rowing us over, said this affair might end in his death; "but," said he, "you will not be brought back alive, will you?" "Not if I can help it," I answered. "And if you are overpowered and return," he asked, "will you conceal my part of the business?" "That I will, so help me God," I replied. "Then I am easy," he answered, "and wish you success." We landed on the Indiana shore, and I began to feel that I was my own master. But in what circumstances of fear and misery still! We were to travel by night, and rest by day, in the woods and bushes. We were thrown absolutely upon our own poor and small resources, and were to rely on our own strength alone. The population was not so numerous as now, nor so well disposed to the slave. We dared look to no one for help. But my courage was equal to the occasion, and we trudged on cautiously and steadily, and as fast as the darkness, and the feebleness of my wife and boys would allow.

It was nearly a fortnight before we reached Cincinnati; and a day or two previous to getting there, our provisions were used up, and I had the misery to hear the cry of hunger and exhaustion from those I loved so dearly. It was necessary to run the risk of exposure by day-light upon the road; so I sprung upon it boldly from our hiding place one morning, and turned towards the south, to prevent the suspicion of my going the other way. I approached the first house I saw, and asked if they would sell me a little bread and meat. No, they had nothing for black fellows. At the next I succeeded better, but had to make as good a bargain as I could, and that was not very successful, with a man who wanted to see how little he could give me for my quarter of a dollar. As soon as I had succeeded in making a purchase, I followed the road, still towards the south, till I got out of sight of the house, and then darted into the woods again, and returned northward, just out of sight of the road. The food which I bought, such as it was, put new life and strength into my wife and children when I got back to them again, and we at length arrived safe at Cincinnati. There we were kindly received and entertained for several days, my wife and little ones were refreshed, and then we were carried on our way thirty miles in a wagon.

We followed the same course as before, of travelling by night, and resting by day, till we arrived at the Scioto, where we had been told we should strike the military road of General Hull, in the last war with Great Britain, and might then safely travel by day. We found the road, accordingly, by the large sycamore and elm which marked its beginning, and entered upon it with fresh spirits early in the day. Nobody had told us that it was cut through the wilderness, and I had neglected to provide any food, thinking we should soon come to some habitation, where we could be supplied. But we travelled on all day without seeing one, and laid down at night, hungry and weary enough. I thought I heard the howling of wolves, and the terror inspired by this, and the exertions I used to keep them off, by making as much noise as I could, took away all power of sleeping, till day-light, and rendered a little delay inevitable. In the morning we were as hungry as ever, but had nothing to relieve our appetites but a little piece of dried beef. I divided some of this all round, and then started for a second day's trip in the wilderness. It was a hard trial, and this day is a memorable one in my life. The road was rough, of course, being neglected, and the logs lying across it constantly; the under-brush was somewhat cleared away, and that was about all to mark the track. As we went wearily on, I was a little ahead of my wife and the boys, when I heard them call to me, and, turning round, saw that my wife had fallen over a log, and was prostrate on the ground. "Moth-er's dying," cried Tom; and when I reached her, it seemed really so. She had fainted. I did not know but it might be fatal, and was half distracted with the fear and the uncertainty. In a few minutes, how-ever, she recovered sufficiently to take a few mouthfuls of the beef, and this, with a little rest, revived her so much that she bravely set out once more.

We had not gone far, and I suppose it was about three o'clock in the afternoon, when we discerned some persons approaching us at no great distance. We were instantly on the alert, as we could hardly expect them to be friends. The advance of a few paces showed me they were Indians, with packs on their shoulders; and they were so near that if they were hostile, it would be useless to try to escape. So I walked along boldly, till we came close upon them. They were bent down with their burdens, and had not raised their eyes till now; and when they did so, and saw me coming towards them, they looked at me in a frightened sort of way for a moment, and then, setting up a peculiar howl, turned round, and ran as fast as they could. There were three or four of them, and what they were afraid of I could not imagine, unless they supposed I was the devil, whom they had perhaps heard of as black. But even then one would have thought my wife and children might have reassured them. However, there was no doubt they were well frightened, and we heard their wild and prolonged howl, as they ran, for a mile or more. My wife was alarmed too, and thought they were merely running back to collect more of a party, and then to come and murder us, and she wanted to turn back. I told her they were numerous enough to do that, if they wanted to, without help; and that as for turning back, I had had quite too much of the road behind us, and that it would be a ridiculous thing that both parties should run away. If they were disposed to run, I would follow. We did follow on, and soon the noise was stopped; and, as we advanced, we could discover Indians peeping at us from behind the trees, and dodging out of our sight, if they thought we were looking at them. Presently we came upon their wigwams, and saw a fine looking, stately Indian, with his arms folded, waiting for us to approach. He was apparently the chief, and, saluting us civilly, he soon discovered that we were human beings, and spoke to his young men, who were scattered about, and made them come in, and give up their foolish fears. And now curiosity seemed to prevail. Each one wanted to touch the children, who were shy as partridges, with their long life in the woods; and as they shrunk away, and uttered a little cry of alarm, the Indian would jump back too, as if he thought they would bite him. However, a little while sufficed to make them understand what we were, and whither we were going, and what we needed; and as little, to set them about supplying our wants, feeding us bountifully, and giving us a comfortable wigwam for our night's rest. The next day we resumed our march, and found, from the Indians, that we were only about twenty-five miles from the lake. They sent some of their young men to point out the place where we were to turn off, and parted from us with as much kindness as possible.

In passing over the part of Ohio near the lake, where such an extensive plain is found, we came to a spot overflowed by a stream, across which the road passed. I forded it first, with the help of a sounding-pole, and then taking the children on my back, first, the two little ones, and then the others, one at a time, and, lastly, my wife, I succeeded in getting them all safely across, where the ford was one hundred to one hundred and fifty yards wide, and the deepest part perhaps four feet deep. At this time the skin was worn from my back to an extent almost equal to the size of my knapsack.

One night more was passed in the woods, and in the course of the next forenoon we came out upon the wide plain, without trees, which lies south and west of Sandusky city. We saw the houses of the village, and kept away from them for the present, till I should have an opportunity to reconnoitre a little. When about a mile from the lake, I hid my companions in the bushes, and pushed forward. Before I had gone far, I observed on the left, on the opposite side from the town, something which looked like a house, between which and a vessel, a number of men were passing and repassing with activity. I promptly decided to approach them; and, as I drew near, I was hailed by one of the number, who asked me if I wanted to work. I told him yes; and it was scarcely a minute before I had hold of a bag of corn, which, like the rest, I emptied into the hold of the vessel lying at anchor a few rods off. I got into the line of laborers hurrying along the plank next to the only colored man I saw engaged, and soon entered into conversation with him; in the course of which I inquired of him where they were going, the best route to Canada, who was the captain, and other particulars interesting to me, and communicated to him where I came from, and whither I wished to go. He told the captain, who called me to one side, and by his frank look and manner soon induced me to acknowledge my condition and purpose. I found I had not mistaken him. He sympathized with me, at once, most heartily; and offered to take me and my family to Buffalo, whither they were bound, and where they might arrive the next evening, if the favorable wind continued, of which they were hurrying to take advantage. Never did men work with a better will, and soon two or three hundred bushels were thrown on board, the hatches were fastened down, the anchor raised, and the sails hoisted. The captain had agreed to send a boat for me, after sundown, rather than take me on board at the landing; as there were Kentucky spies, he said, on the watch for slaves, at Sandusky, who might get a glimpse of me, if I brought my party out of the bush by daylight. I watched the vessel, as she left her moorings, with intense interest, and began to fear that she would go without me, after all; she stretched off to so great a distance, as it seemed to me, before she rounded to. At length, however, I saw her come up to the wind, and lower a boat for the shore; and, in a few minutes, my black friend and two sailors jumped out upon the beach. They went with me, immediately, to bring my wife and children. But what was my alarm when I came back to the place where I had left them, to find they had gone! For a moment, my fears were overpowering; but I soon discerned them, in the fading twilight, at no great distance. My wife had been alarmed by my long absence, and thought I must have been discovered by some of our watchful enemies, and had given up all for lost. Her fears were not removed by seeing me returning with three other men; and she tried to hide herself. It was not without difficulty that I satisfied her all was right, for her agitation was so great that she could not, at once, understand what I said. However, this was soon over, and the kindness of my companions facilitated the matter very much. Before long, we were all on the way to the boat, and it did not require much time or labor to embark our luggage. A short row brought us to the vessel, and, to my astonishment, we were welcomed on board, with three hearty cheers; for the crew were as much pleased as the captain, with the help they were giving us to escape. A fine run brought us to Buffalo the next evening, but it was too late to cross the river that night. The next morning we dropped down to Black Rock, and the friendly captain, whose name I have gratefully remembered as Captain Burnham, put us on board the ferry-boat to Waterloo, paid the passage money, and gave me a dollar at parting. He was a Scotchman, and had done enough to win my enduring gratitude, to prove himself a kind and generous man, and to give me a pleasant association with his dialect and his country.

When I got on the Canada side, on the morning of the 28th of October, 1830, my first impulse was to throw myself on the ground, and giving way to the riotous exultation of my feelings, to execute sundry antics which excited the astonishment of those who were looking on. A gentleman of the neighborhood, Colonel Warren, who happened to be present, thought I was in a fit, and as he inquired what was the matter with the poor fellow, I jumped up and told him I was free. "O," said he, with a hearty laugh, "is that it? I never knew freedom make a man roll in the sand before." It is not much to be wondered at, that my certainty of being free was not quite a sober one at the first moment; and I hugged and kissed my wife and children all round, with a vivacity which made them laugh as well as myself. There was not much time to be lost, though, in frolic, even at this extraordinary moment. I was a stranger, in a strange land, and had to look about me at once, for refuge and resource. I found a lodging for the night; and the next morning set about exploring the interior for the means of support.

Source: Henson, Josiah. *The Life of Josiah Henson.*
Boston: Arthur D. Phelps, 1849, pp. 50–59.

Discussion Questions

1. Why was Levi Coffin so difficult to frighten or intimidate?
2. What do you find most admirable about Coffin? Why?
3. Why do you think most escaped slaves stayed in the free states rather than going on to Canada or leaving the United States altogether?
4. What do you admire most about Levi Coffin, and why?
5. What was the source of his extreme self-confidence?
6. Compare and contrast William Still and Levi Coffin: how do you account for their differences as supporters of the Underground Railroad?
7. Do you think you could have escaped slavery by mailing yourself to a free state? Why or why not?
8. Why do you think Still chose the word "resurrection" to describe Henry Box Brown's emergence from the box he mailed himself in?
9. Compare and contrast Josiah Henson to George Harris in *Uncle Tom's Cabin;* in particular, to what extent do you think he might have been in Stowe's mind as she wrote her most famous novel?
10. Do you admire Henson more than, say, Frederick Douglass, in that the former escaped with his family but the latter did not have to worry about that when he escaped?
11. Henson and his family encountered some Indians during their escape from slavery: how different might American history have been if poor whites, slaves, and Indians had united against white elites instead of fighting each other?
12. Why do you think the Indians were at first afraid of the Hensons but then became friendly toward them?

Suggested Readings

Ashton, Jean. 1977. *Harriet Beecher Stowe: A Reference Guide.* Boston: G. K. Hall Company.

Belasco, Susan. 2009. *Stowe in Her Own Time: A Biographical Chronicle of Her Life, Drawn from Recollections, Interviews, and Memoirs.* Iowa City: University of Iowa Press.

Gossett, Thomas R. 1985. *"Uncle Tom's Cabin" and American Culture.* Dallas, TX: Southern Methodist University Press.

Hedrick, Joan. 1994. *Harriet Beecher Stowe: A Life.* New York: Oxford University Press.

Hildreth, Margaret Holbrook. 1976. *Harriet Beecher Stowe: A Bibliography.* North Haven, CT: Archon Books.

Rugoff, Milton. 1981. *The Beechers: An American Family in the Nineteenth Century.* New York: HarperCollins.

Weinstein, Cindy. 2004. *The Cambridge Companion to Harriet Beecher Stowe.* New York: Cambridge University Press.

White, Barbara A. 2003. *The Beecher Sisters.* New Haven, CT: Yale University Press.

Areas for Research

A particularly interesting area of research is to compare Stowe's *Uncle Tom's Cabin* with the numerous anti-Tom novels that appeared after it. What aspects of Stowe's novel do they concentrate on and why? What is suggested by the fact that some anti-Tom literature was written by Northern writers? Explain why none of these books sold in anything like the number of copies of Stowe's novel that sold. On the other hand, what is revealing about the fact that many of the attacks on *Uncle Tom's Cabin* retain so much that is faithful to it?

Also rich in possibilities is research into how much of *Uncle Tom's Cabin* has an historical basis. Were there really slaves as saintly as Uncle Tom, or does he seem to be more of a figment of Stowe's imagination designed to reassure white readers that black male slaves were not a threat to them? How accurate are Stowe's stereotypes about black people and emotion?

Research into the Fugitive Slave Law of 1850 reveals much about white outrage toward it in the North. Before it, there was a lot of indifference in the North toward slavery in the South. How could one law change feelings so much, even to the point of supporting a civil war eleven years later?

How rigorously was it enforced in the North? How many Northerners paid fines and served prison sentences for breaking that law?

It is interesting, also, to look into Stowe's support of the colonization of African Americans at the end of *Uncle Tom's Cabin,* a position she later renounced. Many African Americans vigorously opposed the idea, although a small minority did return to Africa. In the 1920s Marcus Garvey led a return-to-Africa movement. What does research show as the reasons the idea has never really taken hold in the black community? Why was a later black writer, Langston Hughes, shocked at his reception when he visited Africa?

WHY WE READ *UNCLE TOM'S CABIN* TODAY

One of the key reasons we read *Uncle Tom's Cabin* is its historical influence. It made its Northern readers much more aware of the horrible effects of slavery on the slaves and their masters, and it did so in highly personal terms. Northern mothers and fathers could readily grasp the unbearable pain of separating families, a horror Stowe emphasizes in powerful ways in her novel, perhaps most in Eliza's escape with her son and Lucy's suicide when her baby is sold away from her. These incidents brought their experiences home to Northern readers in ways they could not avoid. Stowe's novel helped cultivate feelings in the North that would support the Civil War nine years after it was first published in book form in 1852. It may be misleading to say *Uncle Tom's Cabin* was a cause of the war, but it is accurate to say that it helped prepare a state of mind in the North that made the possibility of the war understandable. Stowe articulated feelings and ideas that Northerners had sensed but had not put into words.

It is also read because it is the source of so much material in popular culture in the United States. The name "Simon Legree" remains a synonym for extreme cruelty, just as "Uncle Tom" remains one for excessive humility and for passivity in the face of racial oppression. Stowe's racial theories about African Americans and Anglo Saxons also survive in the United States today: She believed Anglo Saxons were known for their logic and rationality, whereas African Americans were particularly susceptible to their imaginations and childlike simplicity. Contemporary readers are sometimes surprised that someone who was opposed to slavery was so taken in by stereotypes and dangerous lies.

Of particular interest now is the debate over why a novel that is so oriented toward obvious appeals to readers' feelings has gained ground in some quarters where modernism still has prestige. In other words, a third

UNCLE TOM'S CABIN

ELIZA'S ESCAPE

This is the most famous scene in *Uncle Tom's Cabin*, designed to appeal to the hearts of mothers whom Stowe hoped to enlist in the cause of abolition. (Library of Congress)

reason *Uncle Tom's Cabin* is read is to show that modernism (a literary movement that prized understatement, irony, and indirection; e.g., some of Ernest Hemingway's novels qualified as modernistic) was not attempting to change the world, whereas that is precisely Stowe's intention in *Uncle Tom's Cabin*. She was not trying to anticipate Hemingway, but she was trying to end slavery; Hemingway's assumption that less is more influenced literary history but not history. The tentativeness of T. S. Eliot's narrator in the modernistic "The Love Song of J. Alfred Prufrock" would have been unsuitable to an overtly political and sentimental novel like Stowe's; she wrote in a style calculated to please readers in the 1850s, not the 1920s, when many writers were rejecting sentimental literature.

A related reason *Uncle Tom's Cabin* continues to be read is that some contemporary critics do praise its literary qualities. The suspense, for instance, of whether or not Eliza and her son will successfully escape slave hunters still works for many of today's readers, as does their anxiety over whether or not Uncle Tom will survive Simon Legree's cruel punishment. And they are genuinely moved by the pathos of the death of Eva, the daughter of Augustine St. Clare, Uncle Tom's second owner. The plot is successful for such readers, regardless of the censures of critics who disapprove of literature they view as propagandistic. And some contemporary readers admire Stowe's ability to manage numerous shreds of plot in a dexterous manner.

V

Incidents in the Life of a Slave Girl (1861)

HISTORICAL BACKGROUND

Incidents in the Life of a Slave Girl reflects key aspects of nineteenth-century American history, particularly slavery. When Harriet Jacobs's novel was published in 1861, slavery had been entrenched for well over two hundred years. Slavery was the foundation of society in the South and the major form of wealth for the masters of large plantations. In other words, it was not going to be abolished voluntarily because it was the basis of the social and economic power of the planter aristocracy, which was determined to hold on to its slavery-based privileges, regardless of the cost. Slaves, however capable and impressive they might be, remained commodities that could be bought and sold at the will of their owners. They could not vote, be legally married, live where they wanted to, run for political office, learn to read and write (in most Southern states), or serve on juries. Given what was at stake, it is clear that war was the only way legal slavery could have ended. It was also clear that the only way to maintain the system of slavery was through the use of violence, because no one would submit to such a system unless coerced.

This image represents what Harriet Jacobs could well have faced if she had not tricked Dr. Norcom into thinking she had fled north instead of hiding in the garret of her grandmother's house for seven years. (The British Library/Robana via Getty Images)

Nineteenth-century American history can be seen as a fight between those who wanted to uphold the system of slavery and those who wanted to abolish it. Much of the fight used legal and political weapons. In 1808 Congress prohibited the African slave trade, but the law was often flouted, and, in any case, the internal slave trade continued until the end of the Civil War in 1865. In 1820 a compromise regarding the spreading of slavery outside the South, known as the Missouri Compromise, prohibited slavery in the United States north of 36 degrees longitude, and Missouri was admitted as a slave state. The House of Representatives, a few years later, passed a gag rule that required all antislavery petitions to be tabled (it was lifted in 1844). Not long before *Incidents* was published in 1861, Henry David Thoreau, the author of *Walden and "Civil Disobedience,"* defied the poll tax to protest slavery. In 1850 Congress passed another compromise, one that required that fugitive slaves be returned to their owners; violations of this law could include substantial fines and imprisonment. Seven years later, the Supreme Court ruled, in the *Dred Scott* (an African American slave) decision, that neither the Constitution nor the Bill of Rights applied to African Americans, and that the Missouri Compromise was not constitutional. The election of Abraham Lincoln to the presidency in 1860 meant the end of slavery, because Lincoln's goals were the preservation of the Union (South Carolina seceded from the Union in the same year) and the destruction of slavery, since it was the basis of Southern society; he needed the approximately 186,000 African American troops, many from the South, to defeat the Confederacy.

Legal and political strategies regarding slavery continued during and after the Civil War (1861–1865). Lincoln delivered the Emancipation

Proclamation on January 1, 1863, which declared slavery illegal in states rebelling against the Union. Toward the end of 1865, the Thirteenth Amendment was passed by Congress: it abolished slavery in the United States. The next year, the Civil Rights Act granted citizenship to everyone born in the United States, and in 1896, the Supreme Court, in *Plessy vs. Ferguson*, approved segregation as long as facilities were separate but equal, an impossible distinction in reality, but one that had legal standing until the 1960s.

In the *Dred Scott* decision of 1857, the Supreme Court ruled that black people had no rights that a white man had to respect, an idea that Dr. Norcom heartily endorsed. (Bettmann/Corbis)

Such a contentious legal and political battle also included other methods, some violent and some nonviolent, of overturning or supporting slavery, which is the central fact of nineteenth-century American history. For instance, a few years after Jacobs was born in 1813, Levi Coffin, whose work appears in this volume (in IV. *Uncle Tom's Cabin* (1852)), established the Underground Railroad, a system for enabling slaves to escape from the South to the North or Canada. One of the most famous slave insurrections occurred in Charleston, South Carolina, in 1822, under the leadership of Denmark Vesey. In 1829, David Walker, a free black clothes dealer in Boston, encouraged African Americans in his appeal to end slavery by any means necessary, and he made his case in a very aggressive manner. Two years later, when Jacobs was eighteen, two key events occurred: Nat Turner led the most famous slave insurrection in American history; it erupted in Virginia and terrified whites. This rebellion figures prominently in *Incidents in the Life of a Slave Girl*. In the same year, William Lloyd Garrison, the most famous of all the white abolitionists (people who wanted to abolish slavery), began publishing *The Liberator*. In it, he demanded the immediate emancipation of the slaves; he wanted the North to secede, which could have been disaster for African Americans in the South.

When Jacobs was a young woman, the American Anti-Slavery Society was founded (1833). In 1852 the novel that President Lincoln supposedly said caused the Civil War, *Uncle Tom's Cabin,* was published. Like Harriet Jacobs's *Incidents in the Life of a Slave Girl* (1861), it appealed to the hearts of Northern mothers, who then, Jacobs hoped, appealed to their husbands to end slavery. In 1859, John Brown made his famous raid on Harpers Ferry in Virginia, for which he was hanged. In other words, nineteenth-century American history can be seen as the inexorable move toward the destruction of slavery; Jacobs's *Incidents* is a key document in this history.

ABOUT HARRIET JACOBS

Harriet Jacobs (1813–1897) did not know when she was a little girl growing up in Edenton, North Carolina, that she was a slave. When she was six, she began to understand that she did not enjoy the same status as white children did. When she was six she also lost her mother and moved in with her mother's owner, a woman who taught her how to read and write, a crucial event for the author of *Incidents in the Life of a Slave Girl.* Another key event in her early life was the death of her mother's owner, because the latter's will left Harriet to the former's five-year-old niece, but a physician named Dr. James Norcom claimed that a codicil to the niece's will (the niece died soon after inheriting Harriet) left Harriet to his daughter. This transfer is what put the young Harriet in the nearly total control of the ruthless sexual predator, Dr. Norcom, referred to as Dr. Flint in *Incidents.*

In several ways, Dr. Norcom is the key figure in the young Harriet Jacobs's life because his interminable pursuit of her for sexual purposes resulted in her writing her only book. He enjoyed harassing her and making his wife jealous as a result, because that was flattering to his ego. What he did not count on was Harriet's resourcefulness: she countered his advances by choosing her lover, and of course it was not Dr. Norcom, but rather a young white lawyer named Samuel Tredwell Sawyer, who promised to free their children, which turned out to be a lie (thus the suggestive fictional name Mr. Sands in the book).

Dr. Norcom also figured prominently in Harriet's life in that he inadvertently provided Harriet with a means to reveal her remarkable character. His treating her as an opportunity for sexual plunder led her to realize the absolute horror and brutality of slavery for black women especially, but his treatment of her also led to her realization that she could fight back but that this fighting back (by rejecting him and choosing Mr. Sands) left her exposed to extreme social censure, especially by her grandmother, because of the pressure for women in nineteenth-century United States to have no sexual experience outside of marriage. Jacobs boldly and openly flouted this social convention and by doing so gained a measure of autonomy, an autonomy that Dr. Norcom found intolerable.

In 1835, when Harriet Jacobs was in her early twenties, she escaped, but she spent the next seven years hiding in a small attic in her grandmother's house so she could at least see and hear her two children, Louisa and Joseph. This heartbreaking arrangement would have been particularly moving to Northern white mothers, who could easily imagine how they would feel in the same circumstances. All these seven years, Dr. Norcom assumed the young woman he wanted to be his concubine had fled to the North, which was exactly what she wanted him to think. Jacobs was a genius at getting the upper hand over a white man and her owner, who thought he had the upper hand.

In 1842, she escaped and made her way to Philadelphia and New York. There she became very active in the abolitionist cause. A few years later she moved to Rochester, New York, where she was encouraged to write *Incidents* by Amy Post, a powerful voice in feminist and antislavery circles at the time. Unfortunately, the publisher went out of business, resulting in Jacobs's publishing it privately in a run of five hundred copies; the book soon disappeared from public interest after its initial publication in 1861, the same year the Civil War started, but since the 1980s, it has been one of the most frequently discussed books in American literature.

Jacobs had to worry, especially after 1850, when the Fugitive Slave Law was passed (it required stiff penalties for anyone in the South or North who helped runaway slaves escape) that Dr. Norcom or his agents would apprehend her and bring her back to Edenton, North Carolina. What finally solved this problem was the purchase of Jacobs by the wife of the writer Nathaniel Parker Willis. She spent the rest of her life in the abolitionist cause, and after the Civil War ended in 1865, in the cause of equality for United States' new citizens, the freed slaves.

HISTORICAL EXPLORATIONS

Nat Turner's Rebellion

The most famous slave insurrection in American history, which figures prominently in Chapter XII of *Incidents in the Life of a Slave Girl,* was Nat Turner's Rebellion of 1831. Turner led an uprising in Southampton County, Virginia, which is about forty miles from Edenton, North Carolina,

Jacobs devotes Chapter XII to Nat Turner's Rebellion (1831), a slave revolt that terrified whites in and around Edenton, North Carolina, where Jacobs lived at the time. (Getty Images)

the setting for Jacobs's book. Turner and his followers killed perhaps fifty-five white people, many of them children and infants; the number of black people killed by execution or mob violence may have been several times that number. Turner was the last participant in the rebellion captured, having concealed himself for two months, after which he was hanged. One of the results of the event was that it undermined the preposterous fantasy that the slaves were happy and contented; another consequence was the passage of laws throughout the South prohibiting instruction in reading and writing for slaves (Turner himself was literate); a third was hysteria among some whites about future violent challenges to the institution of slavery.

Turner believed he was destined for some great accomplishment because of his visions, one of which involved the fighting of black and white belligerents. Given that, and with his sharp mind and refusal to mix with society, he had a mystery about him that captured the interest of other slaves. Turner and his men used swords and axes rather than muskets, because they wanted to avoid attracting an immediate white response, although Turner knew whites would soon enough be terrorized, which was one of his goals. His insurrection continues to spark interest: the publication of

William Styron's novel *The Confessions of Nat Turner* (1967) generated considerable controversy, particularly about Styron's interpretation of Turner's character and motivations.

The effects of Turner's rebellion in Edenton were numerous, according to Jacobs in *Incidents*. Poor whites took advantage of the opportunity to search black people's homes in disrespectful ways, to indulge their thirst for at least temporary power, as they did not own slaves. The poor whites especially liked to lord it over free blacks, such as Harriet Jacobs's grand-mother, who was living more comfortably than the former.

Introduction to Thomas R. Gray, *The Confessions of Nat Turner* (1831)

This document has to be read with caution, keeping in mind that Gray was a white attorney, a man who identified with the slaveowning class (he was a former slaveowner himself), and hardly a dispassionate observer and recorder, which he claims to be. Readers should also be skeptical of his suggestion that Turner is a deranged fanatic, not a rational agent other black people might have the chance to emulate. Gray claims that he is repeating Turner's words, but this is hard to believe, especially in the bland recital of who killed whom and how, over and over, as if Turner and his followers were mere homicidal robots. The Turner we get from Gray is a Turner constructed by Gray's racist imagination, which could not entertain the rational basis of Turner's attitude toward slavery.

From Thomas R. Gray, *The Confessions of Nat Turner* (1831)

Agreeable to his own appointment, on the evening he was committed to prison, with permission of the jailer, I visited NAT on Tuesday the 1st November, when, without being questioned at all, commenced his narrative in the following words:—

SIR,—You have asked me to give a history of the motives which induced me to undertake the late insurrection, as you call it—To do so I must go back to the days of my infancy, and even before I was born. I was thirty-one years of age the 2d of October last, and born the property of Benj. Turner, of this county. In my childhood a circumstance occurred which made an indelible impression on my mind, and laid the ground work of that enthusiasm, which has terminated so fatally to many, both white and black, and for which I am about to atone at the gallows. It is here necessary to relate this circumstance—trifling as it may seem, it was the commencement of that belief which has grown with time, and even now, sir, in this dungeon, helpless and forsaken as I am, I cannot divest myself of. Being at play with other children, when three or four years old, I was telling them something, which my mother overhearing, said it had happened before I was born—I stuck to my story, however, and related some things which went, in her opinion, to confirm it—others being called on were greatly astonished, knowing that these things had happened, and caused them to say in my hearing, I surely would be a prophet, as the Lord had shewn me things that had happened before my birth. And my father and mother strengthened me in this my first impression, saying in my presence, I was intended for some great purpose, which they had always thought from certain marks on my head and breast—[a parcel of excrescences which I believe are not at all uncommon, particularly among negroes, as I have seen several with the same. In this case he has either cut them off or they have nearly disappeared]—My grand mother, who was very religious, and to whom I was much attached—my master, who belonged to the church, and other religious persons who visited the house, and whom I often saw at prayers, noticing the singularity of my manners, I suppose, and my uncommon intelligence for a child, remarked I had too much sense to be raised, and if I was, I would never be of any service to any one as a slave—To a mind like mine, restless, inquisitive and observant of everything that was passing, it is easy to suppose that religion was the subject to which it would be directed, and although this subject principally occupied my thoughts—there was nothing that I saw or heard of to which my attention was not directed—The manner in which I learned to read and write, not only had great influence on my own mind, as I acquired it with the most perfect ease, so much so, that I have no recollection whatever of learning the alphabet—but to the astonishment of the family, one day, when a book was shewn me to keep me from crying, I began spelling the names of different objects—this was a source of wonder to all in the neighborhood, particularly the blacks—and this learning was constantly improved at all opportunities—when I got large enough to go to work, while employed, I was reflecting on many things that would present themselves to my imagination, and whenever an opportunity occurred of looking at a book, when the school children were getting their lessons, I would find many things that the fertility of my own imagination had depicted to me before; all my time, not devoted to my master's service, was spent either in prayer, or in making experiments in casting different things in molds made of earth, in attempting to make paper, gunpowder, and many other experiments, that although I could not perfect, yet convinced me of its practicability if I had the means. I was not addicted to stealing in my youth, nor have ever been—Yet such was the confidence of the negroes in the neighborhood, even at this early period of my life, in my superior judgment, that they would often carry me with them when they were going on any roguery, to plan for them. Growing up among them, with this confidence in my superior judgment, and when this, in their opinions, was perfected by Divine inspiration, from the circumstances already alluded to in my infancy, and which belief was ever afterwards zealously inculcated by the austerity of my life and manners, which became the subject of remark by white and black.—Having soon discovered to be great, I must appear so, and therefore studiously avoided mixing in society, and wrapped myself in mystery, devoting my time to fasting and prayer—By this time, having arrived to man's estate, and hearing the scriptures commented on at meetings, I was struck with that particular passage which says: "Seek ye the kingdom of Heaven and all things shall be added unto you." I reflected much on this passage, and prayed daily for light on this subject—As I was praying one day at my plough, the spirit spoke to me, saying "Seek ye the kingdom of Heaven and all things shall be added unto you." *Question*—what do you mean by the Spirit. *Ans.* The Spirit that spoke to the prophets in former days—and I was greatly astonished, and for two years prayed continually, whenever my duty would permit—and then again I had the same revelation, which fully confirmed me in the impression that I was ordained for some great purpose in the hands of the Almighty. Several years rolled round, in which many events occurred to strengthen me in this my belief. At this time I reverted in my mind to the remarks made of me in my childhood, and the things that had been shewn me—and as it had been said of me in my childhood by those by whom I had been taught to pray, both white and black, and in whom I had the greatest confidence, that I had too much sense to be raised, and if I was, I would never be of any use to any one as a slave. Now finding I had arrived to man's estate, and was a slave, and these revelations being made known to me, I began to direct my attention to this great object, to fulfill the purpose for which, by this time, I felt assured I was intended. Knowing the influence I had obtained over the minds of my fellow servants, (not by the means of conjuring and such like tricks—for to them I always spoke of such things with contempt) but by the communion of the Spirit whose revelations I often communicated to them, and they believed and said my wisdom came from God. I now began to prepare them for my purpose, by telling them something was about to happen that would terminate in fulfilling the great promise that had been made to me—About this time I was placed under an overseer, from whom I ran away—and after remaining in the woods thirty days, I returned, to the astonishment of the negroes on the plantation, who thought I had made my escape to some other part of the country, as my father had done before. But the reason of my return was, that the Spirit appeared to me and said I had my wishes directed to the things of this world, and not to the kingdom of Heaven, and that I should return to the service of my earthly master—"For he who knoweth his Master's will, and doeth it not, shall be beaten with many stripes, and thus, have I chastened you." And the negroes found fault, and murmured against me, saying that if they had my sense they would not serve any master in the world. And about this time I had a vision—and I saw white spirits and black spirits engaged in battle, and the sun was darkened—the thunder rolled in the Heavens, and blood flowed in streams—and I heard a voice saying, "Such is your luck, such you are called to see, and let it come rough or smooth, you must surely bare it." I now withdrew myself as much as my situation would permit, from the intercourse of my fellow servants, for the avowed purpose of serving the Spirit more fully—and it appeared to me, and reminded me of the things it had already shown me, and that it would then reveal to me the knowledge of the elements, the revolution of the planets, the operation of tides, and changes of the seasons. After this revelation in the year 1825, and the knowledge of the elements being made known to me, I sought more than ever to obtain true holiness before the great day of judgment should appear, and then I began to receive the true knowledge of faith. And from the first steps of righteousness until the last, was I made perfect; and the Holy Ghost was with me, and said, "Behold me as I stand in the Heavens"—and I looked and saw the forms of men in different attitudes—and there were lights in the sky to which the children of darkness gave other names than what they really were—for they were the lights of the Saviour's hands, stretched forth from east to west, even as they were extended on the cross on Calvary for the redemption of sinners. And I wondered greatly at these miracles, and prayed to be informed of a certainty of the meaning thereof—and shortly afterwards, while laboring in the field, I discovered drops of blood on the corn as though it were dew from heaven—and I communicated it to many, both white and black, in the neighborhood—and I then found on the leaves in the woods hieroglyphic characters, and numbers, with the forms of men in different attitudes, portrayed in blood, and representing the figures I had seen before in the heavens. And now the Holy Ghost had revealed itself to me, and made plain the miracles it had shown me—For as the blood of Christ had been shed on this earth, and had ascended to heaven for the salvation of sinners, and was now returning to earth again in the form of dew—and as the leaves on the trees bore the impression of the figures I had seen in the heavens, it was plain to me that the Saviour was about to lay down the yoke he had borne for the sins of men, and the great day of judgment was at band. About this time I told these things to a white man, (Etheldred T. Brantley) on whom it had a wonderful effect—and he ceased from his wickedness, and was attacked immediately with a cutaneous eruption, and blood oozed from the pores of his skin, and after praying and fasting nine days, he was healed, and the Spirit appeared to me again, and said, as the Saviour had been baptised so should we be also—and when the white people would not let us be baptised by the church, we went down into the water together, in the sight of many who reviled us, and were baptised by the Spirit—After this I rejoiced greatly, and gave thanks to God. And on the 12th of May, 1828, I heard a loud noise in the heavens, and the Spirit instantly appeared to me and said the Serpent was loosened, and Christ had laid down the yoke he had borne for the sins of men, and that I should take it on and fight against the Serpent, for the time was fast approaching when the first should be last and the last should be first. *Ques.* Do you not find yourself mistaken now? *Ans.* Was not Christ crucified? And by signs in the heavens that it would make known to me when I should commence the great work—and until the first sign appeared, I should conceal it from the knowledge of men—And on the appearance of the sign, (the eclipse of the sun last February) I should arise and prepare myself, and slay my enemies with their own weapons. And immediately on the sign appearing in the heavens, the seal was removed from my lips, and I communicated the great work laid out for me to do, to four in whom I had the greatest confidence, (Henry, Hark, Nelson, and Sam)—It was intended by us to have begun the work of death on the 4th July last—Many were the plans formed and rejected by us, and it affected my mind to such a degree, that I fell sick, and the time passed without our coming to any determination how to commence— Still forming new schemes and rejecting them, when the sign appeared again, which determined me not to wait longer.

Since the commencement of 1830, I had been living with Mr. Joseph Travis, who was to me a kind master, and placed the greatest confidence in me; in fact, I had no cause to complain of his treatment to me. On Saturday evening, the 20th of August, it was agreed between Henry, Hark and myself, to prepare a dinner the next day for the men we expected, and then to concert a plan, as we had not yet determined on any. Hark, on the following morning, brought a pig, and Henry brandy, and being joined by Sam, Nelson, Will and Jack, they prepared in the woods a dinner, where, about three o'clock, I joined them.

Q. **Why were you so backward in joining them.**
A. The same reason that had caused me not to mix with them for years before.

I saluted them on coming up, and asked Will how came he there, he answered, his life was worth no more than others, and his liberty as dear to him. I asked him if he thought to obtain it? He said he would, or lose his life. This was enough to put him in full confidence. Jack, I knew, was only a tool in the hands of Hark, it was quickly agreed we should commence at home (Mr. J. Travis') on that night, and until we had armed and equipped ourselves, and gathered sufficient force, neither age nor sex was to be spared, (which was invariably adhered to.) We remained at the feast until about two hours in the night, when we went to the house and found Austin; they all went to the cider press and drank, except myself. On returning to the house, Hark went to the door with an axe, for the purpose of breaking it open, as we knew we were strong enough to murder the family, if they were awaked by the noise;

but reflecting that it might create an alarm in the neighborhood, we determined to enter the house secretly, and murder them whilst sleeping. Hark got a ladder and set it against the chimney, on which I ascended, and hoisting a window, entered and came down stairs, unbarred the door, and removed the guns from their places. It was then observed that I must spill the first blood. On which, armed with a hatchet, and accompanied by Will, I entered my master's chamber, it being dark, I could not give a death blow, the hatchet glanced from his head, he sprang from the bed and called his wife, it was his last word, Will laid him dead, with a blow of his axe, and Mrs. Travis shared the same fate, as she lay in bed. The murder of this family, five in number, was the work of a moment, not one of them awoke; there was a little infant sleeping in a cradle, that was forgotten, until we had left the house and gone some distance, when Henry and Will returned and killed it; we got here, four guns that would shoot, and several old muskets, with a pound or two of powder. We remained some time at the barn, where we paraded; I formed them in a line as soldiers, and after carrying them through all the manoeuvres I was master of, marched them off to Mr. Salathul Francis', about six hundred yards distant. Sam and Will went to the door and knocked. Mr. Francis asked who was there, Sam replied, it was him, and he had a letter for him, on which he got up and came to the door, they immediately seized him, and dragging him out a little from the door, he was dispatched by repeated blows on the head; there was no other white person in the family. We started from there for Mrs. Reese's, maintaining the most perfect silence on our march, where finding the door unlocked, we entered, and murdered Mrs. Reese in her bed, while sleeping; her son awoke, but it was only to sleep the sleep of death, he had only time to say who is that, and he was no more. From Mrs. Reese's we went to Mrs. Turner's, a mile distant, which we reached about sunrise, on Monday morning. Henry, Austin, and Sam, went to the still, where, finding Mr. Peebles, Austin shot him, and the rest of us went to the house; as we approached, the family discovered us, and shut the door. Vain hope! Will, with one stroke of his axe, opened it, and we entered and found Mrs. Turner and Mrs. Newsome in the middle of a room, almost frightened to death. Will immediately killed Mrs. Turner, with one blow of his axe. I took Mrs. Newsome by the hand, and with the sword I had when I was apprehended, I struck her several blows over the head, but not being able to kill her, as the sword was dull. Will turning around and discovering it, despatched her also. A general destruction of property and search for money and ammunition, always succeeded the murders. By this time my company amounted to fifteen, and nine men mounted, who started for Mrs. Whitehead's, (the other six were to go through a by way to Mr. Bryant's and rejoin us at Mrs. Whitehead's,) as we approached the house we discovered Mr. Richard Whitehead standing in the cotton patch, near the lane fence; we called him over into the lane, and Will, the executioner, was near at hand, with his fatal axe, to send him to an untimely grave. As we pushed on to the house, I discovered some one run round the garden, and thinking it was some of the white family, I pursued them, but finding it was a servant girl belonging to the house, I returned to commence the work of death, but they whom I left, had not been idle; all the family were already murdered, but Mrs. Whitehead and her daughter Margaret. As I came round to the door I saw Will pulling Mrs. Whitehead out of the house, and at the step he nearly severed her head from her body, with his broad axe. Miss Margaret, when I discovered her, had concealed herself in the corner, formed by the projection of the cellar cap from the house; on my approach she fled, but was soon overtaken, and after repeated blows with a sword, I killed her by a blow on the head, with a fence rail. By this time, the six who had gone by Mr. Bryant's, rejoined us, and informed me they had done the work of death assigned them. We again divided, part going to Mr. Richard Porter's, and from thence to Nathaniel Francis', the others to Mr. Howell Harris', and Mr. T. Doyles. On my reaching Mr. Porter's, he had escaped with his family. I understood there, that the alarm had already spread, and I immediately returned to bring up those sent to Mr. Doyles, and Mr. Howell Harris'; the party I left going on to Mr. Francis', having told them I would join them in that neighborhood. I met these sent to Mr. Doyles' and Mr. Harris' returning, having met Mr. Doyle on the road and killed him; and learning from some who joined them, that Mr. Harris was from home, I immediately pursued the course taken by the party gone on before; but knowing they would complete the work of death and pillage, at Mr. Francis' before I could get there, I went to Mr. Peter Edwards', expecting to find them there, but they had been here also. I then went to Mr. John T. Barrow's, they had been here and murdered him. I pursued on their track to Capt. Newit Harris', where I found the greater part mounted, and ready to start; the men now amounting to about forty, shouted and hurraed as I rode up, some were in the yard, loading their guns, others drinking. They said Captain Harris and his family had escaped, the property in the house they destroyed, robbing him of money and other valuables. I ordered them to mount and march instantly, this was about nine or ten o'clock, Monday morning. I proceeded to Mr. Levi Waller's, two or three miles distant. I took my station in the rear, and as it was my object to carry terror and devastation wherever we went, I placed fifteen or twenty of the best armed and most to be relied on, in front, who generally approached the houses as fast as their horses could run; this was for two purposes, to prevent their escape and strike terror to the inhabitants—on this account I never got to the houses, after leaving Mrs. Whitehead's, until the murders were committed, except in one case. I sometimes got in sight in time to see the work of death completed, viewed the mangled bodies as they lay, in silent satisfaction, and immediately started in quest of other victims—Having murdered Mrs. Waller and ten children, we started for Mr. William Williams'—having killed him and two little boys that were there; while engaged in this, Mrs. Williams fled and got some distance from the house, but she was pursued, overtaken, and compelled to get up behind one of the company, who brought her back, and after showing her the mangled body of her lifeless husband, she was told to get down and lay by his side, where she was shot dead. I then started for Mr. Jacob Williams, where the family were murdered—Here we found a young man named Drury, who had come on business with Mr. Williams—he was pursued, overtaken and shot. Mrs. Vaughan was the next place we visited—and after murdering the family here, I determined on starting for Jerusalem—Our number amounted now to fifty or sixty, all mounted and armed with guns, axes, swords and clubs—On reaching Mr. James W. Parkers' gate, immediately on the road leading to Jerusalem, and about three miles distant, it was proposed to me to call there, but I objected, as I knew he was gone to Jerusalem, and my object was to reach there as soon as possible; but some of the men having relations at Mr. Parker's it was agreed that they might call and get his people. I remained at the gate on the road, with seven or eight; the others going across the field to the house, about half a mile off. After waiting some time for them, I became impatient, and started to the house for them, and on our return we were met by a party of white men, who had pursued our blood-stained track, and who had fired on those at the gate, and dispersed them, which I new [*sic*] nothing of, not having been at that time rejoined by any of them—Immediately on discovering the whites, I ordered my men to halt and form, as they appeared to be alarmed—The white men, eighteen in number, approached us in about one hundred yards, when one of them fired, (this was against the positive orders of Captain Alexander P. Peete, who commanded, and who had directed the men to reserve their fire until within thirty paces) And I discovered about half of them retreating, I then ordered my men to fire and rush on them; the few remaining stood their ground until we approached within fifty yards, when they fired and retreated. We pursued and overtook some of them who we thought we left dead; (they were not killed) after pursuing them about two hundred yards, and rising a little hill, I discovered they were met by another party, and had haulted, and were re-loading their guns, (this was a small party from Jerusalem who knew the negroes were in the field, and had just tied their horses to await their return to the road, knowing that Mr. Parker and family were in Jerusalem, but knew nothing of the party that had gone in with Captain Peete; on hearing the firing they immediately rushed to the spot and arrived just in time to arrest the progress of these barbarous villians[*sic*], and save the lives of their friends and fellow citizens.) Thinking that those who retreated first, and the party who fired on us at fifty or sixty yards distant, had all only fallen back to meet others with ammunition. As I saw them reloading their guns, and more coming up than I saw at first, and several of my bravest men being wounded, the others became panick [*sic*] struck and squandered over the field; the white men pursued and fired on us several times. Hark had his horse shot under him, and I caught another for him as it was running by me; five or six of my men were wounded, but none left on the field; finding myself defeated here I instantly determined to go through a private way, and cross the Nottoway river at the Cypress Bridge, three miles below Jerusalem, and attack that place in the rear, as I expected they would look for me on the other road, and I had a great desire to get there to procure arms and ammunition. After going a short distance in this private way, accompanied by about twenty men, I overtook two or three who told me the others were dispersed in every direction. After trying in vain to collect a sufficient force to proceed to Jerusalem, I determined to return, as I was sure they would make back to their old neighborhood, where they would rejoin me, make new recruits, and come down again. On my way back, I called at Mrs. Thomas's, Mrs. Spencer's, and several other places, the white families having fled, we found no more victims to gratify our thirst for blood, we stopped at Majr. Ridley's quarter for the night, and being joined by four of his men, with the recruits made since my defeat, we mustered now about forty strong. After placing out sentinels, I laid down to sleep, but was quickly roused by a great racket; starting up, I found some mounted, and others in great confusion; one of the sentinels having given the alarm that we were about to be attacked, I ordered some to ride round and reconnoitre, and on their return the others being more alarmed, not knowing who they were, fled in different ways, so that I was reduced to about twenty again; with this I determined to attempt to recruit, and proceed on to rally in the neighborhood, I had left. Dr. Blunt's was the nearest house, which we reached just before day; on riding up the yard, Hark fired a gun. We expected Dr. Blunt and his family were at Maj. Ridley's, as I knew there was a company of men there; the gun was fired to ascertain if any of the family were at home; we were immediately fired upon and retreated, leaving several of my men. I do not know what became of them, as I never saw them afterwards. Pursuing our course back and coming in sight of Captain Harris', where we had been the day before, we discovered a party of white men at the house, on which all deserted me but two, (Jacob and Nat,) we concealed ourselves in the woods until near night, when I sent them in search of Henry, Sam, Nelson, and Hark, and directed them to rally all they could, at the place we had had our dinner the Sunday before, where they would find me, and I accordingly returned there as soon as it was dark and remained until Wednesday evening, when discovering white men riding around the place as though they were looking for some one, and none of my men joining me, I concluded Jacob and Nat had been taken, and compelled to betray me. On this I gave up all hope for the present; and on Thursday night after having supplied myself with provisions from Mr. Travis's, I scratched a hole under a pile of fence rails in a field, where I concealed myself for six weeks, never leaving my hiding place but for a few minutes in the dead of night to get water which was very near; thinking by this time I could venture out, I began to go about in the night and eaves drop the houses in the neighborhood; pursuing this course for about a fortnight and gathering little or no intelligence, afraid of speaking to any human being, and returning every morning to my cave before the dawn of day. I know not how long I might have led this life, if accident had not betrayed me, a dog in the neighborhood passing by my hiding place one night while I was out, was attracted by some meat I had in my cave, and crawled in and stole it, and was coming out just as I returned. A few nights after, two negroes having started to go hunting with the same dog, and passed that way, the dog came again to the place, and having just gone out to walk about, discovered me and barked, on which thinking myself discovered, I spoke to them to beg concealment. On making myself known they fled from me. Knowing then they would betray me, I immediately left my hiding place, and was pursued almost incessantly until I was taken a fortnight afterwards by Mr. Benjamin Phipps, in a little hole I had dug out with my sword, for the purpose of concealment, under the top of a fallen tree. On Mr. Phipps' discovering the place of my concealment, he cocked his gun and aimed at me. I requested him not to shoot and I would give up, upon which he demanded my sword. I delivered it to him, and he brought me to prison. During the time I was pursued, I had many hair breadth escapes, which your time will not permit you to relate. I am here loaded with chains, and willing to suffer the fate that awaits me.

I here proceeded to make some inquiries of him after assuring him of the certain death that awaited him, and that concealment would only bring destruction on the innocent as well as guilty, of his own color, if he knew of any extensive or concerted plan. His answer was, I do not. When I questioned him as to the insurrection in North Caro-lina happening about the same time, he denied any knowledge of it; and when I looked him in the face as though I would search his inmost thoughts, he replied, "I see sir, you doubt my word; but can you not think the same ideas, and strange appearances about this time in the heavens might prompt others, as well as myself, to this undertaking." I now had much conversation with and asked him many questions, having forborne to do so previously, except in the cases noted in parenthesis; but during his statement, I had, unnoticed by him, taken notes as to some particular circumstances, and having the advantage of his statement before me in writing, on the evening of the third day that I had been with him, I began a cross examination, and found his statement corroborated by every circumstance coming within my own knowledge or the confessions of others whom had been either killed or executed, and whom he had not seen nor had any knowledge since 22d of August last, he expressed himself fully satisfied as to the impracticability of his attempt. It has been said he was ignorant and cowardly, and that his object was to murder and rob for the purpose of obtaining money to make his escape. It is notorious, that he was never known to have a dollar in his life; to swear an oath, or drink a drop of spirits. As to his ignorance, he certainly never had the advantages of education, but he can read and write, (it was taught him by his parents,) and for natural intelligence and quickness of apprehension, is surpassed by few men I have ever seen. As to his being a coward, his reason as given for not resisting Mr. Phipps, shews the decision of his character. When he saw Mr. Phipps present his gun, he said he knew it was impossible for him to escape as the woods were full of men; he therefore thought it was better to surrender, and trust to fortune for his escape. He is a complete fanatic, or plays his part most admirably. On other subjects he possesses an uncommon share of intelligence, with a mind capable of attaining any thing; but warped and perverted by the influence of early impressions. He is below the ordinary stature, though strong and active, having the true negro face, every feature of which is strongly marked. I shall not attempt to describe the effect of his narrative, as told and commented on by himself, in the condemned hole of the prison. The calm, deliberate composure with which he spoke of his late deeds and intentions, the expression of his fiend-like face when excited by enthusiasm, still bearing the stains of the blood of helpless innocence about him; clothed with rags and covered with chains; yet daring to raise his manacled hands to heaven, with a spirit soaring above the attributes of man; I looked on him and my blood curdled in my veins.

I will not shock the feelings of humanity, nor wound afresh the bosoms of the disconsolate sufferers in this unparalleled and inhuman massacre, by detailing the deeds of their fiend-like barbarity. There were two or three who were in the power of these wretches, had they known it, and who escaped in the most providential manner. There were two whom they thought they left dead on the field at Mr. Parker's, but who were only stunned by the blows of their guns, as they did not take time to re-load when they charged on them. The escape of a little girl who went to school at Mr. Waller's, and where the children were collecting for that purpose, excited general sympathy. As their teacher had not arrived, they were at play in the yard, and seeing the negroes approach, ran up on a dirt chimney, (such as are common to log houses,) and remained there unnoticed during the massacre of the eleven that were killed at this place. She remained on her hiding place till just before the arrival of a party, who were in pursuit of the murderers, when she came down and fled to a swamp, where, a mere child as she was, with the horrors of the late scene before her, she lay concealed until the next day, when seeing a party go up to the house, she came up, and on being asked how she escaped, replied with the utmost simplicity, "The Lord helped her." She was taken up behind a gentleman of the party, and returned to the arms of her weeping mother. Miss Whitehead concealed herself between the bed and the mat that supported it, while they murdered her sister in the same room, without discovering her. She was afterwards carried off, and concealed for protection by a slave of the family, who gave evidence against several of them on their trial. Mrs. Nathaniel Francis, while concealed in a closet heard their blows, and the shrieks of the victims of these ruthless savages; they then entered the closet where she was concealed, and went out without discovering her. While in this hiding place, she heard two of her women in a quarrel about the division of her clothes. Mr. John T. Baron, discovering them approaching his house, told his wife to make her escape, and scorning to fly, fell fighting on his own threshold. After firing his rifle, he discharged his gun at them, and then broke it over the villain who first approached him, but he was overpowered, and slain. His bravery, however, saved from the hands of these monsters, his lovely and amiable wife, who will long lament a husband so deserving of her love. As directed by him, she attempted to escape through the garden, when she was caught and held by one of her servant girls, but another coming to her rescue, she fled to the woods, and concealed herself. Few indeed, were those who escaped their work of death. But fortunate for society, the hand of retributive justice has overtaken them; and not one that was known to be concerned has escaped.

The Commonwealth, vs. Nat Turner.

Charged with making insurrection, and plotting to take away the lives of divers free white persons, &c. on the 22d of August, 1831.

The court composed of —, having met for the trial of Nat Turner, the prisoner was brought in and arraigned, and upon his arraignment pleaded Not guilty; saying to his counsel, that he did not feel so.

On the part of the Commonwealth, Levi Waller was introduced, who being sworn, deposed as follows: (agreeably to Nat's own Confession.)

Col. Trezvant was then introduced, who being Sworn, narrated Nat's Confession to him, as follows: (his Confession as given to Mr. Gray.) The prisoner introduced no evidence, and the case was submitted without argument to the court, who having found him guilty, Jeremiah Cobb, Esq. Chairman, pronounced the sentence of the court, in the following words: "Nat Turner! Stand up. Have you any thing to say why sentence of death should not be pronounced against you?"

Ans. I have not. I have made a full confession to Mr. Gray, and I have nothing more to say.

Attend then to the sentence of the Court. You have been arraigned and tried before this court, and convicted of one of the highest crimes in our criminal code. You have been convicted of plotting in cold blood, the indiscriminate destruction of men, of helpless women, and of infant children. The evidence before us leaves not a shadow of doubt, but that your hands were often imbrued in the blood of the innocent; and your own confession tells us that they were stained with the blood of a master; in your own language, "too indulgent." Could I stop here, your crime would be sufficiently aggravated. But the original contriver of a plan, deep and deadly, one that never can be effected, you managed so far to put it into execution, as to deprive us of many of our most valuable citizens; and this was done when they were asleep, and defenceless; under circumstances shocking to humanity. And while upon this part of the subject, I cannot but call your attention to the poor misguided wretches who have gone before you. They are not few in number—they were your bosom associates; and the blood of all cries aloud, and calls upon you, as the author of their misfortune. Yes! You forced them unprepared, from Time to Eternity. Borne down by this load of guilt, your only justification is, that you were led away by fanaticism. If this be true, from my soul I pity you; and while you have my sympathies, I am, nevertheless called upon to pass the sentence of the court. The time between this and your execution, will necessarily be very short; and your only hope must be in another world. The judgment of the court is, that you be taken hence to the jail from whence you came, thence to the place of execution, and on Friday next, between the hours of 10 A.M. and 2 P.M. be hung by the neck until you are dead! dead! dead and may the Lord have mercy upon your soul.

Source: Gray, Thomas R. *The Confessions of Nat Turner.* Baltimore: Thomas R. Gray, 1831, pp. 7–22.

Introduction to Two Articles from North Carolina— Reporting on Nat Turner: *Raleigh Register,* Sept. 1, 1831, and Reporting on Nat Turner: *North Carolina Star,* Sept. 1, 1831

The two articles reproduced here, one from *Raleigh Register,* the other from *North Carolina Star,* both dated September 1, 1831, reveal the determination to downplay the likelihood of such an insurrection occurring again. The article from the *Star* is particularly concerned to note that "most of these marauders and murderers were runaway slaves, who had broken in upon the white population for robbery and other mischief." In fact, Turner and his men were owned by local whites and did not steal; they were violently rejecting slavery. The paper's white readers do not want to entertain the possibility of organized black resistance to slavery. The first article also hints that "a few white faces" may have been seen among the rebellious blacks: in other words, if there is anything to the idea of the violence having a purpose other than robbery, it would have been connected to a white presence.

The other article names many of the whites who were killed, but only a few of the slaves, as if the blacks are anonymous. It also notes that it is "said that one white man, at least, was found amongst the dead conspirators, disguised and blackened as a negro," as if Turner and the other insurrectionists could not have conceived of such a bold uprising without white influence. And while the whites were "butchered," the blacks were "killed or captured." Like Thomas R. Gray, the white newspaper writers project their racist fantasies upon Turner's rebellion rather than seeing it as an understandable reaction to slavery.

Reporting on Nat Turner: *Raleigh Register,* Sept. 1, 1831

Insurrection and Murder! the disagreeable rumors which were in circulation in this city, at the date of our last publication, in relation to an Insurrection of the Slaves in Southampton county, Va, and a brief notice of which we inserted in a Postscript, turns out to be but too well founded! . . .

From the multiplicity of reports of which this soul harrowing occurrence has given birth, we have endeavored to cull such facts as we believe to be substantiated. These we will succinctly present to our readers, without however vouching for their precise accuracy, though, we have every reason to suppose them correct.—They may serve to allay the anxiety of the public, until something official appears.

On Sunday, the 21st ultimo, there was a negro preaching in the neighborhood of the Cross Keys, in Southampton county, about ten miles from the Court House, at which a black preacher (a slave) named Nat Turner, officiated. What the character of his discourse was, is not stated, but is a fair subject of inference from the fact that the conspiracy broke out the same evening in that neighborhood, and was headed by the preacher himself, in conjunction with a free man of color, called Will Artist. His harangue most probably was the immediate cause of the disturbance, for it seems from all the accounts that: the number of insurgents was few and that there existed nothing like a concerted plan, except in the narrow circle where it began. Perhaps by animating and encouraging the timid with hopes of success, removing the scruples of the religious by grossly prostituting the sacred oracles and inflaming and confirming the resolute, by all the savage fascinations of blood and booty, this mis-called preacher so worked upon the feelings of his auditors that they immediately resolved upon their bloody course. Be this however, as it may, it is certain that on the evening about fifty negroes, headed by the two persons beforenamed, rose in open rebellion and commenced an indiscriminate slaughter of the whites, sparing in their blood thirsty infatuation, neither age, sex, or condition. During that night and the following day, they succeeded in killing more than sixty whites. We have been favored by a gentleman, from the vicinity of the scene of action, with the following list of the individuals butchered, which however does not comprise all, several having fallen whose names could not be procured:

Joseph Travis, wife and three children	5
Lotha Francis	1
William Reese and mother	2
Mrs. Elizabeth Turner and two others	3
Henry Bryant, wife, child &mother-in-law	4
Mrs. C. Whitehead, three daughters, two sons, and one grand son	7
Trajan Doyel	1
John Williams' wife and child	2
Nat'l. Francis two children and overseer	3

Thomas Barrow	1
Levi Waller's eight children, wife and a young lady	10
Francis Feil's two daughters	2
Burnwell Jones' daughter	1
William Williams, wife and two others	4
Jacob Williams' wife, three children and _____ Drury	5
Caswell Worrell's wife and child	2
Mrs. Rebecca Vaughn, two sons, & niece	4
James Story and wife	2
	59

By Wednesday night, the whole band of insurgents, with the exception perhaps of two or three, were either killed or captured. The two leaders were shot and their heads placed upon stakes in the public road. Though many of the accounts differ in their details, they all concur in one point, viz: that the affair is at the end. & that no suspicion is entertained of its having been a general thing. We trust, therefore, that the great excitement into which the country has been thrown, will quickly subside, whilst the prompt manner in which this outrage has been met and the example made, will deter others from making similar attempts. It is very gratifying to us to have it in our power to state, as we can do upon.

It is said that one white man, at least, was found amongst the dead conspirators, disguised and blackened as a negro. . . . If this be true, the fate which overtook him was almost of too mitigated a character. We can think of no crime in the whole range of human enormity so heinous as this. Circumstances may be adduced, by bare possibility, in extenuation of a simple murder, or even of him who should place fire brand in the midst of a populous town—but for the infernal villain who would join our slaves in such an unhallowed and diabolical crusade, there can be no such thing as extenuation.

In closing this hasty account, we regret exceeding to state, that Mr. Shepard Lee, an esteemed member of the Halifax Blues was accidentally shot during an alarm, by a brother member of the Corps. The circumstances seem greatly to have excited the sympathy and regret of the circle, where Mr. Lee was best known.

Source: Reporting on Nat Turner. *Raleigh Register* (September 1, 1831): p. 3.

Reporting on Nat Turner: *North Carolina Star,* Sept. 1, 1831

A letter was received on Tuesday morning from Col. Trezvant, who lives at Jerusalem, in the county of Southampton; stating that an "insurrection" had broken out among the blacks—that several white families had been destroyed; that arms and ammunition were wanting in Southampton, and that a considerable military force might be required to subdue the disturbers. . . .

Another express on the same evening from the Mayor of Petersburg, requested the Governor to Send over arms—which were accordingly dispatched.

No authentic accounts have been received of the character of this unexpected transaction—of the number of blacks collected, of their designs, of the mischief they have done; whether they are the mere runaways who have broken out from the Swamps, or how many slaves of the neighboring plantations have joined—whether they have got together for mere rapine and robbery, or for what. But that these wretches will rue the day on which they broke loose upon the neighboring population, is most certain. A terrible retribution will fall upon their heads. Dearly will they pay for their misdeeds.

Later—We have later accounts, but they are still rumors, still deficient in authenticity. It is said that the leader of the blacks has been shot at the bridge at Jerusalem—that about 20 negroes were on their march to their rendezvous, and attacked by whites—6 killed and several prisoners taken.

It is said that there had been a skirmish between the largest body of blacks, and some few militia—that the negroes had fled into a wood—and the writer of the letter, who gives this account, believes that as soon as the troops are up, they would be completely surrounded and cut off. As ample retribution will be their lot for the blood which they had shed. Rumor had stated the number of their victims as high as 70 or 80, perhaps more—but such stories are always greatly exaggerated. We have no doubt it is in the present instance.

One of the last expresses states, that most, if not all the blacks were runaways, who had broken out of the Swamps, to rob and to mischief—that few, if any, of the plantation hands, had helped them—and in one case, he heard of a master of one of the estates turning out with his slaves, to meet a party coming to attack him—that two of the assailants had been killed, a third wounded, and the rest ran off. He heard of several others being killed. But it is extremely difficult to get at the truth in all such cases.

The Governor received a letter by this express yesterday morning, from Gen. Eppes. Gen. Eppes believes that in a day or two all will be tranquil, that no more troops will be necessary, and perhaps those in service may be discharged, thou there was a party near Southampton Court House, and a small one near Bell field—that things took well.

Late account—An express arrival last night, little before 10 o'clock, with dispatches from Petersburg for the Governor. One of the letters is from Capt. D. H. Branch. He informs that a letter had been received from Jerusalem, written on Wednesday. The writer is said to be an intelligent and respectable man. He states, that he had seen the bodies of all, or most of the whites who had been murdered in that neighborhood, amounting to about 40—most of them women and children! That a skirmish had taken place on Tuesday between the whites and the blacks in the quarter, amounting to about 40—in which no loss was sustained by the whites, and several of the blacks killed, and 6 or 8 of them taken prisoners, and thrown in jail. Capt. B. understands, that the blacks are in two or three detachments—that they have perpetrated in all about 60 murders; that they have lost a considerable part of their force; that their spirits are broken, that their object seems now to be to skulk and that they have lost all further intention of committing further depredations. He is of opinion, from what he understands, that no more troops will be required to repress them; there being a sufficient number to effect that object.

The Express who brought the letter from Petersburg understands that the Richmond Dragoons arrived in Southampton on Wednesday night. The story of the leader being shot down near Jerusalem, is said to be contradicted. It is suggested that he is a negro from North Carolina, and his name has been quoted, we know not on what authority, to be that of Nathaniel Turner.

It is supposed that most of these marauders and murderers were runaway negroes, who had broken in upon the white population for robbery and other mischief. There is no appearance of concert among the slaves, nothing that can deserve the name of insurrection, which it was originally denominated. There is some story of a few white faces being seen, or supposed to be seen, among them. No particular account has been received of the detachment near Belfield; though there were numerous of some of them having been cut or shot down. The number of the bandits had been probably much magnified; if it be true that only forty were engaged in the skirmish near Jerusalem.

There is no doubt that any further danger from them is by this time over, and that they will dearly rue the day when they ever dared to break in upon the peace of the country; and to shed the blood of any one; particularly the women and children.

Source: Reporting on Nat Turner. *North Carolina Star* (September 1, 1831): p. 3.

Introduction to Thomas Wentworth Higginson, "Nat Turner's Insurrection," *The Atlantic* (1861)

Thomas Wentworth Higginson (1823–1911) is best known today for being Emily Dickinson's mentor and editor, but he was also a social activist. He was a strong opponent of slavery and a strong supporter of women's rights. Like so many others, he was energized by the Fugitive Slave Law of 1850 in the cause of abolition, because it made avoiding the issue of slavery impossible for Northerners, who were legally required to help in the pursuit of runaway slaves. Higginson eventually was made a colonel in the 1st South Carolina Volunteers, which was the first black regiment authorized to fight for the Union. After the Civil War he threw himself into numerous efforts to help freed slaves, women, and white working class men gain their rights.

Written thirty years after Turner's rebellion, Higginson's article, which appeared in the newly established *Atlantic Monthly,* presents a much more realistic picture of Nat Turner and his followers. Rather than the deranged fanatic of Thomas R. Gray's *Confession of Nat Turner,* Higginson's Nat Turner is a man who wanted freedom from slavery, the same thing whites in Turner's position would have wanted. He also points out that the horrors of what Turner and his men did were far less than the horrors of suppressing Turner's rebellion, which involved killing perhaps hundreds of black people, many of whom had nothing to do with the insurrection. Higginson contends also that not only was Turner not unique but only the realization of the potential for retribution against whites that could have been found on many other plantations.

From Thomas Wentworth Higginson, "Nat Turner's Insurrection," *The Atlantic* (1861)

DURING the year 1831, up to the twenty-third of August, the Virginia newspapers were absorbed in the momentous problems which then occupied the minds of intelligent American citizens:—What General Jackson should do with the scolds, and what with the disreputables,—Should South Carolina be allowed to nullify? and would the wives of Cabinet Ministers call on Mrs. Eaton? It is an unfailing opiate, to turn over the drowsy files of the "Richmond Enquirer," until the moment when those dry and dusty pages are suddenly kindled into flame by the torch of Nat Turner. Then the terror flares on increasing, until the remotest Southern States are found shuddering at nightly rumors of insurrection,—until far off European colonies, Antigua, Martinique, Caraccas, Tortola, recognize by some secret sympathy the same epidemic alarms,—until the very boldest words of freedom are reported as uttered in the Virginia House of Delegates with unclosed doors,—until an obscure young man named Garrison is indicted at Common Law in North Carolina, and has a price set upon his head by the Legislature of Georgia. The insurrection revived in one agonizing reminiscence all the distresses of Gabriel's Revolt, thirty years before; and its memory endures still fresh, now that thirty added years have brought the more formidable presence of General Butler. It is by no means impossible that the very children or even confederates of Nat Turner may be included at this moment among the contraband articles of Fort Monroe.

In the woods on the plantation of Joseph Travis, upon the Sunday just named, six slaves met at noon for what is called in the Northern States a picnic and in the Southern a barbecue. The bill of fare was to be simple: one brought a pig, and another some brandy, giving to the meeting an aspect so cheaply convivial that no one would have imagined it to be the final consummation of a conspiracy which had been for six months in preparation. In this plot four of the men had been already initiated,—Henry, Hark or Hercules, Nelson, and Sam. Two others were novices, Will and Jack by name. The party had remained together from twelve to three o'clock, when a seventh man joined them,—a short, stout, powerfully built person, of dark mulatto complexion and strongly-marked African features, but with a face full of expression and resolution. This was Nat Turner.

He was at this time nearly thirty-one years old, having been born on the second of October, 1800. He had belonged originally to Benjamin Turner,—whence his last name, slaves having usually no patronymic,—had then been transferred to Putnam Moore, and then to his present owner. He had, by his own account, felt himself singled out from childhood for some great work; and he had some peculiar marks on his person, which, joined to his great mental precocity, were enough to occasion, among his youthful companions, a superstitious faith in his gifts and destiny. He had great mechanical ingenuity also, experimentalized very early in making paper, gunpowder, pottery, and in other arts which in later life he was found thoroughly to understand. His moral faculties were very strong, so that white witnesses admitted that he had never been known to swear an oath, to drink a drop of spirits, or to commit a theft. And in general, so marked were his early peculiarities, that people said "he had too much sense to be raised, and if he was, he would never be of any use as a slave." This impression of personal destiny grew with his growth;—he fasted, prayed, preached, read the Bible, heard voices when he walked behind his plough, and communicated his revelations to the awe-struck slaves. They told him in return, that, "if they had his sense, they would not serve any master in the world."

The biographies of slaves can hardly be individualized; they belong to the class. We know bare facts; it is only the general experience of human beings in like condition which can clothe them with life. The outlines are certain, the details are inferential. Thus, for instance, we know that Nat Turner's young wife was a slave; we know that she belonged to a different master from himself; we know little more than this, but this is much. For this is equivalent to saying that by day or by night that husband had no more power to protect her than the man who lies bound upon a plundered vessel's deck has power to protect his wife on board the pirate-schooner disappearing in the horizon; she may be reverenced, she may be outraged; it is in the powerlessness that the agony lies. There is, indeed, one thing more which we do know of this young woman: the Virginia newspapers state that she was tortured under the lash, after her husband's execution, to make her produce his papers: this is all.

What his private experiences and special privileges or wrongs may have been, it is therefore now impossible to say. Travis was declared to be "more humane and fatherly to his slaves than any man in the county"; but it is astonishing how often this phenomenon occurs in the contemporary annals of slave insurrections. The chairman of the county court also stated, in pronouncing sentence, that Nat Turner had spoken of his master as "only too indulgent"; but this, for some reason, does not appear in his printed Confession, which only says, "He was a kind master, and placed the greatest confidence in me." It is very possible that it may have been so, but the printed accounts of Nat Turner's person look suspicious: he is described in Governor Floyd's proclamation as having a scar on one of his temples, also one on the back of his neck and a large knot on one of the bones of his right arm, produced by a blow; and although these were explained away in Virginia newspapers as being produced by fights with his companions, yet such affrays are entirely foreign to the admitted habits of the man. It must, therefore remain an open question, whether the scars and the knot were produced black hands or by white.

Whatever Nat Turner's experiences of slavery might have been, it is certain that his plans were not suddenly adopted, but that he had brooded over them for years. To this day there are traditions among the Virginia slaves of the keen devices of "Prophet Nat." If he was caught with lime and lamp-black in hand, conning over a half-finished county-map on the barn-door, he was always "planning what to do, if he were blind," or "studying how to get to Mr. Francis's house." When he had called a meeting of slaves, and some poor whites came eavesdropping, the poor whites at once became the subjects for discussion, he incidentally mentioned that the masters had been heard threatening to drive them away; one slave had been ordered to shoot Mr. Jones's pigs, another to tear down Mr. Johnson's fences. The poor whites, Johnson and Jones, ran home see to their homesteads, and were better friends than ever to Prophet Nat.

He never was a Baptist preacher, though such vocation has often been attributed to him. The religious hallucinations narrated in his Confession seem to have been as genuine as the average of such things, and are very well expressed. It reads quite like Jacob Behmen. He saw white spirits and black spirits contending in the skies, the sun was darkened, the thunder rolled. "And the Holy Ghost was with me, and said, 'Behold me as I stand in the heavens!' And I looked and saw the forms of men in different attitudes. And there were lights in the sky, to which the children of darkness gave other names than what they really were; for they were the lights of the Saviour's hands, stretched forth from east to west, even as they were extended on the cross on Calvary, for the redemption of sinners." He saw drops of blood on the corn: this was Christ's blood, shed for man. He saw on the leaves in the woods letters and numbers and figures of men,—the same symbols which he had seen in the skies. On May 12, 1828, the Holy Spirit appeared to him and proclaimed that the yoke of Jesus must fall on him, and he must fight against the Serpent when the sign appeared. Then came an eclipse of the sun in February, 1831: this was the sign; then he must arise and prepare himself, and slay his enemies with their own weapons; then also the seal was removed from his lips, and then he confided his plans to four associates.

When he came, therefore, to the barbecue on the appointed Sunday, and found, not these four only, but two others, his first question to the intruders was, How they came thither. To this Will answered manfully, that his life was worth no more than the others, and "his liberty was as dear to him." This admitted him to confidence, and as Jack was known to be entirely under Hark's influence, the strangers were no bar to their discussion. Eleven hours they remained there, in anxious consultation: one can imagine those terrible dusky faces, beneath the funereal woods, and amid the flickering of pine-knot torches, preparing that stern revenge whose shuddering echoes should ring through the land so long. Two things were at last decided: to begin their work that night, and to begin it with a massacre so swift and irresistible as to create in a few days more terror than many battles, and so spare the need of future bloodshed. "It was agreed that we should commence at home, on that night, and, until we had armed and equipped ourselves and gained sufficient force, neither age nor sex was to be spared: which was invariably adhered to."

John Brown invaded Virginia with nineteen men and with the avowed resolution to take no life but in self-defence. Nat Turner attacked Virginia from within, with six men, and with the determination to spare no life until his power was established. John Brown intended to pass rapidly through Virginia, and then retreat to the mountains. Nat Turner intended to "conquer Southampton County as the white men did in the Revolution, and then retreat, if necessary, to the Dismal Swamp." Each plan was deliberately matured; each was in its way, practicable; but each was defeated by a single false step, as will soon appear.

We must pass over the details of horror, as they occurred during the next twenty-four hours. Swift and stealthy as Indians, the black men passed from house to house,—not pausing, not hesitating, as their terrible work went on. In one thing they were humaner than Indians or than white men fighting against Indians,—there was no gratuitous outrage beyond the death-blow itself, no insult, no mutilation; but in every house they entered, that blow fell on man, woman, and child,—nothing that had a white skin was spared. From every house they took arms and ammunition, and from a few, money; on every plantation they found recruits: those dusky slaves, so obsequious to their master the day before, so prompt to sing and dance before his Northern visitors, were all swift to transform themselves into fiends of retribution now; show them sword or musket and they grasped it, though it were an heirloom from Washington himself. The troop increased from house to house,—first to fifteen, then to forty, then to sixty. Some were armed with muskets, some with axes, some with scythes; some came on their masters' horses. As the numbers increased, they could be divided, and the awful work was carried on more rapidly still. The plan then was for an advanced guard of horsemen to approach each house at a gallop, and surround it till the others came up. Meanwhile what agonies of terror must have taken place within, shared alike by innocent and by guilty! what memories of wrongs inflicted on those dusky creatures, by some,—what innocent participation, by others, in the penance! The outbreak lasted for but forty-eight hours; but during that period fifty-five whites were slain, without the loss of a single slave.

It was admitted in the "Richmond Enquirer" of the time that "indiscriminate massacre was not their intention, after they obtained foothold, and was resorted to in the first instance to strike terror and alarm. Women and children would afterwards have been spared, and men also who ceased to resist." It is reported by some of the contemporary newspapers, that a portion of this abstinence was the result of deliberate consultation among the insurrectionists; that some of them were resolved on taking the white women for wives, but were overruled by Nat Turner. If so, he is the only American slave-leader of whom we know certainly that he rose above the ordinary level of slave vengeance, and Mrs. Stowe's picture of Dred's purposes is then precisely typical of his. "Whom the Lord saith unto us, 'Smite,' them will we smite. We will not torment them with the scourge and fire, nor defile their women as they have done with ours. But we will slay them utterly, and consume them from off the face of the earth."

When the number of adherents had increased to fifty or sixty, Nat Turner judged it time to strike at the county-seat, Jerusalem. Thither a few white fugitives had already fled, and couriers might thence be dispatched for aid to Richmond and Petersburg, unless promptly intercepted. Besides, he could there find arms, ammunition, and money; though they had already obtained, it is dubiously reported, from eight hundred to one thousand dollars. On the way it was necessary to pass the plantation of Mr. Parker, three miles from Jerusalem. Some of the men wished to stop here and enlist some of their friends. Nat Turner objected, as the delay might prove dangerous; he yielded at last, and it proved fatal. He remained at the gate with six or eight men; thirty or forty went to the house, half a mile distant. They remained too long, and he went alone to hasten them. During his absence a party of eighteen white men came up suddenly, dispersing the small guard left at the gate; and when the main body of slaves emerged from the house, they encountered, for the first time, their armed masters. The blacks halted, the whites advanced cautiously within a hundred yards and fired a volley; on its being returned, they broke into disorder, and hurriedly retreated, leaving some wounded on the ground. The retreating whites were pursued, and were saved only by falling in with another band of fresh men from Jerusalem, with whose aid they turned upon the slaves, who in their turn fell into confusion. Turner, Hark, and about twenty men on horseback retreated in some order; the rest were scattered. The leader still planned to reach Jerusalem by a private way, thus evading pursuit; but at last decided to stop for the night, in the hope of enlisting additional recruits.

During the night the number increased again to forty, and they encamped on Major Ridley's plantation. An alarm took place during the darkness,—whether real or imaginary does not appear,—and the men became scattered again. Proceeding to make fresh enlistments with the daylight, they were resisted at Dr. Blunt's house, where his slaves, under his orders, fired upon them, and this, with a later attack from a party of white men near Captain Harris's, so broke up the whole force that they never reunited. The few who remained together agreed to separate for a few hours to see if anything could be done to revive the insurrection, and meet again that evening at their original rendezvous. But they never reached it.

Sadly came Nat Turner at nightfall into those gloomy woods where forty-eight hours before he had revealed the details of his terrible plot to his companions. At the outset all his plans had succeeded; everything was as he predicted: the slaves had come readily at his call, the masters had proved perfectly defenceless. Had he not been persuaded to pause at Parker's plantation, he would have been master before now of the arms and ammunition at Jerusalem; and with these to aid, and the Dismal Swamp for a refuge, he might have sustained himself indefinitely against his pursuers.

Now the blood was shed, the risk was incurred, his friends were killed or captured, and all for what? Lasting memories of terror, to be sure, for his oppressors; but on the other hand, hopeless failure for the insurrection, and certain death for him. What a watch be must have kept that night! To that excited imagination, which had always seen spirits in the sky and blood-drops on the corn and hieroglyphic marks on the dry leaves, how full the lonely forest must have been of signs and solemn warnings! Alone with the fox's bark, the rabbit's rustle, and the screech-owl's scream, the self-appointed prophet brooded over his despair. Once creeping to the edge of the wood, he saw men stealthily approach on horseback. He fancied them some of his companions; but before he dared to whisper their ominous names, "Hark" or "Dred,"—for the latter was the name, since famous, of one of his more recent recruits,—he saw them to be white men, and shrank back stealthily beneath his covert.

There he waited two weary days and two melancholy nights,— long enough to satisfy himself that no one would rejoin him, and that the insurrection had hopelessly failed. The determined, desperate spirits who had shared his plans were scattered forever, and longer delay would be destruction for him also. He found a spot which he judged safe, dug a hole under a pile of fence-rails in a field, and lay there for six weeks, only leaving it for a few moments at midnight to obtain water from a neighboring spring. Food he had previously provided, without discovery, from a house near by.

Meanwhile an unbounded variety of rumors went flying through the State. The express which first reached the Governor announced that the militia were retreating before the slaves. An express to Petersburg further fixed the number of militia at three hundred, and of blacks at eight hundred, and invented a convenient shower of rain to explain the dampened ardor of the whites. Later reports described the slaves as making three desperate attempts to cross the bridge over the Nottoway between Cross Keys and Jerusalem, and stated that the leader had been shot in the attempt. Other accounts put the number of negroes at three hundred, all well mounted and armed, with two or three white men as leaders. Their intention was supposed to be to reach the Dismal Swamp, and they must be hemmed in from that side.

Indeed, the most formidable weapon in the hands of slave-insurgents is always this blind panic they create, and the wild exaggerations which follow. The worst being possible, every one takes the worst for granted. Undoubtedly a dozen armed men could have stifled this insurrection, even after it had commenced operations; but it is the fatal weakness of a slaveholding community, that it can never furnish men promptly for such a purpose. "My first intention was," says one of the most intelligent newspaper narrators of the affair, "to have attacked them with thirty or forty men; but those who had families here were strongly opposed to it."

As usual, each man was pinioned to his own hearth-stone. As usual, aid had to be summoned from a distance, and, as usual, the United States troops were the chief reliance. Colonel House, commanding at Fort Monroe, sent at once three companies of artillery under Lieutenant Colonel Worth, and embarked them on board the steamer Hampton for Suffolk. These were joined by detachments from the United States ships Warren and Natchez, the whole amounting to nearly eight hundred men. Two volunteer companies went from Richmond, four from Petersburg, one from Norfolk, one from Portsmouth, and several from North Carolina. The militia of Norfolk, Nansemond, and Princess Anne Counties, and the United States troops at Old Point Comfort, were ordered to scour the Dismal Swamp, where it was believed that two or three thousand fugitives were preparing to join the insurgents. It was even proposed to send two companies from New York and one from New London to the same point.

When these various forces reached Southampton County, they found all labor paralyzed and whole plantations abandoned. A letter from Jerusalem, dated August 24th, says, "The oldest inhabitant of our county has never experienced such a distressing time as we have had since Sunday night last. . . . Every house, room, and corner in the place is full of women and children, driven from home, who had to take the woods until they could get to this place." "For many miles around their track," says another, "the county is deserted by women and children." Still another writes, "Jerusalem is full of women, most of them from the other side of the river,—about two hundred at Vix's." Then follow descriptions of the sufferings of these persons, many of whom had lain night after night in the woods. But the immediate danger was at an end, the short-lived insurrection was finished, and now the work of vengeance was to begin. In the frank phrase of a North Carolina correspondent,—"The massacre of the whites was over, and the white people had commenced the destruction of the negroes, which was continued after our Men got there, from time to time, as they could fall in with them, all day yesterday." A postscript adds, that "passengers by the Fayetteville stage say, that, by the latest accounts, one hundred and twenty negroes had been killed,"—this being little more than one day's work.

These murders were defended as Nat Turner defended his: a fearful blow must be struck. In shuddering at the horrors of the insurrection, we have forgotten the far greater horrors of its suppression.

The newspapers of the day contain many indignant protests against the cruelties which took place. "It is with pain," says a correspondent of the "National Intelligencer," September 7, 1831, "that we speak of another feature of the Southampton Rebellion; for we have been most unwilling to have our sympathies for the sufferers diminished or affected by their misconduct. We allude to the slaughter of many blacks without trial and under circumstances of great barbarity. . . . We met with an individual of intelligence who told us that he himself had killed between ten and fifteen. . . . We [the Richmond troops] witnessed with surprise the sanguinary temper of the population, who evinced a strong disposition to inflict immediate death on every prisoner."

There is a remarkable official document from General Eppes, the officer in command, to be found in the "Richmond Enquirer" for September 6, 1831. It is an indignant denunciation of precisely these outrages; and though he refuses to give details, he supplies their place by epithets: "revolting,"—"inhuman and not to be justified,"— "acts of barbarity and cruelty,"—"acts of atrocity,"—"this course of proceeding dignifies the rebel and the assassin with the sanctity of martyrdom." And he ends by threatening martial law upon all future transgressors. Such general orders are not issued except in rather extreme cases. And in the parallel columns of the newspaper the innocent editor prints equally indignant descriptions of Russian atrocities in Lithuania, where the Poles were engaged in active insurrection, amid profuse sympathy from Virginia.

The truth is, it was a Reign of Terror. Volunteer patrols rode in all directions, visiting plantations. "It was with the greatest difficulty," said General Brodnax before the House of Delegates, "and at the hazard of personal popularity and esteem, that the coolest and most judicious among us could exert an influence sufficient to restrain an indiscriminate slaughter of the blacks who were suspected." A letter from the Rev. G.W. Powell declares, "There are thousands of troops searching in every direction, and many negroes are killed every day: the exact number will never be ascertained." Petition after petition was subsequently presented to the legislature, asking compensation for slaves thus assassinated without trial.

Men were tortured to death, burned, maimed, and subjected to nameless atrocities. The overseers were called on to point out any slaves whom they distrusted, and if any tried to escape, they were shot down. Nay, worse than this. "A party of horsemen started from Richmond with the intention of killing every colored person they saw in Southampton County. They stopped opposite the cabin of a free colored man, who was hoeing in his little field. They called out, 'Is this Southampton County?' He replied, 'Yes, Sir, you have just crossed the line, by yonder tree.' They shot him dead and rode on." This is from the narrative of the editor of the "Richmond Whig," who was then on duty in the militia, and protested manfully against these outrages. "Some of these scenes," he adds, "are hardly inferior in barbarity to the atrocities of the insurgents."

These were the masters' stories. If even these conceded so much, it would be interesting to hear what the slaves had to report. I am indebted to my honored friend, Lydia Maria Child, for some vivid recollections of this terrible period, as noted down from the lips of an old colored woman, once well known in New York, Charity Bowery. "At the time of the old Prophet Nat," she said, "the colored folks was afraid to pray loud; for the whites threatened to punish 'em dreadfully, if the least noise was heard. The patrols was low drunken whites, and in Nat's time, if they heard any of the colored folks praying or singing a hymn, they would fall upon 'em and abuse 'em, and sometimes kill 'em, afore master or missis could get to 'em. The brightest and best was killed in Nat's time. The whites always suspect such ones. They killed a great many at a place called Duplon. They killed Antonio, a slave of Mr. J. Stanley, whom they shot; then they pointed their guns at him, and told him to confess about the insurrection. He told 'em be didn't know anything about any insurrection. They shot several balls through him, quartered him, and put his head on a pole at the fork of the road leading to the court." (This is no exaggeration, if the Virginia newspapers may be taken as evidence.) "It was there but a short time. He had no trial. They never do. In Nat's time, the patrols would tie up the free colored people, flog 'em, and try to make 'em lie against one another, and often killed them before anybody could interfere. Mr. James Cole, High Sheriff, said, if any of the patrols came on his plantation, he would lose his life in defence of his people. One day he heard a patroller boasting how many niggers he had killed. Mr. Cole said, 'If you don't pack up, as quick as God Almighty will let you, and get out of this town, and never be seen in it again, I'll put you where dogs won't bark at you.' He went off, and wasn't seen in them parts again."

These outrages were not limited to the colored population; but other instances occurred which strikingly remind one of more recent times. An Englishman, named Robinson, was engaged in selling books at Petersburg. An alarm being given, one night, that five hundred blacks were marching towards the town, he stood guard, with others, on the bridge. After the panic had a little subsided, he happened to remark, that "the blacks, as men, were entitled to their freedom, and ought to be emancipated." This led to great excitement, and he was warned to leave town. He took passage in the stage, but the stage was intercepted. He then fled to a friend's house; the house was broken open, and he was dragged forth. The civil authorities, being applied to, refused to interfere. The mob stripped him, gave him a great number of lashes, and sent him on foot, naked, under a hot sun, to Richmond, whence he with difficulty found a passage to New York.

Of the capture or escape of most of that small band who met with Nat Turner in the woods upon the Travis plantation little can now be known. All appear among the list of convicted, except Henry and Will. General Moore, who occasionally figures as second in command, in the newspaper narratives of that day, was probably the Hark or Hercules before mentioned; as no other of the confederates had belonged to Mrs. Travis, or would have been likely to bear her previous name of Moore. As usual, the newspapers state that most, if not all the slaves, were "the property of kind and indulgent masters." Whether in any case they were also the sons of those masters is a point ignored; but from the fact that three out of the seven were at first reported as being white men several different witnesses,— the whole number being correctly given, and the statement therefore probably authentic,—one must suppose that there was an admixture of patrician blood in some of these conspirators.

There is one touching story, in connection with these terrible retaliations, which rests on good authority, that of the Rev. M. B. Cox, a Liberian missionary, then in Virginia. In the hunt which followed the massacre, a slaveholder went into the woods, accompanied by a faithful slave, who had been the means of saving his life during the insurrection. When they had reached a retired place in the forest, the man handed his gun to his master, informing him that he could not live a slave any longer, and requesting him either to free him or shoot him on the spot. The master took the gun, in some trepidation, levelled it at the faithful negro, and shot him through the heart. It is probable that this slaveholder was a Dr. Blunt,—his being the only plantation where the slaves were reported as thus defending their masters. "If this be true," said the "Richmond Enquirer," when it first narrated this instance of loyalty, "great will be the desert of these noble-minded Africans." This "noble-minded African," at least, estimated his own desert at a high standard: he demanded freedom,— and obtained it.

Meanwhile the panic of the whites continued; for, though all others might be disposed of, Nat Turner was still at large. We have positive evidence of the extent of the alarm, although great efforts were afterwards made to represent it as a trifling affair. A distinguished citizen of Virginia wrote three months later to the Hon. W. B. Seabrook of South Carolina,—"From all that has come to my knowledge during and since that affair, I am convinced most fully that every black preacher in the country east of the Blue Ridge was in the secret." "There is much reason to believe," says the Governor's message on December 6th, "that the spirit of insurrection was not confined to Southampton. Many convictions have taken place elsewhere, and some few in distant counties." The withdrawal of the United States troops, after some ten days' service, was a signal for fresh excitement, and an address, numerously signed, was presented to the United States Government, imploring their continued stay. More than three weeks after the first alarm, the Governor sent a supply of arms into Prince William, Fauquier, and Orange Counties. "From examinations which have taken place in other counties," says one of the best newspaper historians of the affair, (in the "Richmond Enquirer" of September 6th,) "I fear that the scheme embraced a wider sphere than I at first supposed." Nat Turner himself, intentionally or otherwise, increased the confusion by denying all knowledge of the North Carolina outbreak, and declaring that he had communicated his plans to his four confederates within six months; while, on the other hand, a slave-girl, sixteen or seventeen years old, belonging to Solomon Parker, testified that she had heard the subject discussed for eighteen months, and that at a meeting held during the previous May some eight or ten had joined the plot.

But the greatest bubble burst in Louisiana. Captain Alexander, an English tourist, arriving in New Orleans at the beginning of September, found the whole city in tumult. Handbills had been issued, appealing to the slaves to rise against their masters, saying that all men were born equal, declaring that Hannibal was a black man, and that they also might have great leaders among them. Twelve hundred stand of weapons were said to have been found in a black man's house; five hundred citizens were under arms, and four companies of regulars were ordered to the city, whose barracks Alexander himself visited.

If such were the alarm in New Orleans, the story, of course, lost nothing by transmission to other Slave States. A rumor reached Frankfort, Kentucky, that the slaves already had possession of the coast, both above and below New Orleans. But the most remarkable circumstance is, that all this seems to have been a mere revival of an old terror, once before excited and exploded. The following paragraph had appeared in the Jacksonville (Georgia) "Observer," during the spring previous:

"FEARFUL DISCOVERY. We were favored, by yesterday's mail, with a letter from New Orleans, of May 1st, in which we find that an important discovery had been made a few days previous in that city. The following is an extract:—'Four days ago, as some planters were digging under ground, they found a square room containing eleven thousand stand of arms and fifteen thousand cartridges, each of the cartridges containing a bullet.' It is said the negroes intended to rise as soon as the sickly season began, and obtain possession of the city by massacring the white population. The same letter states that the mayor had prohibited the opening of Sunday-schools for the instruction of blacks, under a penalty of five hundred dollars for the first offence, and for the second, death."

Such were the terrors that came back from nine other Slave States, as the echo of the voice of Nat Turner; and when it is also known that the subject was at once taken up by the legislatures of other States, where there was no public panic, as in Missouri and Tennessee,—and when, finally, it is added that reports of insurrection had been arriving all that year from Rio Janeiro, Martinique, St. Jago, Antigua, Caraccas, and Tortola, it is easy to see with what prolonged distress the accumulated terror must have weighed down upon Virginia, during the two months that Nat Turner lay hid.

True, there were a thousand men in arms in Southampton County, to inspire security. But the blow had been struck by only seven men before; and unless there were an armed guard in every house, who could tell but any house might at any moment be the scene of new horrors? They might kill or imprison unresisting negroes by day, but could they resist their avengers by night? "The half cannot be told," wrote a lady from another part of Virginia, at this time, "of the distresses of the people. In Southampton County, the scene of the insurrection, the distress beggars description. A gentleman who has been there says that even here, where there has been great alarm, we have no idea of the situation of those in that county. . . . I do not hesitate to believe that many negroes around us would join in a massacre as horrible as that which has taken place, if an opportunity should offer."

Meanwhile the cause of all this terror was made the object of desperate search. On September 17th the Governor offered a reward of five hundred dollars for his capture, and there were other rewards swelling the amount to eleven hundred dollars,—but in vain. No one could track or trap him. On September 30th a minute account of his capture appeared in the newspapers, but it was wholly false. On October 7th there was another, and on October 18th another; yet all without foundation. Worn out by confinement in his little cave, Nat Turner grew more adventurous, and began to move about stealthily by night, afraid to speak to any human being, but hoping to obtain some information that might aid his escape. Returning regularly to his retreat before daybreak, he might possibly have continued this mode of life until pursuit had ceased, had not a dog succeeded where men had failed. The creature accidentally smelt out the provisions hid in the cave, and finally led thither his masters, two negroes, one of whom was named Nelson. On discovering the terrible fugitive, they fled precipitately, when he hastened to retreat in an opposite direction. This was on October 15th, and from this moment the neighborhood was all alive with excitement, and five or six hundred men undertook the pursuit.

It shows a more than Indian adroitness in Nat Turner to have escaped capture any longer. The cave, the arms, the provisions were found; and lying among them the notched stick of this miserable Robinson Crusoe, marked with five weary weeks and six days. But the man was gone. For ten days more he concealed himself among the wheat-stacks on Mr. Francis's plantation, and during this time was reduced almost to despair. Once he decided to surrender himself, and walked by night within two miles of Jerusalem before his purpose failed him. Three times he tried to get out of that neighborhood, but in vain: travelling by day was, of course, out of the question, and by night he found it impossible to elude the patrol. Again and again, therefore, he returned to his hiding-place, and during his whole two months' liberty never went five miles from the Cross Keys. On the 25th of October, he was at last discovered by Mr. Francis, as he was emerging from a stack. A load of buckshot was instantly discharged at him, twelve of which passed through his hat as he fell to the ground. He escaped even then, but his pursuers were rapidly concentrating upon him, and it is perfectly astonishing that he could have eluded them for five days more.

On Sunday, October 30th, a man named Benjamin Phipps, going out for the first time on patrol duty, was passing at noon a clearing in the woods where a number of pine-trees had long since been felled. There was a motion among their boughs; he stopped to watch it; and through a gap in the branches he saw, emerging from a hole in the earth beneath, the face of Nat Turner. Aiming his gun instantly, Phipps called on him to surrender. The fugitive, exhausted with watching and privation, entangled in the branches, armed only with a sword, had nothing to do but to yield; sagaciously reflecting, also, as he afterwards explained, that the woods were full of armed men, and that he had better trust fortune for some later chance of escape, instead of desperately attempting it then. He was correct in the first impression, since there were fifty armed scouts within a circuit of two miles. His insurrection ended where it began; for this spot was only a mile and a half from the house of Joseph Travis.

Torn, emaciated, ragged, "a mere scarecrow," still wearing the hat perforated with buckshot, with his arms bound to his sides, he was driven before the levelled gun to the nearest house, that of a Mr. Edwards. He was confined there that night; but the news had spread so rapidly that within an hour after his arrival a hundred persons had collected, and the excitement became so intense "that it was with difficulty he could be conveyed alive to Jerusalem." The enthusiasm spread instantly through Virginia; Mr. Trezvant, the Jerusalem postmaster, sent notices of it far and near; and Governor Floyd himself wrote a letter to the "Richmond Enquirer" to give official announcement of the momentous capture. When Nat Turner was asked by Mr. T. R. Gray, the counsel assigned him, whether, although defeated, he still believed in his own Providential mission he answered, as simply as one who came thirty years after him, "Was not Christ crucified?" In the same spirit, when arraigned before the court, "he answered, 'Not guilty,' saying to his counsel that he did not feel so." But apparently no argument was made in his favor by his counsel, nor were any witnesses called,—he being convicted on the testimony of Levi Waller, and upon his own confession, which was put in by Mr. Gray, and acknowledged by the prisoner before the six justices composing the court, as being "full, free, and voluntary." He was therefore placed in the paradoxical position of conviction by his own confession, under a plea of "Not guilty." The arrest took place on the thirtieth of October, 1831, the confession on the first of November, the trial and conviction on the fifth, and the execution on the following Friday, the eleventh of November, precisely at noon. He met his death with perfect composure, declined addressing the multitude assembled, and told the sheriff in a firm voice that he was ready. Another account says that he "betrayed no emotion, and even hurried the executioner in the performance of his duty." "Not a limb nor a muscle was observed to move. His body, after his death, was given over to the surgeons for dissection."

While these things were going on, the enthusiasm for the Polish Revolution was rising to its height. The nation was ringing with a peal of joy, on hearing that at Frankfort the Poles had killed fourteen thousand Russians. "The Southern Religious Telegraph" was publishing an impassioned address to Kosciusko; standards were being consecrated for Poland in the larger cities; heroes, like Skrzynecki, Czartoryski, Rozyski, Kaminski, were choking the trump of Fame with their complicated patronymics. These are all forgotten now; and this poor negro, who did not even possess a name, beyond one abrupt monosyllable,—for even the name of Turner was the master's property,—still lives a memory of terror and a symbol of retribution triumphant.

Source: Higginson, Thomas Wentworth, "Nat Turner's Insurrection." *The Atlantic Monthly* 8 (August 1861): 173–187.

Discussion Questions

1. Who did Thomas R. Gray have in mind for his *The Confessions of Nat Turner* and how can you tell?
2. What do you make of Turner's religious visions? Did he imagine them, or did he actually see what he claims to have seen? How can you tell?
3. Why does Gray depict Nat Turner and his men as mindless killers of white people?
4. Explain how Gray can acknowledge Turner's obvious intelligence but deny that his rebellion made plenty of sense.
5. Explain how the judge at Nat Turner's trial could dismiss him as just a fanatic.
6. Why do both newspaper reports of Turner's rebellion downplay the likelihood of Turner being a determined leader?
7. Account for the fact that Higginson's narrative makes much more sense and is much more credible than the other versions of Turner's rebellion.
8. Who is Higginson's target audience, and how can you tell?

9. Why do you think Higginson's version is much more detailed than the other versions are?

10. What difference does it make that Higginson's narrative appeared thirty years after Turner's Rebellion, whereas the other three recountings were contemporary?

11. Why was Higginson able to see Turner as a rational human being who planned his rebellion over a period of years rather than an impulsive fanatic?

12. Higginson provides specific reasons Turner and his followers killed whites (e.g., the sexual victimization of black women by white men), but the other narratives of his rebellion do not: why is the omission strategic and revealing?

13. What do you make of the fact that far more blacks were killed by whites than the number of whites killed by blacks in this incident? And of the fact that the whites considered the blacks particularly prone to violence?

14. Given what Higginson reports, was the white reaction to Turner's Rebellion in Edenton typical of other white responses throughout the South?

15. Who, in fact, in 1831 and now, is by far the greatest threat to the security and safety of white people, blacks or other whites?

16. What is Higginson's opinion of Gray's pamphlet? Was Higginson right?

17. What is so ironic of the whites' condemnation of an insurrection by black men who wanted freedom?

Suggested Readings

Burnham, Michelle. "Loopholes of Resistance: Harriet Jacobs' Slave Narrative and the Critique of Agency in Foucault." *Arizona Quarterly* 49 (1993): 53–73.

Gates, Henry L., Jr. and K. A. Appiah, eds. 1997. *Harriet Jacobs: Critical Perspectives Past and Present.* New York: Amistad.

Greenberg, Kenneth S. 2004. *Nat Turner: A Slave Rebellion in History and Memory.* Oxford: Oxford University Press.

Noble, Marianne, 2000. *The Masochistic Pleasures of Sentimental Literature.* Princeton, NJ: Princeton University Press.

Oates, Stephen B. 2004. *The Fires of Jubilee: Nat Turner's Fierce Rebellion.* New York: Harper Perennial.

Styron, William. 1967. *The Confessions of Nat Turner.* New York: Vintage.

HISTORICAL EXPLORATIONS

The Fugitive Slave Law (1850)

This federal law, as opposed to one of similar intent passed in 1789, had very sharp teeth in it, which is why Harriet Jacobs was so concerned about it when she finally escaped from slavery. The fifth section, for example, stipulated that any marshal or deputy marshal who refused to enforce the provisions of the act would be fined a thousand dollars, a very substantial sum in 1850. Citizens were required to help the marshals in the pursuit of fugitive slaves. The sixth section indicates that fugitives were not to be allowed to testify at their trials or hearings, the seventh that anyone who aided a fugitive in escaping slavery was subject to a fine not to exceed a thousand dollars and a prison sentence not to exceed six months. Section eight reads like an outright bribe in that it says when the evidence results in the return of a runaway, the commissioner handling the case is to be paid ten dollars, but when the evidence does not result in the return, the commissioner is to be paid half that amount. Many Northerners refused to comply with this law, which increased bitterness toward the North in the South. In Harriet Jacobs's case, a friend paid for her so that she would not be subject to the law. A law designed to protect the interests of slaveowners resulted in infuriating Northerners, thus pushing the nation closer to war.

The Fugitive Slave Act, September 18, 1850

The Fugitive Slave Act mandated the return of runaway slaves, regardless of where in the Union they might be at the time of their discovery or capture. Along with the Kansas-Nebraska Act and the ratification of Kansas' admission for free statehood, this legislation is part of the chain of events which culminated in the Civil War.

Section 1: Be it enacted by the Senate and House of Representatives of the United States of America in Congress assembled, That the persons who have been, or may hereafter be, appointed commissioners, in virtue of any act of Congress, by the Circuit Courts of the United States, and Who, in consequence of such appointment, are authorized to exercise the powers that any justice of the peace, or other magistrate of any of the United States, may exercise in respect to offenders for any crime or offense against the United States, by arresting, imprisoning, or bailing the same under and by the virtue of the thirty-third section of the act of the twenty-fourth of September seventeen hundred and eighty-nine, entitled "An Act to establish the judicial courts of the United States" shall be, and are hereby, authorized and required to exercise and discharge all the powers and duties conferred by this act.

Section 2: And be it further enacted, That the Superior Court of each organized Territory of the United States shall have the same power to appoint commissioners to take acknowledgments of bail and affidavits, and to take depositions of witnesses in civil causes, which is now possessed by the Circuit Court of the United States; and all commissioners who shall hereafter be appointed for such purposes by the Superior Court of any organized Territory of the United States, shall possess all the powers, and exercise all the duties, conferred by law upon the commissioners appointed by the Circuit Courts of the United States for similar purposes, and shall moreover exercise and discharge all the powers and duties conferred by this act.

Section 3: And be it further enacted, That the Circuit Courts of the United States shall from time to time enlarge the number of the commissioners, with a view to afford reasonable facilities to reclaim fugitives from labor, and to the prompt discharge of the duties imposed by this act.

Section 4: And be it further enacted, That the commissioners above named shall have concurrent jurisdiction with the judges of the Circuit and District Courts of the United States, in their respective circuits and districts within the several States, and the judges of the Superior Courts of the Territories, severally and collectively, in term-time and vacation; shall grant certificates to such claimants, upon satisfactory proof being made, with authority to take and remove such fugitives from service or labor, under the restrictions herein contained, to the State or Territory from which such persons may have escaped or fled.

Section 5: And be it further enacted, That it shall be the duty of all marshals and deputy marshals to obey and execute all warrants and precepts issued under the provisions of this act, when to them directed; and should any marshal or deputy marshal refuse to receive such warrant, or other process, when tendered, or to use all proper means diligently to execute the same, he shall, on conviction thereof, be fined in the sum of one thousand dollars, to the use of such claimant, on the motion of such claimant, by the Circuit or District Court for the district of such marshal; and after arrest of such fugitive, by such marshal or his deputy, or whilst at any time in his custody under the provisions of this act, should such fugitive escape, whether with or without the assent of such marshal or his deputy, such marshal shall be liable, on his official bond, to be prosecuted for the benefit of such claimant, for the full value of the service or labor of said fugitive in the State, Territory, or District whence he escaped: and the better to enable the said commissioners, when thus appointed, to execute their duties faithfully and efficiently, in conformity with the requirements of the Constitution of the United States and of this act, they are hereby authorized and empowered, within their counties respectively, to appoint, in writing under their hands, any one or more suitable persons, from time to time, to execute all such warrants and other process as may be issued by them in the lawful performance of their respective duties; with authority to such commissioners, or the persons to be appointed by them, to execute process as aforesaid, to summon and call to their aid the bystanders, or posse comitatus of the proper county, when necessary to ensure a faithful observance of the clause of the Constitution referred to, in conformity with the provisions of this act; and all good citizens are hereby commanded to aid and assist in the prompt and efficient execution of this law, whenever their services may be required, as aforesaid, for that purpose; and said warrants shall run, and be executed by said officers, any where in the State within which they are issued.

Section 6: And be it further enacted, That when a person held to service or labor in any State or Territory of the United States, has heretofore or shall hereafter escape into another State or Territory of the United States, the person or persons to whom such service or labor may be due, or his, her, or their agent or attorney, duly authorized, by power of attorney, in writing, acknowledged and certified under the seal of some legal officer or court of the State or Territory in which the same may be executed, may pursue and reclaim such fugitive person, either by procuring a warrant from some one of the courts, judges, or commissioners aforesaid, of the proper cir-cuit, district, or county, for the apprehension of such fugitive from service or labor, or by seizing and arresting such fugitive, where the same can be done without process, and by taking, or causing such person to be taken, forthwith before such court, judge, or commis-sioner, whose duty it shall be to hear and determine the case of such claimant in a summary manner; and upon satisfactory proof being made, by deposition or affidavit, in writing, to be taken and certi-fied by such court, judge, or commissioner, or by other satisfactory testimony, duly taken and certified by some court, magistrate, justice of the peace, or other legal officer authorized to administer an oath and take depositions under the laws of the State or Territory from which such person owing service or labor may have escaped, with a certificate of such magistracy or other authority, as aforesaid, with the seal of the proper court or officer thereto attached, which seal shall be sufficient to establish the competency of the proof, and with proof, also by affidavit, of the identity of the person whose service or labor is claimed to be due as aforesaid, that the person so arrested does in fact owe service or labor to the person or persons claiming him or her, in the State or Territory from which such fugitive may have escaped as aforesaid, and that said person escaped, to make out and deliver to such claimant, his or her agent or attorney, a certifi-cate setting forth the substantial facts as to the service or labor due from such fugitive to the claimant, and of his or her escape from the State or Territory in which he or she was arrested, with authority to such claimant, or his or her agent or attorney, to use such reasonable force and restraint as may be necessary, under the circumstances of the case, to take and remove such fugitive person back to the State or Territory whence he or she may have escaped as aforesaid. In no trial or hearing under this act shall the testimony of such alleged fugitive be admitted in evidence; and the certificates in this and the first [fourth] section mentioned, shall be conclusive of the right of the person or persons in whose favor granted, to remove such fugitive to the State or Territory from which he escaped, and shall prevent all molestation of such person or persons by any process issued by any court, judge, magistrate, or other person whomsoever.

Section 7: And be it further enacted, That any person who shall knowingly and willingly obstruct, hinder, or prevent such claimant, his agent or attorney, or any person or persons lawfully assisting him, her, or them, from arresting such a fugitive from service or labor, either with or without process as aforesaid, or shall rescue, or attempt to rescue, such fugitive from service or labor, from the custody of such claimant, his or her agent or attorney, or other person or persons lawfully assisting as aforesaid, when so arrested, pursuant to the authority herein given and declared; or shall aid, abet, or assist such person so owing service or labor as aforesaid, directly or indirectly, to escape from such claimant, his agent or attorney, or other person or persons legally authorized as aforesaid; or shall harbor or conceal such fugitive, so as to prevent the discovery and arrest of such person, after notice or knowledge of the fact that such person was a fugitive from service or labor as aforesaid, shall, for either of said offences, be subject to a fine not exceeding one thousand dollars, and imprisonment not exceeding six months, by indictment and conviction before the District Court of the United States for the district in which such offence may have been committed, or before the proper court of criminal jurisdiction, if committed within any one of the organized Territories of the United States; and shall moreover forfeit and pay, by way of civil damages to the party injured by such illegal conduct, the sum of one thousand dollars for each fugitive so lost as aforesaid, to be recovered by action of debt, in any of the District or Territorial Courts aforesaid, within whose jurisdiction the said offence may have been committed.

Section 8: And be it further enacted, That the marshals, their deputies, and the clerks of the said District and Territorial Courts, shall be paid, for their services, the like fees as may be allowed for similar services in other cases; and where such services are rendered exclusively in the arrest, custody, and delivery of the fugitive to the claimant, his or her agent or attorney, or where such supposed fugitive may be discharged out of custody for the want of sufficient proof as aforesaid, then such fees are to be paid in whole by such claimant, his or her agent or attorney; and in all cases where the proceedings are before a commissioner, he shall be entitled to a fee of ten dollars in full for his services in each case, upon the delivery of the said certificate to the claimant, his agent or attorney; or a fee of five dollars in cases where the proof shall not, in the opinion of such commissioner, warrant such certificate and delivery, inclusive of all services incident to such arrest and examination, to be paid, in either case, by the claimant, his or her agent or attorney. The person or persons authorized to execute the process to be issued by such commissioner for the arrest and detention of fugitives from service or labor as aforesaid, shall also be entitled to a fee of five dollars each for each person he or they may arrest, and take before any commissioner as aforesaid, at the instance and request of such claimant, with such other fees as may be deemed reasonable by such commissioner for such other additional services as may be necessarily performed by him or them; such as attending at the examination, keeping the fugitive in custody, and providing him with food and lodging during his detention, and until the final determination of such commissioners; and, in general, for performing such other duties as may be required by such claimant, his or her attorney or agent, or commissioner in the premises, such fees to be made up in conformity with the fees usually charged by the officers of the courts of justice within the proper district or county, as near as may be practicable, and paid by such claimants, their agents or attorneys, whether such supposed fugitives from service or labor be ordered to be delivered to such claimant by the final determination of such commissioner or not.

Section 9: And be it further enacted, That, upon affidavit made by the claimant of such fugitive, his agent or attorney, after such certificate has been issued, that he has reason to apprehend that such fugitive will he rescued by force from his or their possession before he can be taken beyond the limits of the State in which the arrest is made, it shall be the duty of the officer making the arrest to retain such fugitive in his custody, and to remove him to the State whence he fled, and there to deliver him to said claimant, his agent, or attorney. And to this end, the officer aforesaid is hereby authorized and required to employ so many persons as he may deem necessary to overcome such force, and to retain them in his service so long as circumstances may require. The said officer and his assistants, while so employed, to receive the same compensation, and to be allowed the same expenses, as are now allowed by law for transportation of criminals, to be certified by the judge of the district within which the arrest is made, and paid out of the treasury of the United States.

Section 10: And be it further enacted, That when any person held to service or labor in any State or Territory, or in the District of Columbia, shall escape therefrom, the party to whom such service or labor shall be due, his, her, or their agent or attorney, may apply to any court of record therein, or judge thereof in vacation, and make satisfactory proof to such court, or judge in vacation, of the escape aforesaid, and that the person escaping owed service or labor to such party. Whereupon the court shall cause a record to be made of the matters so proved, and also a general description of the person so escaping, with such convenient certainty as may be; and a transcript of such record, authenticated by the attestation of the clerk and of the seal of the said court, being produced in any other State, Territory, or district in which the person so escaping may be found, and being exhibited to any judge, commissioner, or other office, authorized by the law of the United States to cause persons escaping from service or labor to be delivered up, shall be held and taken to be full and conclusive evidence of the fact of escape, and that the service or labor of the person escaping is due to the party in such record mentioned. And upon the production by the said party of other and further evidence if necessary, either oral or by affidavit, in addition to what is contained in the said record of the identity of the person escaping, he or she shall be delivered up to the claimant, And the said court, commissioner, judge, or other person authorized by this act to grant certificates to claimants or fugitives, shall, upon the production of the record and other evidences aforesaid, grant to such claimant a certificate of his right to take any such person identified and proved to be owing service or labor as aforesaid, which certificate shall authorize such claimant to seize or arrest and transport such person to the State or Territory from which he escaped: Provided, That nothing herein contained shall be construed as requiring the production of a transcript of such record as evidence as aforesaid. But in its absence the claim shall be heard and determined upon other satisfactory proofs, competent in law.

Source: United States Constitution.

Introduction to Ralph Waldo Emerson's Speech on the Fugitive Slave Law (1851)

Ralph Waldo Emerson (1803–1882) is best known for such famous essays as "Self-Reliance" and "Nature" and for his speech entitled "The American Scholar," as well as for being the central figure in Transcendentalism, a movement that was highly critical of social institutions. But he also

delivered a powerful speech on the Fugitive Slave Law, which he absolutely detested. He was particularly angry that an escaped slave named
Shadrach Minkins was arrested by federal marshals in Boston, the city of
freedom. He was rescued by abolitionists and made his way to Canada, but
Massachusetts's famous senator Daniel Webster had supported the Fugitive Slave Law; this is why Emerson considers him a traitor to the cause
of freedom in his speech. On the other hand, Emerson acknowledges that
those Bostonians who supported the return of Shadrach Minkins to his
owner are evidence of how shaky the foundations of freedom are, even
in the city of freedom: "The famous town of Boston is his [Shadrach
Minkins'] hound." Declaring that black slavery is "the greatest calamity
in the Universe," Emerson goes on to say that people have an obligation
to disobey an immoral law, a position Jacobs agreed with. Another telling
point he makes, one that *Incidents* echoes, is "How can a law be enforced
that fines pity, and imprisons charity?"

From Ralph Waldo Emerson's Speech on the Fugitive Slave Law (1851)

FELLOW CITIZENS: I accepted your invitation to speak to you
on the great question of these days, with very little consideration of
what I might have to offer: for there seems to be no option. The last
year has forced us all into politics, and made it a paramount duty to
seek what it is often a duty to shun. We do not breathe well. There
is infamy in the air. I have a new experience. I wake in the morning
with a painful sensation, which I carry about all day, and which, when
traced home, is the odious remembrance of that ignominy which has
fallen on Massachusetts, which robs the landscape of beauty, and
takes the sunshine out of every hour. I have lived all my life in this
state, and never had any experience of personal inconvenience from
the laws, until now. They never came near me to any discomfort
before. I find the like sensibility in my neighbors; and in that class
who take no interest in the ordinary questions of party politics. There
are men who are as sure indexes of the equity of legislation and of the
same state of public feeling, as the barometer is of the weight of the
air, and it is a bad sign when these are discontented, for though they
snuff oppression and dishonor at a distance, it is because they are

Perhaps the most famous of all the Transcendentalists, Emerson eventually condemned slavery in strong terms, particularly the Fugitive Slave law of 1850, which Jacobs is extremely concerned about in her novel. (Library of Congress)

more impressionable: the whole population will in a short time be as painfully affected.

Every hour brings us from distant quarters of the Union the expression of mortification at the late events in Massachusetts, and at the behavior of Boston. The tameness was indeed shocking. Boston, of whose fame for spirit and character we have all been so proud; Boston, whose citizens, intelligent people in England told me they could always distinguish by their culture among Americans; the Boston of the American Revolution, which figures so proudly in John Adams's Diary, which the whole country has been reading; Boston, spoiled by prosperity, must bow its ancient honor in the dust, and make us irretrievably ashamed. In Boston, we have said with such lofty confidence, no fugitive slave can be arrested, and now, we must transfer our vaunt to the country, and say, with a little less confidence, no fugitive man can be arrested here; at least we can brag thus until tomorrow, when the farmers also may be corrupted.

The tameness is indeed complete. The only haste in Boston, after the rescue of Shadrach, last February, was, who should first put his name on the list of volunteers in aid of the marshal. I met the smoothest of Episcopal Clergymen the other day, and allusion being made to Mr. Webster's treachery, he blandly replied, "Why, do you know I think that the great action of his life." It looked as if in the city and the suburbs all were involved in one hot haste of terror,—presidents of colleges, and professors, saints, and brokers, insurers, lawyers, importers, manufacturers: not an unpleasing sentiment, not a liberal recollection, not so much as a snatch of an old song for freedom, dares intrude on their passive obedience.

The panic has paralyzed the journals, with the fewest exceptions, so that one cannot open a newspaper without being disgusted by new records of shame. I cannot read longer even the local good news. When I look down the columns at the titles of paragraphs, "Education in Massachusetts," "Board of Trade," "Art Union," "Revival of Religion," what bitter mockeries! The very convenience of property, the house and land we occupy, have lost their best value, and a man looks gloomily at his children, and thinks, "What have I done that you should begin life in dishonor?" Every liberal study is discredited,—literature and science appear effeminate, and the hiding of the head. The college, the churches, the schools, the very shops and factories are discredited; real estate, every kind of wealth, every branch of industry, every avenue to power, suffers injury, and the value of life is reduced. Just now a friend came into my house and said, "If this law shall be repealed I shall be glad that I have lived; if not I shall be sorry that I was born." What kind of law is that which extorts language like this from the heart of a free and civilized people?

One intellectual benefit we owe to the late disgraces. The crisis had the illuminating power of a sheet of lightning at midnight. It showed truth. It ended a good deal of nonsense we had been wont to hear and to repeat, on the 19th of April, the 17th of June, the 4th of July. It showed the slightness and unreliableness of our social fabric, it showed what stuff reputations are made of, what straws we dignify by office and title, and how competent we are to give counsel and help in a day of trial. It showed the shallowness of leaders; the divergence of parties from their alleged grounds; showed that men would not stick to what they had said, that the resolutions of public bodies, or the pledges never so often given and put on record of public men, will not bind them. The fact comes out more plainly that you cannot rely on any man for the defence of truth, who is not constitutionally or by blood and temperament on that side. A man of a greedy and unscrupulous selfishness may maintain morals when they are in fashion: but he will not stick. However close Mr. Wolf's nails have been pared, however neatly he has been shaved, and tailored, and set up on end, and taught to say, "Virtue and Religion," he cannot be relied on at a pinch: he will say, morality means pricking a vein. The popular assumption that all men loved freedom, and believed in the Christian religion, was found hollow American brag; only persons who were known and tried benefactors are found standing for freedom: the sentimentalists went down-stream. I question the value of our civilization, when I see that the public mind had never less hold of the strongest of all truths. The sense of injustice is blunted,—a sure sign of the shallowness of our intellect. I cannot accept the railroad and telegraph in exchange for reason and charity. It is not skill in iron locomotives that makes so fine civility, as the jealousy of liberty. I cannot think the most judicious tubing a compensation for metaphysical debility. What is the use of admirable law-forms, and political forms, if a hurricane of party feeling and a combination of monied interests can beat them to the ground? What is the use of courts, if judges only quote authorities, and no judge exerts original jurisdiction, or recurs to first principles? What is the use of a Federal Bench, if its opinions are the political breath of the hour? And what is the use of constitutions, if all the guaranties provided by the jealousy of ages for the protection of liberty are made of no effect, when a bad act of Congress finds a willing commissioner? The levity of the public mind has been shown in the past year by the most extravagant actions. Who could have believed it, if foretold that a hundred guns would be fired in Boston on the passage of the Fugitive Slave Bill? Nothing proves the want of all thought, the absence of standard in men's minds, more than the dominion of party. Here are humane people who have tears for misery, an open purse for want; who should have been the defenders of the poor man, are found his embittered enemies, rejoicing in his rendition,—merely from party ties. I thought none, that was not ready to go on all fours, would back this law. And yet here are upright men, *compotes mentis,* [of sound mind] husbands, fathers, trustees, friends, open, generous, brave, who can see nothing in this claim for bare humanity, and the health and honor of their native State, but canting fanaticism, sedition and "one idea." Because of this preoccupied mind, the whole wealth and power of Boston—two hundred thousand souls, and one hundred and eighty millions of money—are thrown into the scale of crime: and the poor black boy, whom the fame of Boston had reached in the recesses of a vile swamp, or in the alleys of Savannah, on arriving here finds all this force employed to catch him. The famous town of Boston is his master's hound. The learning of the universities, the culture of elegant society, the acumen of lawyers, the majesty of the Bench, the eloquence of the Christian pulpit, the stoutness of Democracy, the respectability of the Whig party[Daniel Webster's party] are all combined to kidnap him.

The crisis is interesting as it shows the self-protecting nature of the world and of the Divine laws. It is the law of the world,—as much immorality as there is, so much misery. The greatest prosperity will in vain resist the greatest calamity. You borrow the succour of the devil and he must have his fee. He was never known to abate a penny of his rents. In every nation all the immorality that exists breeds plagues. But of the corrupt society that exists we have never been able to combine any pure prosperity. There is always something in the very advantages of a condition which hurts it. Africa has its malformation; England has its Ireland; Germany its hatred of classes; France its love of gunpowder; Italy its Pope; and America, the most prosperous country in the Universe, has the greatest calamity in the Universe, negro slavery.

Let me remind you a little in detail how the natural retribution acts in reference to the statute which Congress passed a year ago. For these few months have shown very conspicuously its nature and impracticability. It is contravened:

1. By the sentiment of duty. An immoral law makes it a man's duty to break it, at every hazard. For virtue is the very self of every man. It is therefore a principle of law that an immoral contract is void, and that an immoral statute is void. For, as laws do not make right, and are simply declaratory of a right which already existed, it is not to be presumed that they can so stultify themselves as to command injustice.

It is remarkable how rare in the history of tyrants is an immoral law. Some color, some indirection was always used. If you take up the volumes of the "Universal History," you will find it difficult searching. The precedents are few. It is not easy to parallel the wickedness of this American law. And that is the head and body of this discontent, that the law is immoral.

Here is a statute which enacts the crime of kidnapping,—a crime on one footing with arson and murder. A man's right to liberty is as inalienable as his right to life.

Pains seem to have been taken to give us in this statute a wrong pure from any mixture of right. If our resistance to this law is not right, there is no right. This is not meddling with other people's affairs: this is hindering other people from meddling with us. This is not going crusading into Virginia and Georgia after slaves, who, it is alleged, are very comfortable where they are:—that amiable argument falls to the ground: but this is befriending in our own State, on our own farms, a man who has taken the risk of being shot, or burned alive, or cast into the sea, or starved to death, or suffocated in a wooden box, to get away from his driver: and this man who has run the gauntlet of a thousand miles for his freedom, the statute says, you men of Massachusetts shall hunt, and catch, and send back again to the dog-hutch he fled from.

It is contrary to the primal sentiment of duty, and therefore all men that are born are, in proportion to their power of thought and their moral sensibility, found to be the natural enemies of this law. The resistance of all moral beings is secured to it. I had thought, I confess, what must come at last would come at first, a banding of all men against the authority of this statute. I thought it a point on which all sane men were agreed, that the law must respect the public morality. I thought that all men of all conditions had been made sharers of a certain experience, that in certain rare and retired moments they had been made to see how man is man, or what makes the essence of rational beings, namely, that whilst animals have to do with eating the fruits of the ground, men have to do with rectitude, with benefit, with truth, with something which is, independent of appearances: and that this tie makes the substantiality of life, this, and not their ploughing, or sailing, their trade or the breeding of families. I thought that every time a man goes back to his own thoughts, these angels receive him, talk with him, and that, in the best hours, he is uplifted in virtue of this essence, into a peace and into a power which the material world cannot give: that these moments counterbalance the years of drudgery, and that this owning of a law, be it called morals, religion, or godhead, or what you will, constituted the explanation of life, the excuse and indemnity for the errors and calamities which sadden it. In long years consumed in trifles, they remember these moments, and are consoled. I thought it was this fair mystery, whose foundations are hidden in eternity, which made the basis of human society, and of law; and that to pretend anything else, as that the acquisition of property was the end of living, was to confound all distinctions, to make the world a greasy hotel, and, instead of noble motives and inspirations, and a heaven of companions and angels around and before us, to leave us in a grimacing menagerie of monkeys and idiots. All arts, customs, societies, books, and laws, are good as they foster and concur with this spiritual element: all men are beloved as they raise us to it; hateful as they deny or resist it. The laws especially draw their obligation only from their concurrence with it.

I am surprised that lawyers can be so blind as to suffer the principles of Law to be discredited. A few months ago, in my dismay at hearing that the Higher Law was reckoned a good joke in the courts, I took pains to look into a few law-books. I had often heard that the Bible constituted a part of every technical law library, and that it was a principle in law that immoral laws are void.

I found, accordingly, that the great jurists, Cicero, Grotius, Coke, Blackstone, Burlamaqui, Montesquieu, Vattel, Burke, Mackintosh, Jefferson, [all theorists of the Law] do all affirm this. I have no intention to recite these passages I had marked:—such citation indeed seems to be something cowardly (for no reasonable person needs a quotation from Blackstone to convince him that white cannot be legislated to be black), and shall content myself with reading a single passage. Blackstone admits the sovereignty "antecedent to any positive precept, of the law of Nature," among whose principles are, "that we should live on, should hurt nobody, and should render unto every one his due," etc. "No human laws are of any validity, if contrary to this." "Nay, if any human law should allow or enjoin us to commit a crime" (his instance is murder), "we are bound to transgress that human law; or else we must offend both the natural and divine." Lord Coke held that where an Act of Parliament is against common right and reason, the common law shall control it, and adjudge it to be void. Chief Justice Hobart, Chief Justice Holt, and Chief Justice Mansfield [all English chief justices] held the same.

Lord Mansfield, in the case of the slave Somerset, wherein the dicta of Lords Talbot and Hardwicke had been cited, to the effect of carrying back the slave to the West Indies, said, "I care not for the supposed *dicta* of judges, however eminent, if they be contrary to all principle." Even the *Canon Law* [law based on religious authority] says (*in malis promissis non expedit servare fidem*), "Neither allegiance nor oath can bind to obey that which is wrong."

No engagement (to a sovereign) can oblige or even authorize a man to violate the laws of Nature. All authors who have any conscience or modesty agree that a person ought not to obey such commands as are evidently contrary to the laws of God. Those governors of places who bravely refused to execute the barbarous orders of Charles IX. [French king who ordered the killing of Huguenot Protestants on St. Bartholomew's Day] for the famous "Massacre of St. Bartholomew," have been universally praised; and the court did not dare to punish them, at least openly. "Sire," said the brave Orte, governor of Bayonne, in his letter, "I have communicated your majesty's command to your faithful inhabitants and warriors in the garrison, and I have found there only good citizens, and brave soldiers; not one hangman: therefore, both they and I must humbly entreat your majesty to be pleased to employ your arms and lives in things that are possible, however hazardous they may be, and we will exert ourselves to the last drop of our blood."

The practitioners should guard this dogma well, as the palladium of the profession, as their anchor in the respect of mankind. Against a principle like this, all the arguments of Mr. Webster are the spray of a child's squirt against a granite wall.

2. It is contravened by all the sentiments. How can a law be enforced that fines pity, and imprisons charity? As long as men have bowels, they will disobey. You know that the Act of Congress of September 18, 1850, is a law which every one of you will break on the earliest occasion. There is not a manly Whig, or a manly Democrat, of whom, if a slave were hidden in one of our houses from the hounds, we should not ask with confidence to lend his wagon in aid of his escape, and he would lend it. The man would be too strong for the partisan.

And here I may say that it is absurd, what I often hear, to accuse the friends of freedom in the North with being the occasion of the new stringency of the Southern slave-laws. If you starve or beat the orphan, in my presence, and I accuse your cruelty, can I help it? In the words of Electra in the Greek tragedy, "'T is you that say it, not I. You do the deeds, and your ungodly deeds find me the words." Will you blame the ball for rebounding from the floor, blame the air for rushing in where a vacuum is made or the boiler for exploding under pressure of steam? These facts are after laws of the world, and so is it law, that, when justice is violated, anger begins. The very defence which the God of Nature has provided for the innocent against cruelty is the sentiment of indignation and pity in the bosom of the beholder. Mr. Webster tells the President that "he has been in the North, and he has found no man, whose opinion is of any weight, who is opposed to the law." Oh, Mr. President, trust not the information! The gravid old Universe goes spawning on; the womb conceives and the breasts give suck to thousands and millions of hairy babes formed not in the image of your statute, but in the image of the Universe; too many to be bought off; too many than they can be rich, and therefore peaceable; and necessitated to express first or last every feeling of the heart. You can keep no secret, for whatever is true some of them will unreasonably say. You can commit no crime, for they are created in their sentiments conscious of and hostile to it; and unless you can suppress the newspaper, pass a law against book-shops, gag the English tongue in America, all short of this is futile. This dreadful English Speech is saturated with songs, proverbs and speeches that flatly contradict and defy every line of Mr. Mason's [Mason was the author of the Fugitive Slave Law] statute. Nay, unless you can draw a sponge over those seditious Ten Commandments which are the root of our European and American civilization; and over that eleventh commandment, "Do unto others as you would have them do to you," your labor is vain.

3. It is contravened by the written laws themselves, because the sentiments, of course, write the statutes. Laws are merely declaratory of the natural sentiments of mankind, and the language of all permanent laws will be in contradiction to any immoral enactment. And thus it happens here: Statute fights against Statute. By the law of Congress March 2, 1807, it is piracy and murder, punishable with death, to enslave a man on the coast of Africa. By law of Congress September, 1850, it is a high crime and misdemeanor, punishable with fine and imprisonment, to resist the reënslaving a man on the coast of America. Off soundings, it is piracy and murder to enslave him. On soundings, it is fine and prison not to reënslave. What kind of legislation is this? What kind of constitution which covers it? And yet the crime which the second law ordains is greater than the crime which the first law forbids under penalty of the gibbet. For it is a greater crime to reënslave a man who has shown himself fit for freedom, than to enslave him at first, when it might be pretended to be a mitigation of his lot as a captive in war.

4. It is contravened by the mischiefs it operates. A wicked law cannot be executed by good men, and must be by bad. Flagitious men must be employed, and every act of theirs is a stab at the public peace. It cannot be executed at such a cost, and so it brings a bribe in its hand. This law comes with infamy in it, and out of it. It offers a bribe in its own clauses for the consummation of the crime. To serve it, low and mean people are found by the groping of the government. No government ever found it hard to pick up tools for base actions. If you cannot find them in the huts of the poor, you shall find them in the palaces of the rich. Vanity can buy some, ambition others, and money others. The first execution of the law, as was inevitable, was a little hesitating; the second was easier; and the glib officials became, in a few weeks, quite practised and handy at stealing men. But worse, not the officials alone are bribed, but the whole community is solicited. The scowl of the community is attempted to be averted by the mischievous whisper, "Tariff and Southern market, if you will be quiet: no tariff and loss of Southern market, if you dare to murmur." I wonder that our acute people who have learned that the cheapest police is dear schools, should not find out that an immoral law costs more than the loss of the custom of a Southern city.

The humiliating scandal of great men warping right into wrong was followed up very fast by the cities. New York advertised in Southern markets that it would go for slavery, and posted the names of merchants who would not. Boston, alarmed, entered into the same design. Philadelphia, more fortunate, had no conscience at all, and, in this auction of the rights of mankind, rescinded all its legislation against slavery. And the Boston "Advertiser," and the "Courier," in these weeks, urge the same course on the people of Massachusetts. Nothing remains in this race of roguery but to coax Connecticut or Maine to outbid us all by adopting slavery into its constitution.

Great is the mischief of a legal crime. Every person who touches this business is contaminated. There has not been in our lifetime another moment when public men were personally lowered by their political action. But here are gentlemen whose believed probity was the confidence and fortification of multitudes, who, by fear of public opinion, or through the dangerous ascendency of Southern manners, have been drawn into the support of this foul business. We poor men in the country who might once have thought it an honor to shake hands with them, or to dine at their boards, would now shrink from their touch, nor could they enter our humblest doors. You have a law which no man can obey, or abet the obeying, without loss of self-respect and forfeiture of the name of gentleman. What shall we say of the functionary by whom the recent rendition was made? If he has rightly defined his powers, and has no authority to try the case, but only to prove the prisoner's identity, and remand him, what office is this for a reputable citizen to hold? No man of honor can sit on that bench. It is the extension of the planter's whipping-post; and its incumbents must rank with a class from which the turnkey, the hangman and the informer are taken, necessary functionaries, it may be, in a state, but to whom the dislike and the ban of society universally attaches.

5. These resistances appear in the history of the statute, in the retributions which speak so loud in every part of this business, that I think a tragic poet will know how to make it a lesson for all ages. Mr. Webster's measure was, he told us, final. It was a pacification, it was a suppression, a measure of conciliation and adjustment. These were his words at different times: "there was to be no parleying more;" it was "irrepealable." Does it look final now? His final settlement has dislocated the foundations. The state-house shakes likes a tent. His pacification has brought all the honesty in every house, all scrupulous and good-hearted men, all women, and all children, to accuse the law. It has brought United States swords into the streets, and chains round the court-house. "A measure of pacification and union." What is its effect? To make one sole subject for conversation and painful thought throughout the continent, namely, slavery. There is not a man of thought or of feeling but is concentrating his mind on it. There is not a clerk but recites its statistics; not a politician but is watching its incalculable energy in the elections; not a jurist but is hunting up precedents; not a moralist but is prying into its quality; not an economist but is computing its profit and loss: Mr. Webster can judge whether this sort of solar microscope brought to bear on his law is likely to make opposition less. The only benefit that has accrued from the law is its service to education. It has been like a university to the entire people. It has turned every dinner-table into a debating-club, and made every citizen a student of natural law. When a moral quality comes into politics, when a right is invaded, the discussion draws on deeper sources: general principles are laid bare, which cast light on the whole frame of society. And it is cheering to

behold what champions the emergency called to this poor black boy; what subtlety, what logic, what learning, what exposure of the mischief of the law; and, above all, with what earnestness and dignity the advocates of freedom were inspired. It was one of the best compensations of this calamity.

But the Nemesis works underneath again. It is a power that makes noonday dark, and draws us on to our undoing; and its dismal way is to pillory the offender in the moment of his triumph. The hands that put the chain on the slave are in that moment manacled. Who has seen anything like that which is now done? The words of John Randolph, [member of House of Representatives; represented Virginia] wiser than he knew, have been ringing ominously in all echoes for thirty years, words spoken in the heat of the Missouri debate. "We do not govern the people of the North by our black slaves, but by their own white slaves. We know what we are doing. We have conquered you once, and we can and will conquer you again. Ay, we will drive you to the wall, and when we have you there once more, we will keep you there and nail you down like base money." These words resounding ever since from California to Oregon, from Cape Florida to Cape Cod, come down now like the cry of Fate, in the moment when they are fulfilled. By white slaves, by a white slave, are we beaten. Who looked for such ghastly fulfilment, or to see what we see? Hills and Halletts, servile editors by the hundred, we could have spared. But him, our best and proudest, the first man of the North, in the very moment of mounting the throne, irresistibly taking the bit in his mouth and the collar on his neck, and harnessing himself to the chariot of the planters.

The fairest American fame ends in this filthy law. Mr. Webster cannot choose but regret his law. He must learn that those who make fame accuse him with one voice; that those who have no points to carry that are not identical with public morals and generous civilization, that the obscure and private who have no voice and care for none, so long as things go well, but who feel the disgrace of the new legislation creeping like miasma into their homes, and blotting the daylight,—those to whom his name was once dear and honored, as the manly statesman to whom the choicest gifts of Nature had been accorded, disown him: that he who was their pride in the woods and mountains of New England is now their mortification,—they have torn down his picture from the wall, they have thrust his speeches into the chimney. No roars of New York mobs can drown this voice in Mr. Webster's ear. It will outwhisper all the salvos of the "Union Committees'" cannon. But I have said too much on this painful topic. I will not pursue that bitter history.

But passing from the ethical to the political view, I wish to place this statute, and we must use the introducer and substantial author of the bill as an illustration of the history. I have as much charity for Mr. Webster, I think, as any one has. I need not say how much I have enjoyed his fame. Who has not helped to praise him? Simply he was the one eminent American of our time, whom we could produce as a finished work of Nature. We delighted in his form and face, in his voice, in his eloquence, in his power of labor, in his concentration, in his large understanding, in his daylight statement, simple force; the facts lay like the strata of a cloud, or like the layers of the crust of the globe. He saw things as they were, and he stated them so. He has been by his clear perceptions and statements in all these years the best head in Congress, and the champion of the interests of the Northern seaboard: but as the activity and growth of slavery began to be offensively felt by his constituents, the senator became less sensitive to these evils. They were not for him to deal with: he was the commercial representative. He indulged occasionally in excellent expression of the known feeling of the New England people: but, when expected and when pledged, he omitted to speak, and he omitted to throw himself into the movement in those critical moments when his leadership would have turned the scale. At last, at a fatal hour, this sluggishness accumulated to downright counteraction, and, very unexpectedly to the whole Union, on the 7th March, 1850, in opposition to his education, association, and to all his own most explicit language for thirty years, he crossed the line, and became the head of the slavery party in this country.

Mr. Webster perhaps is only following the laws of his blood and constitution. I suppose his pledges were not quite natural to him. Mr. Webster is a man who lives by his memory, a man of the past, not a man of faith or of hope. He obeys his powerful animal nature;— and his finely developed understanding only works truly and with all its force, when it stands for animal good; that is, for property. He believes, in so many words, that government exists for the protection of property. He looks at the Union as an estate, a large farm, and is excellent in the completeness of his defence of it so far. He adheres to the letter. Happily he was born late,—after the independence had been declared, the Union agreed to, and the constitution settled. What he finds already written, he will defend. Lucky that so much had got well written when he came. For he has no faith in the power of self-government; none whatever in extemporizing a government. Not the smallest municipal provision, if it were new, would receive his sanction. In Massachusetts, in 1776, he would, beyond all question, have been a refugee. He praises Adams and Jefferson [second and third presidents of the United States], but it is a past Adams and Jefferson that his mind can entertain. A present Adams and Jefferson he would denounce. So with the eulogies of liberty in his writings,—they are sentimentalism and youthful rhetoric. He can celebrate it, but it means as much from him as from Metternich or Talleyrand [European politicians]. This is all inevitable from his constitution. All the drops of his blood have eyes that look downward. It is neither praise nor blame to say that he has no moral perception, no moral sentiment, but in that region—to use the phrase of the phrenologists—a hole in the head. The scraps of morality to be gleaned from his speeches are reflections of the mind of others; he says what he hears said, but often makes signal blunders in their use. In Mr. Webster's imagination the American Union was a huge Prince Rupert's drop [molten glass dropped into water, which creates tadpole-shaped glass easily broken at the thin end but strong in the big end], which, if so much as the smallest end be shivered off, the whole will snap into atoms. Now the fact is quite different from this. The people are loyal, law-loving, law-abiding. They prefer order, and have no taste for misrule and uproar.

The destiny of this country is great and liberal, and is to be greatly administered. It is to be administered according to what is, and is to be, and not according to what is dead and gone. The union of this people is a real thing, an alliance of men of one flock, one language, one religion, one system of manners and ideas. I hold it to be a real and not a statute union. The people cleave to the Union, because they see their advantage in it, the added power of each.

I suppose the Union can be left to take care of itself. As much real union as there is, the statutes will be sure to express; as much disunion as there is, no statute can long conceal. Under the Union I suppose the fact to be that there are really two nations, the North and the South. It is not slavery that severs them, it is climate and temperament. The South does not like the North, slavery or no slavery, and never did. The North likes the South well enough, for it knows its own advantages. I am willing to leave them to the facts. If they continue to have a binding interest, they will be pretty sure to find it out: if not, they will consult their peace in parting. But one thing appears certain to me, that, as soon as the constitution ordains an immoral law, it ordains disunion. The law is suicidal, and cannot be obeyed. The Union is at an end as soon as an immoral law is enacted. And he who writes a crime into the statute-book digs under the foundations of the Capitol to plant there a powder-magazine, and lays a train.

I pass to say a few words to the question, What shall we do?

1. What in our federal capacity is our relation to the nation?
2. And what as citizens of a state?

I am an Unionist as we all are, or nearly all, and I strongly share the hope of mankind in the power, and therefore, in the duties of the Union; and I conceive it demonstrated,—the necessity of common sense and justice entering into the laws. What shall we do? First, abrogate this law; then, proceed to confine slavery to slave states, and help them effectually to make an end of it. Or shall we, as we are advised on all hands, lie by, and wait the progress of the census? But will Slavery lie by? I fear not. She is very industrious, gives herself no holidays. No proclamations will put her down. She got Texas and now will have Cuba, and means to keep her majority. The experience of the past gives us no encouragement to lie by. Shall we call a new Convention, or will any expert statesman furnish us a plan for the summary or gradual winding up of slavery, so far as the Republic is its patron? Where is the South itself? Since it is agreed by all sane men of all parties (or was yesterday) that slavery is mischievous, why does the South itself never offer the smallest counsel of her own? I have never heard in twenty years any project except Mr. Clay's. [U.S. Senator from Kentucky who supported the return of slaves to Africa]. Let us hear any project with candor and respect. Is it impossible to speak of it with reason and good nature? It is really the project fit for this country to entertain and accomplish. Everything invites emancipation. The grandeur of the design, the vast stake we hold; the national domain, the new importance of Liberia; the manifest interest of the slave states; the religious effort of the free states; the public opinion of the world;—all join to demand it.

We shall one day bring the States shoulder to shoulder and the citizens man to man to exterminate slavery. Why in the name of common sense and the peace of mankind is not this made the subject of instant negotiation and settlement? Why not end this dangerous dispute on some ground of fair compensation on one side, and satisfaction on the other to the conscience of the free states? It is really the great task fit for this country to accomplish, to buy that property of the planters, as the British nation bought the West Indian slaves. I say buy,—never conceding the right of the planter to own, but that we may acknowledge the calamity of his position, and bear a countryman's share in relieving him; and because it is the only practicable course, and is innocent. Here is a right social or public function, which one man cannot do, which all men must do. 'T is said it will cost two thousand millions of dollars. Was there ever any contribution that was so enthusiastically paid as this will be? We will have a chimney-tax. We will give up our coaches, and wine, and watches. The churches will melt their plate. The father of his country shall wait, well pleased, a little longer for his monument; Franklin for his, the Pilgrim Fathers for theirs, and the patient Columbus for his. The mechanics will give, the needle-women will give; the children will have cent-societies. Every man in the land will give a week's work to dig away this accursed mountain of sorrow once and forever out of the world.

Nothing is impracticable to this nation, which it shall set itself to do. Were ever men so endowed, so placed, so weaponed? Their power of territory seconded by a genius equal to every work. By new arts the earth is subdued, roaded, tunnelled, telegraphed, gaslighted; vast amounts of old labor disused; the sinews of man being relieved by sinews of steam. We are on the brink of more wonders. The sun paints; presently we shall organize the echo, as now we do the shadow. Chemistry is extorting new aids. The genius of this people, it is found, can do anything which can be done by men. These thirty nations are equal to any work, and are every moment stronger. In twenty-five years they will be fifty millions. Is it not time to do something besides ditching and draining, and making the earth mellow and friable? Let them confront this mountain of poison,—bore, blast, excavate, pulverize, and shovel it once for all, down into the bottomless Pit. A thousand millions were cheap.

But grant that the heart of financiers, accustomed to practical figures, shrinks within them at these colossal amounts, and the embarrassments which complicate the problem; granting that these contingencies are too many to be spanned by any human geometry, and that these evils are to be relieved only by the wisdom of God working in ages,—and by what instrument, whether Liberia, whether flax-cotton, whether the working out this race by Irish and Germans, none can tell, or by what sources God has guarded his law; still the question recurs, What must we do? One thing is plain, we cannot answer for the Union, but we must keep Massachusetts true. It is of unspeakable importance that she play her honest part. She must follow no vicious examples. Massachusetts is a little state: countries have been great by ideas. Europe is little compared with Asia and Africa; yet Asia and Africa are its ox and its ass. Europe, the least of all the continents, has almost monopolized for twenty centuries the genius and power of them all. Greece was the least part of Europe. Attica a little part of that,—one tenth of the size of Massachusetts. Yet that district still rules the intellect of men. Judaea was a petty country. Yet these two, Greece and Judaea, furnish the mind and the heart by which the rest of the world is sustained; and Massachusetts is little, but, if true to it self, can be the brain which turns about the behemoth.

I say Massachusetts, but I mean Massachusetts in all the quarters of her dispersion; Massachusetts, as she is the mother of all the New England states, and as she sees her progeny scattered over the face of the land, in the farthest South, and the uttermost West. The immense power of rectitude is apt to be forgotten in politics. But they who have brought the great wrong on the country have not forgotten it. They avail themselves of the known probity and honor of Massachusetts, to endorse the statute. The ancient maxim still holds that never was any injustice effected except by the help of justice. The great game of the government has been to win the sanction of Massachusetts to the crime. Hitherto they have succeeded only so far as to win Boston to a certain extent. The behavior of Boston was the reverse of what it should have been: it was supple and officious, and it put itself into the base attitude of pander to the crime. It should have placed obstruction at every step. Let the attitude of the states be firm. Let us respect the Union to all honest ends. But also respect an older and wider union, the law of Nature and rectitude.

Massachusetts is as strong as the Universe, when it does that. We will never intermeddle with your slavery,—but you can in no wise be suffered to bring it to Cape Cod and Berkshire. This law must be made inoperative. It must be abrogated and wiped out of the statute-book; but whilst it stands there, it must be disobeyed. We must make a small state great, by making every man in it true. It was the praise of Athens, "She could not lead countless armies into the field, but she knew how with a little band to defeat those who could." Every Roman reckoned himself at least a match for a Province. Every Dorian [ancient Greek ethnic group] did. Every Englishman in Australia, in South Africa, in India, or in whatever barbarous country their forts and factories have been set up,—represents London, represents the art, power and law of Europe. Every man educated at the Northern school carries the like advantages into the South. For it is confounding distinctions to speak of the geographic sections of this country as of equal civilization. Every nation and every man bows, in spite of himself, to a higher mental and moral existence; and the sting of the late disgraces is that this royal position of Massachusetts was foully lost, that the well-known sentiment of her people was not expressed. Let us correct this error. In this one fastness let truth be spoken and right done. Here let there be no confusion in our ideas. Let us not lie, not steal, nor help to steal, and let us not call stealing by any fine name, such as "Union" or "Patriotism." Let us know that not by the public, but by ourselves, our safety must be bought. That is the secret of Southern power, that they rest not on meetings, but on private heats and courages.

It is very certain from the perfect guaranties in the constitution, and the high arguments of the defenders of liberty, which the occasion called out, that there is sufficient margin in the statute and the law for the spirit of the Magistrate to show itself, and one, two, three occasions have just now occurred, and past, in either of which, if one man had felt the spirit of Coke or Mansfield or Parsons [author of *The Law of Contracts* (1857], and read the law with the eye of freedom, the dishonor of Massachusetts had been prevented, and a limit set to these encroachments forever.

Source: Emerson, Ralph Waldo. *The Complete Works of Ralph Waldo Emerson: Miscellaneous,* Volume 11. Boston: Houghton & Mifflin, 1904, unnumbered pages.

Introduction to Frederick Douglass's Speech on the Fugitive Slave Law (1852)

Frederick Douglass was the author of one of the premier slave narratives, *Narrative of the Life of Frederick Douglass* (1845), as well as one of the most important abolitionists. An outstanding public orator, he was asked to speak at the National Free Soil Convention at Pittsburgh on August 11, 1852. The National Free Soil Party was a one-issue party based on the nonexpansion of slavery into free territories. In his fiery speech, Douglass openly supports not only the killing of slaveowners, suggesting he felt confident that feelings in the North were moving toward the Civil War, but also the killing of slave kidnappers acting under the power the Fugitive Slave Law provided them. The audience's enthusiastic response to Douglass's candid acknowledgement that violence may be on the horizon indicates his confidence that slavery would eventually be destroyed. The Fugitive Slave Law turned out to be a disaster for slaveowners, as Douglass seems to sense here: it forced every American, slaveowner or not, to be complicit in the evils of slavery.

From Frederick Douglass's Speech on the Fugitive Slave Law (1852)

Gentlemen, I take it that you are in earnest, and mean all you say by this call, and therefore I will address you. I am taken by surprise, but I never withhold a word on such an occasion as this. The object of this Convention is to organize a parry, not merely for the present, but a party identified with eternal principles and therefore permanent. I have come here, not so much of a free soiler as others have come. I am, of course, for circumscribing and damaging slavery in every way I can. But my motto is extermination—not only in New Mexico, but in New Orleans—not only in California but in South Carolina. No where has God ordained that this beautiful land shall be cursed with bondage by enslaving men. Slavery has no rightful existence anywhere. The slaveholders not only forfeit their right to liberty, but to life itself.—[Applause.] The earth is God's, and it ought to be covered with righteousness, and not slavery. We expect this great National Convention to lay down some such principle as this.

What we want is not a temporary organization, for a temporary want, but a firm, fixed, immovable, liberty party. Had the old liberty parry continued true to its principles, we never should have seen such a hell born enactment as the Fugitive Slave Law.

In making your Platform, nothing is to be gained by a timid policy. The more closely we adhere to principle, the more certainly will we command respect. Both National Conventions [of the Whig and Democratic parties] acted in open contempt of the antislavery sentiment of the North, by incorporating, as the corner stone of their two platforms, the infamous law to which I have alluded—a law which, I think, will never be repealed—it is too bad to be repealed—a law fit only to trampled under foot, (suiting the action to the word). The only way to make the Fugitive Slave Law a dead letter is to make half a dozen or more dead kidnappers. [Laughter and applause.] A half dozen more dead kidnappers carried down South would cool the ardor of Southern gentlemen, and keep their rapacity in check. That is perfectly right as long as the colored man has no protection. The colored men's rights are less than those of a jackass. No man can take away a jackass without submitting the matter to twelve men in any part of this country. A black man may be carried away without any reference to a jury. It is only necessary to claim him, and that some villain should swear to his identity. There is more protection there for a horse, for a donkey, or anything, rather than a colored man—who is, therefore, justified in the eye of God, in maintaining his right with his arm.

A Voice.—Some of us do not believe that doctrine.

Douglass.—The man who takes the office of a bloodhound ought to be treated as a bloodhound; and I believe that the lines of eternal justice are sometimes so obliterated by a course of long continued oppression that it is necessary to revive them by deepening their traces with the blood of a tyrant. [Much applause.] This Fugitive Slave Law had the support of the Lords, and the Coxes, the Tyngs, the Sharps [prominent slaveowning families] and the flats. [Laughter.] It is nevertheless a degradation and a scandalous outrage on religious liberty; and if the American people were not sunk into degradation too deep for one possessing so little eloquence as I do to describe, they would feel it, too. This vile, infernal law does not interfere with singing of psalms, or anything of that kind, but with the weightier matters of the law, judgment, mercy, and faith. It makes it criminal for you, sir, to carry out the principles of Christianity. It forbids you the right to do right—forbids you to show mercy—forbids you to follow the example of the good Samaritan [in the Bible he believed in treating everyone as his neighbor].

Had this law forbidden any of the rites of religion, it would have been a very different thing. Had it been a law to strike at baptism, for instance, it would have been denounced from a 1000 pulpits, and woe to the politician who did not come to the rescue.—But, I am spending my strength for nought; what care we for religious liberty? what are we—an unprincipled set of knaves. [Laughter.] You feel it to be so. Not a man of you that looks a fellow Democrat or Whig in the face, but knows it. But it has been said that this law is constitutional— if it were, it would be equally the legitimate sphere of government to repeal it. I am proud to be one of the disciples of Gerrit Smith, [a leading abolitionist and member of the Free Soil Party] and this is his doctrine; and he only utters what all law writers have said who have risen to any eminence. Human government is for the protection of rights; and when human government destroys human rights, it ceases to be a government, and becomes a foul and blasting conspiracy; and is entitled to no respect whatever.

It has been said that our fathers entered into a covenant for this slavecatching. Who were your daddies? [Laughter.] I take it they were men, and so are you. You are the sons of your fathers; and if you find your fathers exercising any rights that you don't find among your rights, you may be sure that they have transcended their limits. If they have made a covenant that you should do that which they have no right to do themselves, they transcended their own authority, and surely it is not binding on you. If you look over the list of your rights, you do not find among them any right to make a slave of your brother. [Many cries of "no, no, no—and so say we, all of us."]

Well, you have just as good a right to do so as your fathers had. It is a fundamental truth that every man is the rightful owner of his own body. If you have no right to the possession of another man's body your fathers had no such right. But suppose that they have written in a constitution that they have a right, you and I have no right to conform to it. Suppose you and I had made a deed to give away two or three acres of blue sky; would the sky fall—and would anybody be able to plough it? You will say that this is an absurdity, and so it is. The binding quality of law, is its reasonableness. I am safe, therefore, in saying, that slavery cannot be legalized at all. I hope, therefore, that you will take the ground that this slavery is a system, not only of wrong, but is of a lawless character, and cannot be christianized nor legalized. [Applause.]

Can you hear me in that end of the hall now? [Laughter and applause.] I trust that this Convention will be the means of laying before the country the principles of the Liberty Party [a party that strongly opposed slavery] which I have the honor to represent, to some extent, on this floor. Slavery is such a piracy that it is known neither to law nor gospel—it is neither human nor divine—a monstrosity that cannot be legalized. If they took this ground it would be the handwriting on the wall to the Belshazzars [Babylonian king who saw the writing on the wall] of the South. It would strip the crime of its legality, and all the forms of law would shrink back with horror from it. As I have always an object when speaking on such subjects as this, I wish you to supply yourselves with Gerrit Smith's pamphlet on civil government, which I now hold in my hand. I thought you doubted the impossibility of legalizing slavery. [Cries of no.]

Could a law be made to pass away any of your individual rights? No. And so neither can a law be made to pass away the right of the black man. This is more important than most of you seem to think. You are about to have a party, but I hope not such a party as will gather up the votes, here and there, to be swallowed up at a meal by the great parties. I think I know what some leading men are now thinking. We hear a great deal of the independent, free democracy—at one time independent and another time dependent—but I want always to be independent, and not hurried to and fro into the ranks of Whigs or Democrats. [the two dominant political parties at the time] It has been said that we ought to take the position to gain the greatest number of voters, but that is wrong.

We have had enough of that folly. It was said in 1848 that Martin Van Buren [American president, 1837–1841] would carry a strong vote in New York; he did so but he almost ruined us. He merely looked at us as into the pigpen to see how the animal grew; but the table was the final prospect in view; he regarded the Free Soil party as a fatling to be devoured. [Great laughter.] Numbers should not be looked to so much as right. The man who is right is a majority. He who has God and conscience on his side, has a majority against the universe. Though he does not represent the present state, he represents the future state. If he does not represent what we are, he represents what we ought to be. In conclusion, this party ought to extend a hand to the noble, self-sacrificing patriot—glorious Kossuth. [Hungarian politician widely admired in America at the time for his support of freedom] But I am a voting delegate, and must now go to the convention. You will excuse me for breaking off so abruptly.

Source: Frederick Douglass' Paper. August 11, 1852.

Discussion Questions

1. Why did the Fugitive Slave Law infuriate many Northern whites?
2. What do you think you would have done if you had lived in the North in the 1850s and encountered a fugitive slave? Why?
3. Was Harriet Jacobs right to be so worried about it in her own case and that of her children?
4. Why do you think that law basically used bribery to encourage people to return runaway slaves to their owners?
5. How risky do you think it was for Ralph Waldo Emerson to oppose the Fugitive Slave Law in his speech? Why?
6. Why did Emerson oppose the Fugitive Slave Law in particular so vigorously? Were there not other laws on the books that were equally offensive or worse?
7. Why did the case of Shadrach Minkins make such a strong impression on Emerson?
8. How does Emerson defend his claim that the Fugitive Slave Law corrupts everything?
9. Why does Emerson claim the Fugitive Slave Law is obviously wrong and immoral but then goes on at length to prove that it is?
10. Why do you think Emerson links breaking the Fugitive Slave Law with manliness?
11. It is clear in Frederick Douglass's speech that he no longer thinks voluntary or gradual emancipation will end slavery; why do you think he changed his mind?
12. Do you agree with Douglass that killing slave hunters was justified? Why or why not?

13. Do you agree with him that the Fugitive Slave Law made it a criminal act "to carry out the principles of Christianity"?
14. If Douglass is right that slavery cannot be Christianized, how would you account for the fact that many people who regarded themselves as devout Christians thought it was a Christian concept?
15. Do you agree with Douglass that a man who is right is a majority?

Suggested Readings

Burnham, Michelle. "Loopholes of Resistance: Harriet Jacobs' Slave Narrative and the Critique of Agency in Foucault." *Arizona Quarterly* 49 (1993): 53–73.

McKay, Nellie Y. 1991. "The Girls Who Became the Women: Childhood Memories in the Autobiographies of Harriet Jacobs, Mary Church Terrell, and Anne Moody." *Tradition and the Talents of Women.* Ed. Florence Howe. Urbana and Chicago: University of Illinois Press, 106–124.

Mills, Bruce. 1994. *Cultural Reformation: Lydia Maria Child and the Literature of Reform.* Athens: University of Georgia Press.

Sánchez-Eppler, Karen. 1993. *Touching Liberty: Abolition, Feminism, and the Politics of the Body.* Berkeley: University of California Press.

Yellin, Jean Fagin. 2004. *Harriet Jacobs: A Life.* New York: Basic Books.

Yellin, Jean Fagin, et al., eds. 2008. *The Harriet Jacobs Family Papers.* Chapel Hill: The University of North Carolina Press.

HISTORICAL EXPLORATIONS

Nineteenth-Century Views of Slavery

Nineteenth-century views of slavery differed widely, depending on the perspective of the observer. Except for Booker T. Washington in *Up from Slavery,* it is rare to find a black apologist for slavery, and Washington described it as a "school" for black people because he wanted to reassure Southern whites that the ex-slaves were not bitter or angry; he took this position because he wanted the financial support of white businessmen in his efforts to establish Tuskegee Institute, as it used to be called. He knew that angry, frightened whites would not have provided this support.

Generally speaking, then, black views of slavery in the nineteenth century were of course negative. The best source for this evidence is slave narratives, written or spoken. Many of the spoken ones were published in the 1930s as part of the Federal Writers Project: they must be read between the lines, though, because many of the interviewers were white, and the interviews were conducted seventy years after legal slavery ended in 1865, so some ex-slaves' recollections were cloudy. But these oral narratives make it clear that slavery was an abomination beyond measure, even if some masters were "kind" and that there is no way to justify the ownership of human beings.

The written slave narratives, and other works about slavery by black writers, are our primary source of information about views of slavery in nineteenth-century United States. Frederick Douglass makes the essential point in his famous speech on slavery delivered on July 5, 1852, instead of July 4: everyone knows that slavery is wrong for him or her. In other words, who would want to be a slave? The answer is self-evident, but Douglass wisely proceeds to demolish the idea of slavery anyway, because he knows all too well that obvious truth has not fared well in a world based on the idea that blacks are inferior to whites.

Earlier in the nineteenth century, in 1829, the black writer David Walker published his *Appeal*. His view of slavery was that it should be ended by whatever means were required, that it was such a horrible institution that it had to be destroyed as soon as possible. This militant view of slavery is the one that eventually prevailed, although over thirty years passed before the Civil War began in 1861.

Black women also provided written views of slavery in the nineteenth century, Harriet Jacobs's *Incidents in the Life of a Slave Girl* (1861) now considered the most important. Jacobs dramatized the truth that slavery for black women was even worse than it was for black men because the former were

David Walker frequently racializes Christianity, as in this black religious figure stretching his hands toward liberty and justice rather than heaven, an idea Harriet Jacobs was very comfortable with. (Library of Congress)

not only slaves but also the sexual prey of white men. Black women were involved in slavery in a very personal way that black men were not. Harriet Jacobs spent her adolescence resisting Dr. Flint's efforts to make her his concubine. Sojourner Truth gave speeches that were later published, making it clear that although slavery was an abomination for all slaves, it was especially difficult for black women because they were victims of gender-based discrimination as well as racial prejudice.

Nineteenth-century white writers also expressed various views on slavery, besides the ones collected here. In some ways the most provocative and controversial views are those of Herman Melville in *Benito Cereno* (1855). Debate continues over whether or not Melville means to suggest that Babo, the leader of a slave revolt on board a ship once commanded by the Spanish captain Benito Cereno, is a stereotype of black depravity or an understandably vengeful African leading other Africans against the Spanish captain and his crew. Other readers question why the Africans should be expected to be any less violent than whites would have been in the same situation. That is, why should Babo and his men be held to higher standards than nonblacks might be? The ending is especially disturbing and ambiguous because when the American captain Amasa Delano asks Benito Cereno why he is still in a state of despair, even after the revolt has been put down and Babo decapitated, Cereno replies cryptically, "the negro [*sic*]," which could mean, among other possibilities, a particular black man, such as Babo, or black men in general and their potential threat to whites in the future.

Introduction to Angela Emily Grimké, *An Appeal to the Christian Women of the South* (1836)

Although Grimké grew up in a wealthy, privileged, slaveowning family in South Carolina, she, even as a little girl, was deeply offended by slavery. With her sister Sarah, she devoted much of her life to the abolition of slavery, beginning with writing a letter to William Lloyd Garrison, which he published in his abolitionist newspaper. She was forced to leave the Society of Friends because, as an outspoken abolitionist who delivered public lectures condemning slavery, she was too radical even for that group. Her husband, Theodore Weld, was also highly active in the abolitionist cause. Her pamphlet, *An Appeal to the Christian Women of the South*, was burned in some quarters; it is the only known example of a white Southern woman declaring publicly and in print her rejection of slavery. Grimké shrewdly uses the Christian beliefs of her audience so that they cannot easily reject her argument. Using numerous Biblical references, allusions, and quotations, she insists that her readers contrast their supposed Christian values with their tolerance of slavery. Like Harriet Jacobs, she hopes gender will trump race in her readers' minds and hearts.

From Angela Emily Grimké, *An Appeal to the Christian Women of the South* (1836)

The Ladies' Anti-Slavery Society of Boston was called last fall, to a severe trial of their faith and constancy. They were mobbed by "the gentlemen of property and standing," in that city at their anniversary meeting, and their lives were jeopardized by an infuriated crowd; but their conduct on that occasion did credit to our sex, and affords a full assurance that they will never abandon the cause of the slave. The pamphlet, Right and Wrong in Boston, issued by them in which a particular account is given of that "mob of broad cloth in broad day," does equal credit to the head and the heart of her who wrote it. I wish my Southern sisters could read it; they would then understand that the women of the North have engaged in this work from a sense of *religious duty,* and that nothing will ever induce them to take their hands from it until it is fully accomplished. They feel no hostility to you, no bitterness or wrath; they rather sympathize in your trials and difficulties; but they well know that the first thing to be done to help you, is to pour in the light of truth on your minds, to urge you to reflect on, and pray over the subject. This is all *they* can do for you, *you* must work out your own deliverance with fear and trembling, and with the direction and blessing of God, *you can do it.* Northern women may labor to produce a correct public opinion at the North, but if Southern women sit down in listless indifference and criminal idleness, public opinion cannot be rectified and purified at the South. It is manifest to every reflecting mind, that slavery must be abolished; the era in which we live, and the light which is overspreading the whole world on this subject, clearly show that the time cannot be distant when it will be done. Now there are only two ways in which it can be effected, by moral power or physical force, and it is for you to choose which of these you prefer. Slavery always has, and always will produce insurrections wherever it exists, because it is a violation of the natural order of things, and no human power can much longer perpetuate it. The opposers of abolitionists fully believe this; one of them remarked to me not long since, there is no doubt there will be a most terrible overturning at the South in a few years, such cruelty and wrong, must be visited with Divine vengeance soon. Abolitionists believe, too, that this must inevitably be the case if you do not repent, and they are not willing to leave you to perish without entreating you, to save yourselves from destruction; Well may they say with the apostle, "am I then your enemy because I tell you the truth," and warn you to flee from impending judgments.

But why, my dear friends, have I thus been endeavoring to lead you through the history of more than three thousand years, and to point you to that great cloud of witnesses who have gone before, "from works to rewards?" Have I been seeking to magnify the sufferings, and exalt the character of woman, that she "might have praise of men?" No! no! my object has been to arouse *you,* as the wives and mothers, the daughters and sisters, of the South, to a sense of your duty as *women,* and as Christian women, on that great subject, which has already shaken our country, from the St. Lawrence and the lakes, to the Gulf of Mexico, and from the Mississippi to the shores of the Atlantic; *and will continue mightily to shake it,* until the polluted temple of slavery fall and crumble into ruin. I would say unto each one of you, "what meanest thou, O sleeper! arise and call upon thy God, if so be that God will think upon us that we perish not." Perceive you not that dark cloud of vengeance which hangs over our boasting Republic? Saw you not the lightnings of Heaven's wrath, in the flame which leaped from the Indian's torch to the roof of yonder dwelling, and lighted with its horrid glare the darkness of midnight? Heard you not the thunders of Divine anger, as the distant roar of the cannon came rolling onward, from the Texian country, where Protestant American Rebels are fighting with Mexican Republicans—for what? For the re-establishment of *slavery;* yes! of American slavery in the bosom of a Catholic Republic, where that system of robbery, violence, and wrong, had been legally abolished for twelve years. Yes! citizens of the United States, after plundering Mexico of her land, are now engaged in deadly conflict, for the privilege of fastening chains, and collars, and manacles—upon whom? upon the subjects of some foreign prince? No! upon native born American Republican citizens, although the fathers of these very men declared to the whole world, while struggling to free themselves the three penny taxes of an English king, that they believed it to be a *self-evident* truth that *all men* were created equal, and had an *unalienable right to liberty.*

Well may the poet exclaim in bitter sarcasm,

"The fustian flag that proudly waves
In solemn mockery o'er a *land of slaves.*"

Can you not, my friends, understand the signs of the times; do you not see the sword of retributive justice hanging over the South, or are you still slumbering at your posts?—Are there no Shiphrahs, no Puahs among you, who will dare in Christian firmness and Christian meekness, to refuse to obey the *wicked laws* which require *woman to enslave, to degrade and to brutalize woman?* Are there no Miriams, who would rejoice to lead out the captive daughters of the Southern States to liberty and light? Are there no Huldahs there who will dare to *speak the truth* concerning the sins of the people and those judgments, which it requires no prophet's eye to see, must follow if repentance is not speedily sought? Is there no Esther among you who will plead for the poor devoted slave? Read the history of this Persian queen, it is full of instruction; she at first refused to plead for the Jews; but, hear the words of Mordecai, "Think not within thyself, that *thou* shalt escape in the king's house more than all the Jews, for *if thou altogether holdest thy peace at this time,* then shall there enlargement and deliverance arise to the Jews from another place: but *thou and thy father's house shall be destroyed.*" Listen, too, to her magnanimous reply to this powerful appeal; "*I will* go in, unto the king, which is *not* according to law, and if I perish, I perish." Yes! if there were but *one* Esther at the South, she *might* save her country from ruin; but let the Christian women there arise, at [*sic*] the Christian women of Great Britain did, in the majesty of moral power, and that salvation is certain. Let them embody themselves in societies, and send petitions up to their different legislatures, entreating their husbands, fathers, brothers and sons, to abolish the institution! of slavery; no longer to subject *woman* to the scourge and the chain, to mental darkness and moral degradation; no longer to tear husbands from their wives, and children from their parents; no longer to make men, women, and children, work *without wages;* no longer to make their lives bitter in hard bondage; no longer to reduce *American citizens* to the abject condition of *slaves,* of "chattels personal;" no longer to barter the *image of God* in human shambles for corruptible things such as silver and gold.

The *women of the South can overthrow* this horrible system of oppression and cruelty, licentiousness and wrong. Such appeals to your legislatures would be irresistible, for there is something in the heart of man which *will bend under moral suasion.* There is a swift witness for truth in his bosom, *which will respond to truth* when it is uttered with calmness and dignity. If you could obtain but six signatures to such a petition in only one state, I would say, send up that petition, and be not in the least discouraged by the scoffs and jeers of the heartless, or the resolution of the house to lay it on the table. It will be a great thing if the subject can be introduced into your legislatures in any way, even by *women,* and *they* will be the most likely to introduce it there in the best possible manner, as a matter of *morals* and *religion,* not of expediency or politics. You may petition, too, the different ecclesiastical bodies of the slave states. Slavery must be attacked with the whole power of truth and the sword of the spirit. You must take it up on *Christian* ground, and fight against it with Christian weapons, whilst your feet are shod with the preparation of the gospel of peace. And *you are now* loudly called upon by the cries of the widow and the orphan, to arise and gird yourselves for this great moral conflict, with the whole armour of righteousness upon the right hand and on the left.

There is every encouragement for you to labor and pray, my friends, because the abolition of slavery as well as its existence, has been the theme of prophecy. "Ethiopia (says the Psalmist) shall stretch forth her hands unto God." And is she not now doing so? Are not the Christian negroes of the south lifting their hands in prayer for deliverance, just as the Israelites did when their redemption was drawing nigh? Are they not sighing and crying by reason of the hard bondage? And think you, that He, of whom it was said, "and God heard their groaning, and their cry came up unto him by reason of the hard bondage," think you that his ear is heavy that he cannot *now* hear the cries of his suffering children? Or that He who raised up a Moses, an Aaron, and a Miriam, to bring them up out of the land of Egypt from the house of bondage, cannot now, with a high hand and a stretched out arm, rid the poor negroes out of the hands of their masters? Surely you believe that his aim is *not* shortened that he cannot save. And would not such a work of mercy redound to his glory? But another string of the harp of prophecy vibrates to the song of deliverance: "But they shall sit every man under his vine, and under his fig-tree, and *none shall make them afraid;* for the mouth of the Lord of Hosts hath spoken it." The *slave* never can do this as long as he is a *slave;* whilst he is a "chattel personal" he can own *no* property; but the time *is to come* when *every* man is to sit under *his own* vine and *his own* fig-tree, and no domineering driver, or irresponsible master, or irascible mistress, shall make him afraid of the chain or the whip. Hear, too, the sweet tones of another string: "Many shall run to and fro, and *knowledge* shall be *increased.*" Slavery is an insurmountable barrier to the increase of knowledge in every community where it exists*; slavery, then, must be abolished before this prediction can be fulfiled.* The last chord I shall touch, will be this, "They shall not hurt nor destroy in all my holy mountain."

Slavery, then, must be overthrown before the prophecies can be accomplished, but how are they to be fulfiled? Will the wheels of the millennial car be rolled onward by miraculous power? No! God designs to confer this holy privilege upon *man;* it is through *his* instrumentality that the great and glorious work of reforming the world is to be done. And see you not how the mighty engine of *moral power* is dragging in its rear the Bible and peace societies, anti-slavery and temperance, sabbath schools, moral reform, and missions? or to adopt another figure, do not these seven philanthropic associations compose the beautiful tints in that bow of promise which spans the arch of our moral heaven? Who does not believe, that if these societies were broken up, their constitutions burnt, and the vast machinery with which they are laboring to regenerate mankind was stopped, that the black clouds of vengeance would soon burst over our world, and every city would witness the fate of the devoted cities of the plain? Each one of these societies is walking abroad through the earth scattering the seeds of truth over the wide field of our world, not with the hundred hands of a Briareus, but with a hundred thousand.

Source: Grimké, Angela E. *An Appeal to the Christian Women of the South.* New York: American Anti-Slavery Society, 1836, pp. 19–21.

Introduction to Lydia Maria Child, *An Appeal in Favor of That Class of Americans Called Africans* (1836)

Lydia Maria Child (1802–1880), who helped Harriet Jacobs with editing *Incidents in the Life of a Slave Girl* and with finding a publisher for it, was an extremely impressive nineteenth-century figure. She spoke out boldly in favor of women's rights, the rights of African Americans, and the rights of Native Americans. She was absolutely opposed to slavery and absolutely in favor of abolition. For all this, she was subjected to severe rejection and condemnation, but that did not stop her efforts toward social progress.

Born in Medford, Massachusetts, she grew up in a strict Calvinist home but rejected its Calvinism and numerous other versions of Christianity in her lifelong search for religious truth. In an early work, *Hobomok* (1824), she depicted love between a Native American, Hobomok, and a young white woman, an endorsement that reappeared in her support for marriage between blacks and whites as a way to end white racism. Such a view was considered beyond the pale by many of her white contemporaries.

Twelve years later she published *An Appeal in Favor of That Class of Americans Called Africans,* which is often considered to be the first learned treatise on slavery in the United States. She calmly but boldly insists on the emancipation of the slaves, along with their being granted the rights to formal education, interracial marriage, and the right to vote; she also emphasized that the racial situation in the United States was a problem caused by whites, not blacks. She was implying that if whites could relinquish their preposterous notions of racial privilege, there would not be a racial problem. Her position has been echoed repeatedly ever since.

She spent the rest of her life publishing numerous books, including novels, antislavery tracts, collections of her letters, and short stories. She is being rediscovered now for more than being the author of "Over the River and Through the Wood," the work she is most famous for. She is being recognized as one of the foremost spokespersons for the rights of everyone, a remarkable position for a nineteenth-century writer to take. She was approximated 150 years ahead of her time.

From Lydia Maria Child, *An Appeal in Favor of That Class of Americans Called Africans* (1836)

The palliator of slavery assures the abolitionists that their benevolence is perfectly quixotic—that the negroes are happy and contented, and have no desire to change their lot. An answer to this may, as I have already said, be found in the Judicial Reports of slaveholding States, in the vigilance of their laws, in advertisements for runaway slaves, and in the details of their own newspapers. The West India planters make the same protestations concerning the happiness of their slaves; yet the cruelties proved by undoubted and unanswerable testimony are enough to sicken the heart. It is said that slavery is a great deal worse in the West Indies than in the United States; but I believe precisely the reverse of this proposition has been true within late years; for the English government have been earnestly trying to atone for their guilt, by the introduction of laws expressly framed to guard the weak and defenceless. A gentleman who has been a great deal among the planters of both countries, and who is by no means favorable to anti-slavery, gives it as his decided opinion that the slaves are better off in the West Indies, than they are in the United States. It is true we hear a great deal more about West Indian cruelty than we do about our own. English books and periodicals are continually full of the subject; and even in the colonies, newspapers openly denounce the hateful system, and take every opportunity to prove the amount of wretchedness it produces. In this country, we have not, until very recently, dared to publish any thing upon the subject. Our books, our reviews, our newspapers, our almanacs, have all been silent, or exerted their influence on the wrong side. The negro's crimes are repeated, but his sufferings are never told. Even in our geographies it is taught that the colored race must always be degraded. Now and then anecdotes of cruelties committed in the slaveholding States are told by individuals who witnessed them; but they are almost always afraid to give their names to the public, because the Southerners will call them "a disgrace to the soil," and the Northerners will echo the sentiment. The promptitude and earnestness with which New-England has aided the slaveholders in repressing all discussions which they were desirous to avoid, has called forth many expressions of gratitude in their public speeches, and private conversation; and truly we have well earned Randolph's favorite appellation, "the white slaves of the North," by our tameness and servility with regard to a subject where good feeling and good principle alike demand a firm and independent spirit.

We are told that the Southerners will of themselves do away with slavery, and they alone understand how to do it. But it is an obvious fact that all their measures have tended to perpetuate the system; and even if we have the fullest faith that they mean to do their duty, the belief by no means absolves us from doing ours. The evil is gigantic; and its removal requires every heart and head in the community.

It is said that our sympathies ought to be given to the masters, who are abundantly more to be pitied than the slaves. If this be the case, the planters are singularly disinterested not to change places with their bondmen. Our sympathies have been given to the masters—and to those masters who seemed most desirous to remain for ever in their pitiable condition. There are hearts at the South sincerely desirous of doing right in this cause; but their generous impulses are checked by the laws of their respective States, and the strong disapprobation of their neighbors. I know a lady in Georgia who would, I believe, make any personal sacrifice to instruct her slaves, and give them freedom; but if she were found guilty of teaching the alphabet, or manumitting her slaves, fines and imprisonment would be the consequence; if she sold them, they would be likely to fall into hands less merciful than her own. Of such slave-owners we cannot speak with too much respect and tenderness. They are comparatively few in number, and stand in a most perplexing situation; it is a duty to give all our sympathy to them. It is mere mockery to say, what is so often said, that the Southerners, as a body, really wish to abolish slavery. If they wished it, they certainly would make the attempt. When the majority heartily desire a change, it is effected, be the difficulties what they may. The Americans are peculiarly responsible for the example they give; for in no other country does the unchecked voice of the people constitute the whole of government.

We must not be induced to excuse slavery by the plausible argument that England introduced it among us. The wickedness of beginning such a work unquestionably belongs to her; the sin of continuing it is certainly our own. It is true that Virginia, while a province, did petition the British government to check the introduction of slaves into the colonies; and their refusal to do so was afterward enumerated among the public reasons for separating from the mother country: but it is equally true that when we became independent, the Southern States stipulated that the slave-trade should not be abolished by law until 1808.

The strongest and best reason that can be given for our supineness on the subject of slavery, is the fear of dissolving the Union. The Constitution of the United States demands our highest reverence. Those who approve, and those who disapprove of particular portions, are equally bound to yield implicit obedience to its authority. But we must not forget that the Constitution provides for any change that may be required for the general good. The great machine is constructed with a safety-valve, by which any rapidly increasing evil may be expelled whenever the people desire it.

If the Southern politicians are determined to make a Siamese question of this also—if they insist that the Union shall not exist without slavery—it can only be said that they join two things, which have no affinity with each other, and which cannot permanently exist together. They chain the living and vigorous to the diseased and dying; and the former will assuredly perish in the infected neighborhood.

The universal introduction of free labor is the surest way to consolidate the Union, and enable us to live together in harmony and peace. If a history is ever written entitled "The Decay and Dissolution of the North American Republic," its author will distinctly trace our downfall to the existence of slavery among us.

There is hardly any thing bad, in politics or religion, that has not been sanctioned or tolerated by a suffering community, because certain powerful individuals were able to identify the evil with some other principle long consecrated to the hearts and consciences of men.

Under all circumstances, there is but one honest course; and that is to do right, and trust the consequences to Divine Providence. "Duties are ours; events are God's." Policy, with all her cunning, can devise no rule so safe, salutary, and effective, as this simple maxim.

We cannot too cautiously examine arguments and excuses brought forward by those whose interest or convenience is connected with keeping their fellow-creatures in a state of ignorance and brutality; and such we shall find in abundance, at the North as well as the South. I have heard the abolition of slavery condemned on the ground that New-England vessels would not be employed to export the produce of the South, if they had free laborers of their own. This objection is so utterly bad in its spirit, that it hardly deserves an answer. Assuredly it is a righteous plan to retard the progress of liberal principles, and "keep human nature for ever in the stocks," that some individuals may make a few hundred dollars more per annum! Besides the experience of the world abundantly proves that all such forced expedients are unwise. The increased prosperity of one country, or of one section of a country, always contributes, in some form or other, to the prosperity of other states. To "love our neighbor as ourselves," is, after all, the shrewdest way of doing business.

In England, the abolition of the traffic was long and stoutly resisted, in the same spirit, and by the same arguments, that characterize the defence of the system here; but it would now be difficult to find a man so reckless, that he would not be ashamed of being called a slave-dealer. Public opinion has nearly conquered one evil, and if rightly directed, it will ultimately subdue the other.

Is it asked what can be done? I answer, much, very much, can be effected, if each individual will try to deserve the commendation bestowed by our Saviour on the woman of old—"She hath done what she could."

The Friends,—always remarkable for fearless obedience to the inward light of conscience,—early gave an example worthy of being followed. At their annual meeting in Pennsylvania, in 1688, many individuals urged the incompatibility of slavery and Christianity; and their zeal continued until, in 1776, all Quakers who bought or sold a slave, or refused to emancipate those they already owned, were excluded from communion with the society. Had it not been for the early exertions of these excellent people, the fair and flourishing State of Pennsylvania might now, perchance, be withering under the effects of slavery. To this day, the Society of Friends, both in England and America, omit no opportunity, public or private, of discountenancing this bad system; and the Methodists (at least in England) have earnestly labored in the same glorious cause.

The famous Anthony Benezet, a Quaker in Philadelphia, has left us a noble example of what may be done for conscience' sake. Being a teacher, he took effectual care that his scholars should have ample knowledge and Christian impressions concerning the nature of slavery; he caused articles to be inserted in the almanacs likely to arrest public attention upon the subject; he talked about it, and wrote letters about it; he published and distributed tracts at his own expense; if any person was going a journey, his first thought was how he could make him instrumental in favor of his benevolent purposes; he addressed a petition to the Queen for the suppression of the slave-trade; and another to the good Countess of Huntingdon, beseeching that the rice and indigo plantations belonging to the orphan-house, which she had endowed near Savannah, in Georgia, might not be cultivated by those who encouraged the slave-trade; he took care to increase the comforts and elevate the character of the colored people within his influence; he zealously promoted the establishment of an African school, and devoted much of the two last years of his life to personal attendance upon his pupils. By fifty years of constant industry he had amassed a small fortune; and this was left after the decease of his widow, to the support of the African school.

Similar exertions, though on a less extensive scale, were made by the late excellent John Kenrick, of Newton, Mass. For more than thirty years the constant object of his thoughts, and the chief purpose of his life, was the abolition of slavery. His earnest conversation aroused many other minds to think and act upon the subject. He wrote letters, inserted articles in the newspapers, gave liberal donations, and circulated pamphlets at his own expense.

Cowper contributed much to the cause when he wrote the "Negro's Complaint," and thus excited the compassion of his numerous readers. Wedgewood aided the work, when he caused cameos to be struck, representing a kneeling African in chains, and thus made even capricious fashion an avenue to the heart. Clarkson assisted by patient investigation of evidence; and Fox and Wilberforce by eloquent speeches. Mungo Park gave his powerful influence by the kind and liberal manner in which he always represented the Africans. The Duchess of Devonshire wrote verses and caused them to be set to music; and wherever those lines were sung, some hearts were touched in favor of the oppressed. This fascinating woman made even her far-famed beauty serve in the cause of benevolence. Fox was returned for Parliament through her influence, and she is said to have procured more than one vote, by allowing the yeomanry of England to kiss her beautiful cheek.

All are not able to do so much as Anthony Benezet and John Kenrick have done; but we can all do something. We can speak kindly and respectfully of colored people upon all occasions; we can repeat to our children such traits as are honorable in their character and history; we can avoid making odious caricatures of negroes; we can teach boys that it is unmanly and contemptible to insult an unfortunate class of people by the vulgar outcry of "Nigger!—Nigger!" Even Mahmoud of Turkey rivals us in liberality—for he long ago ordered a fine to be levied upon those who called a Christian a dog; and in his dominions the prejudice is so great that a Christian must be a degraded being. A residence in Turkey might be profitable to those Christians who patronize the eternity of prejudice; it would afford an opportunity of testing the goodness of the rule, by showing how it works both ways.

If we are not able to contribute to African schools, or do not choose to do so, we can at least refrain from opposing them. If it be disagreeable to allow colored people the same rights and privileges as other citizens, we can do with our prejudice, what most of us often do with better feeling—we can conceal it.

Our almanacs and newspapers can fairly show both sides of the question; and if they lean to either party, let it not be to the strongest. Our preachers can speak of slavery, as they do of other evils. Our poets can find in this subject abundant room for sentiment and pathos. Our orators (provided they do not want office) may venture an allusion to our *in*-"glorious institutions."

The union of individual influence produces a vast amount of moral force, which is not the less powerful because it is often unperceived. A mere change in the direction of our efforts, without any increased exertion, would in the course of a few years, produce an entire revolution of public feeling. This slow but sure way of doing good is almost the only means by which benevolence can effect its purpose.

Sixty thousands petitions have been addressed to the English parliament on the subject of slavery, and a large number of them were signed by women. The same steps here would be, with one exception, useless and injudicious; because the general government has no control over the legislatures of individual States. But the District of Columbia forms an exception to this rule. There the United States have power to abolish slavery; and it is the duty of the citizens to petition year after year, until a reformation is effected. But who will present remonstrances against slavery? The Hon. John Q. Adams was intrusted with fifteen petitions for the abolition of slavery in the District of Columbia; yet clearly as that gentleman sees and defines the pernicious effects of the system, he offered the petitions only to protest against them! Another petition to the same effect, intrusted to another Massachusetts representative, was never noticed at all. "Brutus is an honorable man:—So are they all—all honorable men." Nevertheless, there is, in this popular government, a subject on which it is impossible for the people to make themselves heard.

By publishing this book I have put my mite into the treasury. The expectation of displeasing all classes has not been unaccompanied with pain. But it has been strongly impressed upon my mind that it was a duty to fulfil this task; and worldly considerations should never stifle the voice of conscience.

Source: Child, Lydia Maria. *An Appeal in Favor of That Class of Americans Called Africans.* New York: John S. Taylor, 1836, pp. 211–216.

Introduction to John C. Calhoun, "Slavery a Positive Good" (1837)

John C. Calhoun (1782–1850) was one of the most prominent politicians in the nineteenth-century United States, serving in the House of Representatives and the Senate, and twice as vice president. A native of South Carolina, he was a strong supporter of slavery and the Fugitive Slave Law and a strong opponent of abolition. Not only did he not see slavery as evil, he saw it as a "positive good," arguing that is was in the best interests of blacks and whites. As one of the primary defenders of the rights of plantation owners, he feared, though, that the slaveowning South was doomed unless it woke up to the threat abolition and emancipation represented. In his famous speech defending slavery, delivered to the Senate on February 6, 1837, he maintained that Congress had no right to even debate abolition, because he believed slavery was a matter of states' rights. He did not think abolition and a united United States could coexist, and in that he was correct. To Calhoun it was unthinkable that there could be equality between blacks and whites or between the wealthy and the poor. He regarded privilege and inequality as a natural state of affairs, which should be respected as such. But as his speech makes clear, he is aware that his position might well be subjected to a violent challenge, which is why he advises the white, slaveowning South to wake up.

From John C. Calhoun, "Slavery a Positive Good" (1837)

I do not belong, said Mr. C., to the school which holds that aggression is to be met by concession. Mine is the opposite creed, which teaches that encroachments must be met at the beginning, and that those who act on the opposite principle are prepared to become slaves. In this case, in particular I hold concession or compromise to be fatal. If we concede an inch, concession would follow concession—compromise would follow compromise, until our ranks would be so broken that effectual resistance would be impossible. We must meet the enemy on the frontier, with a fixed determination of maintaining our position at every hazard. Consent to receive these insulting petitions, and the next demand will be that they be referred to a committee in order that they may be deliberated and acted upon. At the last session we were modestly asked to receive them, simply to lay them on the table, without any view to ulterior action. . . . I then said, that the next step would be to refer the petition to a committee, and I already see indications that such is now the intention. If we yield, that will be followed by another, and we will thus proceed, step by step, to the final consummation of the object of these petitions. We are now told that the most effectual mode of arresting the progress of abolition is, to reason it down; and with this view it is urged that the petitions ought to be referred to a committee. That is the very ground which was taken at the last session in the other House, but instead of arresting its progress it has since advanced more rapidly than ever. The most unquestionable right may be rendered doubtful, if once admitted to be a subject of controversy, and that would be the case in the present instance. The subject is beyond the jurisdiction of Congress—they have no right to touch it in any shape or form, or to make it the subject of deliberation or discussion. . . .

As widely as this incendiary spirit has spread, it has not yet infected this body, or the great mass of the intelligent and business portion of the North; but unless it be speedily stopped, it will spread and work upwards till it brings the two great sections of the Union into deadly conflict. This is not a new impression with me. Several years since, in a discussion with one of the Senators from Massachusetts (Mr. Webster), before this fell spirit had showed itself, I then predicted that the doctrine of the proclamation and the Force Bill—that this Government had a right, in the last resort, to determine the extent of its own powers, and enforce its decision at the point of the bayonet, which was so warmly maintained by that Senator, would at no distant day arouse the dormant spirit of abolitionism. I told him that the doctrine was tantamount to the assumption of unlimited power on the part of the Government, and that such would be the impression on the public mind in a large portion of the Union. The consequence would be inevitable. A large portion of the Northern States believed slavery to be a sin, and would consider it as an obligation of conscience to abolish it if they should feel themselves in any degree responsible for its continuance, and that this doctrine would necessarily lead to the belief of such responsibility. I then predicted that it would commence as it has with this fanatical portion of society, and that they would begin their operations on the ignorant, the weak, the young, and the thoughtless—and gradually extend upwards till they would become strong enough to obtain political control, when he and others holding the highest stations in society, would, however reluctant, be compelled to yield to their doctrines, or be driven into obscurity. But four years have since elapsed, and all this is already in a course of regular fulfilment.

Standing at the point of time at which we have now arrived, it will not be more difficult to trace the course of future events now than it was then. They who imagine that the spirit now abroad in the North, will die away of itself without a shock or convulsion, have formed a very inadequate conception of its real character; it will continue to rise and spread, unless prompt and efficient measures to stay its progress be adopted. Already it has taken possession of the pulpit, of the schools, and, to a considerable extent, of the press; those great instruments by which the mind of the rising generation will be formed.

However sound the great body of the non-slaveholding States are at present, in the course of a few years they will be succeeded by those who will have been taught to hate the people and institutions of nearly one-half of this Union, with a hatred more deadly than one hostile nation ever entertained towards another. It is easy to see the end. By the necessary course of events, if left to themselves, we must become, finally, two people. It is impossible under the deadly hatred which must spring up between the two great nations, if the present causes are permitted to operate unchecked, that we should continue under the same political system. The conflicting elements would burst the Union asunder, powerful as are the links which hold it together. Abolition and the Union cannot coexist. As the friend of the Union I openly proclaim it—and the sooner it is known the better. The former may now be controlled, but in a short time it will be beyond the power of man to arrest the course of events. We of the South will not, cannot, surrender our institutions. To maintain the existing relations between the two races, inhabiting that section of the Union, is indispensable to the peace and happiness of both. It cannot be subverted without drenching the country in blood, and extirpating one or the other of the races. Be it good or bad, [slavery] has grown up with our society and institutions, and is so interwoven with them that to destroy it would be to destroy us as a people. But let me not be understood as admitting, even by implication, that the existing relations between the two races in the slaveholding States is an evil:—far otherwise; I hold it to be a good, as it has thus far proved itself to be to both, and will continue to prove so if not disturbed by the fell spirit of abolition. I appeal to facts. Never before has the black race of Central Africa, from the dawn of history to the present day, attained a condition so civilized and so improved, not only physically, but morally and intellectually.

In the meantime, the white or European race, has not degenerated. It has kept pace with its brethren in other sections of the Union where slavery does not exist. It is odious to make comparison; but I appeal to all sides whether the South is not equal in virtue, intelligence, patriotism, courage, disinterestedness, and all the high qualities which adorn our nature.

But I take higher ground. I hold that in the present state of civilization, where two races of different origin, and distinguished by color, and other physical differences, as well as intellectual, are brought together, the relation now existing in the slaveholding States between the two, is, instead of an evil, a good—a positive good. I feel myself called upon to speak freely upon the subject where the honor and interests of those I represent are involved. I hold then, that there never has yet existed a wealthy and civilized society in which one portion of the community did not, in point of fact, live on the labor of the other. Broad and general as is this assertion, it is fully borne out by history. This is not the proper occasion, but, if it were, it would not be difficult to trace the various devices by which the wealth of all civilized communities has been so unequally divided, and to show by what means so small a share has been allotted to those by whose labor it was produced, and so large a share given to the non-producing classes. The devices are almost innumerable, from the brute force and gross superstition of ancient times, to the subtle and artful fiscal contrivances of modern. I might well challenge a comparison between them and the more direct, simple, and patriarchal mode by which the labor of the African race is, among us, commanded by the European. I may say with truth, that in few countries so much is left to the share of the laborer, and so little exacted from him, or where there is more kind attention paid to him in sickness or infirmities of age. Compare his condition with the tenants of the poor houses in the more civilized portions of Europe—look at the sick, and the old and infirm slave, on one hand, in the midst of his family and friends, under the kind superintending care of his master and mistress, and compare it with the forlorn and wretched condition of the pauper in the poorhouse. But I will not dwell on this aspect of the question; I turn to the political; and here I fearlessly assert that the existing relation between the two races in the South, against which these blind fanatics are waging war, forms the most solid and durable foundation on which to rear free and stable political institutions. It is useless to disguise the fact. There is and always has been in an advanced stage of wealth and civilization, a conflict between labor and capital. The condition of society in the South exempts us from the disorders and dangers resulting from this conflict; and which explains why it is that the political condition of the slaveholding States has been so much more stable and quiet than that of the North. . . . Surrounded as the slaveholding States are with such imminent perils, I rejoice to think that our means of defense are ample, if we shall prove to have the intelligence and spirit to see and apply them before it is too late. All we want is concert, to lay aside all party differences and unite with zeal and energy in repelling approaching dangers. Let there be concert of action, and we shall find ample means of security without resorting to secession or disunion. I speak with full knowledge and a thorough examination of the subject, and for one see my way clearly. . . . I dare not hope that anything I can say will arouse the South to a due sense of danger; I fear it is beyond the power of mortal voice to awaken it in time from the fatal security into which it has fallen.

Source: Calhoun, John C. *Speeches of John C. Calhoun,* ed. Richard R. Cradle. New York: D. Appleton, 1853, pp. 625–633.

Discussion Questions

1. How would you account for the fact that Grimké strongly disagreed with other upper-class white women in the nineteenth-century South about slavery? To put the question another way, should we avoid generalizations about groups of people? Is that possible?
2. Why is Grimké wise to avoid harsh condemnations of members of her audience who do not share her views?
3. Why does she put so much emphasis on gender and motherhood?
4. Explain her heavy reliance on the Bible in her attacks on slavery: why that particular document in an appeal to Southern white women?
5. Does she think slaves should be taught to read, and if so, taught to read what in particular?
6. Why might some white *women* like Grimké and Lydia Maria Child have had insightful views of slavery and racism?
7. Keeping in mind that the Civil War started twenty-five years after Child's treatise on slavery appeared, how farsighted was she in her prediction that the North and the South could not coexist as long as there was slavery in the South?
8. What do you admire most about Child's treatise? Least? Why?
9. Why does Child hold the Quakers in such high regard? Do you know any? Are they like the ones Child mentions?
10. Do you agree with Child, when she says at the end of her excerpt, that "worldly considerations should never stifle the voice of conscience"? Do you know anyone who lives this way consistently?
11. How would you account for John C. Calhoun's outrageous views on black people and slavery? Do you think he really believed them or was just trying to be sensational? Why?
12. Does Calhoun think the Southern way of life is doomed because of any inherent flaws?
13. Does he conflate "natural" with "cultural" when he claims white control over blacks is "natural"? Or the control of the poor by the rich is "natural"?
14. Does he think the masters had every right to protect their privileges? Why or why not?
15. Would Calhoun have agreed that blacks had a right to control whites if the racial situation in the South had been the reverse of what it was?

16. Do you know anyone with views similar to Calhoun's, or have such people died out?

Suggested Readings

Accomando, Christina. "'The Laws Were Laid Down to Me Anew': Harriet Jacobs and the Reframing of Legal Fictions." *African American Review* 32 (1998): 229–244.

Bartholomaus, Craig. " 'What Would You Be?' Racial Myths and Cultural Sameness in *Incidents in the Life of a Slave Girl*." *College Language Association Journal* 39 (1995): 179–194.

Brown, Gillian. 1992. *Domestic Individualism: Imagining the Self in Nineteenth-Century America.* Berkeley: University of California Press.

Fleischner, Jennifer. 1996. *Mastering Slavery: Memory, Family, and Identity in Women's Slave Narratives.* New York: New York University Press.

Foster, Frances Smith. 1993. *Written by Herself: Literary Production by African American Women,* 1746–1892. Bloomington: Indiana University Press.

Garfield, Deborah M. and Rafia Zafar, eds. 1996. *Harriet Jacobs and "Incidents in the Life of a Slave Girl": New Critical Essays.* New York: Cambridge University Press.

Kaplan, Carla. 1996. *The Erotics of Talk: Women's Writing and Feminist Paradigms.* New York: Oxford University Press.

Karcher, Carolyn L. 1994. *The First Woman in the Republic: A Cultural Biography of Lydia Maria Child.* Durham, NC: Duke University Press.

Mullen, Harryette. 1992. "Runaway Tongue: Resistant Orality in *Uncle Tom's Cabin, Our Nig, Incidents in the Life of a Slave Girl, and Beloved.*" *The Culture of Sentiment.* Ed. Shirley Samuels. New York: Oxford University Press, 244–264, 332–335.

Painter, Nell Irvin. 1994. "Three Southern Women and Freud: A Non-Exceptionalist Approach to Race, Class, and Gender in the Slave South." *Feminist Revision History.* Ed. Ann-Louise Shapiro. New Brunswich, NJ: Rutgers University Press, 195–216.

Ryan, Susan M. 2003. *The Grammar of Good Intentions: Race and the Antebellum Culture of Benevolence.* Ithaca, NY: Cornell University Press.

Smith, Valerie. 1987. *Self-Discovery and Authority in Afro-American Narrative.* Cambridge, MA: Harvard University Press.

Spelman, Elizabeth V. 1997. *Fruits of Sorrow: Framing Our Attention to Suffering.* Boston: Becon Press.

Taves, Ann. "Spiritual Purity and Sexual Shame: Religious Themes in the Writings of Harriet Jacobs." *Church History* (March 1987): 59–72.

Yellin, Jean Fagin. "Written by Herself: Harriet Jacobs' Slave Narrative." *American Literature* 53 (November 1981): 379–486.

Zafar, Rafia and Deborah M. Garfield, eds. 1996. *Harriet Jacobs and "Incidents in the Life of a Slave Girl": New Critical Essays.* Cambridge: Cambridge University Press.

Areas for Research

A fascinating area of research on *Incidents* is to compare the historical record with Jacobs's version of it. Did she really hide in her grandmother's attic for seven years to stay near her son and daughter? Was the historical Dr. Flint, Dr. James Norcom, really as Jacobs depicts him? Was Mr. Sands (Samuel Tredwell Sawyer in actuality) as hardhearted toward Jacobs and their children as he is depicted (consider the implications of his fictional last name and Dr. Flint's)? If the historical record supports Jacobs's answer to these questions, how would you account for their being raised?

Also fruitful is a close look at the Fugitive Slave Law of 1850, which today is an empty phrase for most people, but at the time generated intense hostility in the North toward the South and vice versa. Many Northerners preferred to think of slavery, if and when they did consider it, as a social institution peculiar to the South. But the new law forced Americans north of the Mason-Dixon Line to admit slavery was very much a part of their lives, with serious consequences for them if they violated it. Research will reveal a wide range of responses: comparing and contrasting those responses will indicate the complicated feelings the law provoked in the North.

In addition, the various responses to abolition will yield interesting results for researchers. Huck Finn, for example, grew up thinking of abolitionists as at the bottom of the social ladder, whereas of course Jacobs views them and antislavery societies in a different light. There were also deep divisions within the abolitionist movement itself, between those who wanted to abolish slavery slowly and those who wanted it abolished immediately, as William Lloyd Garrison eventually began to think should be done. Some abolitionists believed slavery could be ended without bloodshed, others that war was unavoidable.

Research is especially concentrated now on the role of black women in the resistance to slavery. Until recently, black men such as Frederick Douglass were seen as what should be emphasized. But with the rediscovery of *Incidents in the Life of a Slave Girl,* and a number of other works by African American women, it is becoming much clearer that they played a major role as well. Research will uncover more contributions by black (and white) women in the central movement in nineteenth-century United States: the eradication of slavery.

WHY WE READ *INCIDENTS IN THE LIFE OF A SLAVE GIRL* TODAY

A primary reason for reading *Incidents in the Life of a Slave Girl* is that it helps fill what had been a gap in African American literature: the supposed silence of black women during slavery. While numerous African American men's voices had been preserved, Frederick Douglass's, for example, in *Narrative of the Life of Frederick Douglass* (1845), until the republication of *Incidents* in the 1980s, black women were an absence. Jacobs's voice is often restrained and under tight control, but it was "loud" nevertheless. And it speaks powerfully to black women and women in general in the twenty-first century.

And that is connected to another reason it is read and discussed so much now. One of the implications of *Incidents* is that enslaved black women are not so different from white and nonwhite women who are not slaves, as both of the latter might think, because both are subject to white patriarchy. Jacobs had to be careful about this implication because she wanted the support of white women in the North, but many of them occupied a position in life not so different from Mrs. Flint's, or from modern-day Mrs. Flints.

Incidents is also read because it is such a skillful combination of the slave narrative, such as Douglass's 1845 *Narrative,* and the novel of romance, such as Samuel Richardson's *Pamela* and Charlotte Bronte's *Jane Eyre,* both tales of women pursued relentlessly by the men in their lives. Jacobs sensed that such novels appealed to white women in the North and exploited the opportunity by using the language and form associated with intentionally sentimental, romantic literature. But she also wanted to emphasize that she, like Frederick Douglass, escaped from slavery, thus the reliance on the conventions of the slave narrative. She duplicated Douglass's achievement while including her children in her successful plans, something Douglass did not have to worry about as he was childless when he ran away from slavery.

We read *Incidents,* too, because it is such a rich, detailed picture of the horrors of being an enslaved black woman: as other black writers have suggested, if being an enslaved black man is unspeakably horrible, being an enslaved black woman is even worse, because that involves oppression based on gender as well as race. Harriet Jacobs had to withstand the endless pressure of Dr. Flint's sexual obsession, while withstanding the pressures of white racism and slavery. Only the most resilient temperament could survive such treatment.

VI

Adventures of Huckleberry Finn
(1884)

HISTORICAL BACKGROUND

The historical background to *Adventures of Huckleberry Finn* differs considerably from that of *Narrative of the Life of Frederick Douglass, Uncle Tom's Cabin,* and *Incidents in the Life of a Slave Girl,* because they were published before the Civil War began in 1861, whereas Twain's novel was published about twenty years after it ended, although it is set in 1835 or 1845. Twain has a perspective on slavery that the other three writers could not have had, because it was legal when they wrote their books but illegal when Twain wrote his. He knew when writing his most famous book that President Lincoln's Emancipation Proclamation had not really freed the slaves, something the other three could not have known. He knows in particular that abolishing slavery is the beginning of a long struggle, which is far from over now.

Fifteen years before Twain was born in 1835, the Missouri Compromise was passed by Congress (Twain was born in Hannibal, Missouri). The compromise was to allow Maine to be admitted to the country as a free state, while Missouri gained admission as a slave state. Twain himself was opposed to

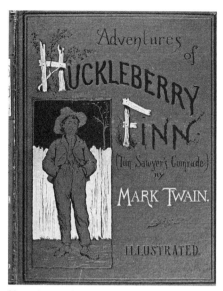

Note the reminder of Tom Sawyer tricking other white boys to whitewash a fence in the *The Adventures of Tom Sawyer* in contrast to the "trick" when Tom "frees" an already free Jim, in *Huckleberry Finn*. (GraphicaArtis/Corbis)

slavery and saw it at first hand. The extent to which he realized blacks were every bit as human as whites, though, is still hotly debated, especially in regard to his depiction of Jim through Huck's eyes in the novel. When Twain was growing up in the 1840s, Congressman David Wilmot tried but failed repeatedly to get a law passed by Congress that would have disallowed slavery in territories ruled by Mexico that the United States might claim after the Mexican-American War. When Twain was in his mid-teens, the Fugitive Slave Law of 1850 did pass; it infuriated Northerners because it required their support, under penalty of law, of the return of runaway slaves (like Jim). Twain was also keenly aware of abolitionism and treats that movement in his novel, in which supporters of abolition are viewed as the lowest of the low in the South.

Twain also knew of the more personal aspects of slavery, such as the breaking up of slave families, as *Huckleberry Finn* powerfully demonstrates: Jim and Huck are both fugitives, Huck from his vicious drunken lout of a father, Jim from slavery, as he attempts to rejoin his wife and children. What makes Tom Sawyer's "freeing" of Jim at the end of the novel so cruel is that he knows Miss Watson has already freed him in her will, but this does not bother Tom because in his view Jim does not have the same feelings toward his family whites had toward theirs; Huck has come to feel otherwise.

About the historical event that ended legal slavery, the Civil War, Twain also felt very strongly (he served briefly in a Confederate unit as he recounts in "A Private History of a Campaign That Failed"). He regarded the South's entry into it as largely based on romantic fictions in regard to chivalry and feudalism, which explains why he names the steamboat that runs aground in *Huckleberry Finn* the Sir Walter Scott, after a Scottish writer of novels based on fantasies about feudalism. Romantic illusions about war and violence are just one of society's lies that Twain attacks in his novels.

The Fifteenth Amendment to the Constitution, which passed in 1870, gave African Americans citizenship in theory, but in reality they got Jim Crow laws. Such laws prohibited blacks from voting, attending decent schools, and living where they wanted to. Perhaps Twain is hinting at this when he has Tom Sawyer and Huck playing at freeing an already free Jim, who is imprisoned on the Phelps's farm toward the end of the novel. In other words, even though Miss Watson has freed Jim, white society hardly treats him like an equal. Unlike Douglass, Stowe, and Jacobs, Twain knew as he wrote his masterpiece that truly ending slavery was going to require a lot more than the Emancipation Proclamation, the Civil War, and the passage of legislation could deliver.

He also knew that the historical period known as Reconstruction was a disaster, in many ways, for black people. For a brief period after the Civil War, some blacks voted and were elected to public office, but the white South soon put a stop to this "reconstruction," just as Tom Sawyer went along with keeping Jim tied up. Twain's view of the aftermath of slavery was much less optimistic than Douglass's, Stowe's, and Jacobs's hopes about slavery's end because he was writing from a post-Reconstruction point of view in *Huckleberry Finn*.

ABOUT MARK TWAIN

Mark Twain (1835–1910) is probably the best-known American author in the world, particularly for *The Adventures of Tom Sawyer* and *Adventures of Huckleberry Finn*. Born in Florida, Missouri, he lived in Hannibal, Missouri, from the ages of four through seventeen. His boyhood is a defining part of his wide experience: he continually returned to it for inspiration and continually used it as an idyllic foil to the world of adult society. But even in his memories of his childhood, he reveals the split between "respectable" boys like Tom Sawyer, who used his imagination for self-aggrandizement, and the "unrespectable" Huck, who used his to empathize with society's victims, like Jim. Huck and Jim knew what it was like to be looked down on, whereas Tom did not. Hannibal is the source for "St. Petersburg" in *Huckleberry Finn*.

Twain's father having died when the author-to-be was only twelve years old, he had to go to work; as a result, he became an apprentice printer for the *Hannibal Courier*, the first of several associations with journalism. As he entered his twenties, Twain learned how to be a steamboat pilot on the Mississippi River, a lucrative and respected position. He took his pen name from the saying "mark twain," which indicated a depth of twelve feet, or safe

Although Twain condemned respectability based on dress, as in the case of Colonel Grangerford, he himself was deeply concerned about it, as this image makes clear. (The Illustrated London News Picture Library)

passage for a steamboat (Twain's real name was Samuel Langhorne Clemens). The Mississippi River figures prominently in *Huckleberry Finn* as an ambiguous symbol many readers have puzzled over. Huck and Jim for the most part get along while they are on the raft, most of their trouble occurring on the shore world; but even on the raft, trouble (or history) intrudes in the form of storms, Huck's cruel joke on Jim, and the duke and the king. Twain's experiences as a steamboat pilot ended with the start of the Civil War in 1861, when traffic on the Mississippi was shut down.

Twain went west to Nevada that same year to work on the *Virginia City Territorial Enterprise.* His first widely recognized publication was "The Celebrated Jumping Frog of Calaveras County" (1865); today's readers are sometimes puzzled at the lighthearted nature of this tall tale's appearance the year the Civil War, the bloodiest war in American history by far, ended. But Twain's work was always characterized by attempts to escape from history as well as bitter acknowledgements of it, sometimes even within the same work, as in the case of *Huckleberry Finn.* It combines good-humored satire on the sentimental poetry of the nineteenth century, in the case of "Ode to Stephen Dowling Bots," with some of the most bitter confrontations with history ever written, as in the case of the killing of Boggs, a town drunk who is shot down in the streets as a mob watches.

Twain published *Innocents Abroad* four years later; it was based on his trip to the Holy Land and was well received. Twain was now only thirty-four and famous. He married the daughter of a wealthy businessman the next year, Olivia Langdon. Her efforts to "reform" him were only partly successful, and many observers of Twain's life and works have noted the tension between candor and being respectable, a tension dramatized most clearly in the contrast between Tom Sawyer and Huck Finn. His two most famous books, *The Adventures of Tom Sawyer* and *Adventures of Huckleberry Finn*, were published in 1876 and 1884, respectively. The former is much less powerful and candid in its engagement with history than the latter, but modern-day readers have noted Twain's notorious hatred of Native Americans in his depiction of Injun Joe. *Huckleberry Finn,* on the other hand, remains one of the most challenging and controversial treatments of American history even written: its use of the most offensive racial epithet in the United States continues to spark debate over whether the book should be banned from school curricula and from libraries. Its satire on small town life in the Mississippi Valley in the 1830s and 1840s is brutal. Twain was appalled at what American history contained but also fascinated by it, particularly the contrast in American history between the country's official values and the reality. Huck refers to the hypocrisy at the heart of American history as "soul buttering and hogwash," an apt phrase that suggests the disgust and bitterness underlying Twain's humor.

In the 1880s Twain also published *The Prince and the Pauper* (1881), *Life on the Mississippi (*1883), and *A Connecticut Yankee in King Arthur's Court* (1889), all popular but nowhere near *Huckleberry Finn* in historical resonance. The year 1894 saw the publication of *Pudd'nhead Wilson,* which did treat the issue of miscegenation. His last years were marked by great fame and numerous honors, such as receiving honorary degrees from Oxford and Yale, but underneath the success there was overwhelming grief and perhaps increasing pessimism. Only one of his four children outlived him, and one of them died in infancy. His wife died in 1904, and although he was often away traveling during their marriage, even when she was sick, he does seem to have loved her deeply and truly. Twain was a very complicated man, with mixed feelings about American history and many other things, including himself.

HISTORICAL EXPLORATIONS

Abolition

In the South in the 1830s and 1840s, the words "abolition" and "abolitionist" were equivalent to obscenities. Early in *Huckleberry Finn,* Huck tells Jim he will not reveal Jim is a fugitive slave, even though he will be called "a low-down abolitionist." As a product of the South in many ways, at this time, Huck unthinkingly assumes that what he agrees to conceal about Jim will mark him as lacking any social stature at all, and this is the case of a person who is already at the bottom of the social ladder, except for the black people underneath him. Twain himself grew up in a slaveowning family in a society that did not challenge slavery, and he therefore saw nothing wrong with it when he was young. But as he matured he began to rethink, possibly as a result of his father-in-law's opposition to slavery and also possibly as a result of meeting Frederick Douglass. In any case, he did come to support the abolition of slavery.

Abolition was not monolithic. Some abolitionists wanted slavery abolished immediately, others over a period of time with financial reparations to former masters (Twain thought if there were to be reparations, they should be paid to former slaves for their uncompensated labor); some abolitionists wanted slavery destroyed by violence if necessary, others by moral persuasion. There were abolitionists in the South until Nat Turner's Rebellion in 1831, which effectively ended white opposition to slavery in the South. Some abolitionist groups were inspired by Evangelical Protestantism, others by Quakerism. And of course there were black abolitionists like Douglass, who thought at first that argument and moral persuasion might work but eventually decided war was the only way slavery could be made illegal.

Examples of abolitionists, and from some perspectives *the* abolitionist, include President Abraham Lincoln. But it should be kept in mind that he had two goals: putting down a rebellion that broke the Union in two and destroying the basis of Southern society, slavery. One result was 186,000 African American troops fighting to end slavery and preserve the Union. Another major figure in the cause of abolition was William Lloyd Garrison, whose "To the Public" is included in this chapter. Garrison wanted the North to secede from the Union, an idea that if adopted might well have resulted in a longer history for American slavery. Many nineteenth-century observers believed that Garrison was more interested

These African American soldiers fighting for the Union in the Civil War could never have been imagined by the Phelpses, who view Jim as a harmless "darky." (Library of Congress)

in pontificating about how evil slavery was than he was in explaining practical ways to end it. His fellow abolitionist, Wendell Phillips, also supported the North's secession from the Union but later came to support Lincoln and the war; he was particularly recognized for his oratorical skills.

Outstanding examples of black abolitionists would have to include Frederick Douglass, David Walker, Harriet Tubman, and Sojourner Truth. After Douglass escaped from Maryland, he went north and dedicated his life to abolishing slavery. As a magnificent public speaker and a powerful writer, he came to see that war was the only alternative if slavery was to be overturned; he urged Lincoln to use black troops in the cause, which Lincoln eventually agreed to. David Walker, on the other hand, in 1829 urged the use of any means necessary to end slavery; he saw early on that to abolish slavery, violence would be required. Two of the most famous black women abolitionists, Sojourner Truth and Harriet Tubman, relied on the spoken word and moral persuasion to end slavery. In her most famous speech, "Arn't a Woman?," Truth added gender equality to support for the abolition of slavery. Harriet Tubman figured prominently in the Underground Railroad, helping hundreds of slaves escape from slavery; she later became active in the cause of women's rights.

In this image of Harriet Tubman and slaves she freed via the Underground Railroad, we are reminded of Huck and Jim as they flee Pap and slavery, on a raft that can be taken as a kind of aboveground "railroad." (Bettmann/Corbis)

Introduction to William Lloyd Garrison, "To the Public" (1831)

Today's best-known abolitionist, William Lloyd Garrison, was not the most effective supporter of the abolition of slavery, but he was the most outspoken, thus his popular reputation as the Massachusetts Madman. Nevertheless, even though his life was threatened, and he was frequently reviled, he never wavered from the cause. His most famous words—"I will not equivocate— I will not excuse—I will not retreat a single inch—AND I WILL BE HEARD"—are from an editorial in *The Liberator,* the abolitionist newspaper he founded. A man of great integrity, he kept the fire burning in the cause of abolition for over thirty years, a remarkable commitment. He liked to remind his New England readers especially that they were inheritors of a glorious tradition of liberty and should remain faithful to it by supporting the end of bondage. He also urged the right of slaves to vote immediately, an idea not all abolitionists upheld, and he apologized for once supporting gradual abolition. As he says in his editorial in *The Liberator,* "tell the mother to gradually extricate her babe from the fire into which it has fallen."

From William Lloyd Garrison, "To the Public" (1831)

In the month of August, I issued proposals for publishing "THE LIBERATOR" in Washington City; but the enterprise, though hailed in different sections of the country, was palsied by public indifference. Since that time, the removal of the Genius of Universal Emancipation [Benjamin Lundy's anti-slavery newspaper] to the Seat of Government has rendered less imperious the establishment of a similar periodical in that quarter.

During my recent tour for the purpose of exciting the minds of the people by a series of discourses on the subject of slavery, every place that I visited gave fresh evidence of the fact, that a greater revolution in public sentiment was to be effected in the free states—and particularly in New-England—than at the south. I found contempt more bitter, opposition more active, detraction more relentless, prejudice more stubborn, and apathy more frozen, than among slave owners themselves. Of course, there were individual exceptions to the contrary. This state of things afflicted, but did not dishearten me. I determined, at every hazard, to lift up the standard of emancipation in the eyes of the nation, within sight of Bunker Hill and in the birth place of liberty.

That standard is now unfurled; and long may it float, unhurt by the spoliations of time or the missiles of a desperate foe—yea, till every chain be broken, and every bondman set free! Let southern oppressors tremble—let their secret abettors tremble—let their northern apologists tremble—let all the enemies of the persecuted blacks tremble.

I deem the publication of my original Prospectus unnecessary, as it has obtained a wide circulation. The principles therein inculcated will be steadily pursued in this paper, excepting that I shall not array myself as the political partisan of any man. In defending the great cause of human rights, I wish to derive the assistance of all religions and of all parties.

Assenting to the "self-evident truth" maintained in the American Declaration of Independence, "that all men are created equal, and endowed by their Creator with certain inalienable rights—among which are life, liberty and the pursuit of happiness," I shall strenuously contend for the immediate enfranchisement of our slave population. In Park-street Church, on the Fourth of July, 1829, in an address on slavery, I unreflectingly assented to the popular but pernicious doctrine of gradual abolition. I seize this opportunity to make a full and unequivocal recantation, and thus publicly to ask pardon of my God, of my country, and of my brethren the poor slaves, for having uttered a sentiment so full of timidity, injustice and absurdity. A similar recantation, from my pen, was published in the Genius of Universal Emancipation at Baltimore, in September, 1829. My conscience in now satisfied.

I am aware, that many object to the severity of my language; but is there not cause for severity? I will be as harsh as truth, and as uncompromising as justice. On this subject, I do not wish to think, or speak, or write, with moderation. No! no! Tell a man whose house is on fire, to give a moderate alarm; tell him to moderately rescue his wife from the hand of the ravisher; tell the mother to gradually extricate her babe from the fire into which it has fallen;—but urge me not to use moderation in a cause like the present. I am in earnest—I will not equivocate—I will not excuse—I will not retreat a single inch—AND I WILL BE HEARD. The apathy of the people is enough to make every statue leap from its pedestal, and to hasten the resurrection of the dead.

It is pretended, that I am retarding the cause of emancipation by the coarseness of my invective, and the precipitancy of my measures. The charge is not true. On this question my influence,—humble as it is,—is felt at this moment to a considerable extent, and shall be felt in coming years—not perniciously, but beneficially—not as a curse, but as a blessing; and posterity will bear testimony that I was right. I desire to thank God, that he enables me to disregard [Proverbs 29:25] "the fear of man which bringeth a snare," and to speak his truth in its simplicity and power.

Source: William Lloyd Garrison, 1805–1879, Volume 1, New York: The Century Company, 1885, pp. 224–226.

Introduction to Henry Highland Garnet, "An Address to the Slaves of the United States" (1843)

Henry Highland Garnet was an extremely outspoken black Presbyterian minister, who gave this speech to the National Negro Convention in 1843 in Buffalo, New York. Years before Frederick Douglass finally realized blood would have to be shed before slavery could be ended, Garnet told his listeners that they should do whatever circumstances required to destroy the enslavement of black people. He especially emphasizes that black men should not tolerate the sexual abuse of black women, any more than white men would have, had whites been enslaved by blacks. And he shrewdly repeats Patrick Henry's famous cry, "Give me liberty or give me death," to suggest black men, in overthrowing slavery, will be repeating what white patriots had done in the American Revolution: in other words, black men would be following a basic American tradition, the resistance of tyranny. He points out, too, that violent black resistance to slavery will be the further development of a black American history full of earlier black heroes, including Denmark Veasey and Nat Turner. His recommendation failed to pass at the convention by only one vote. In later life he pushed for African Americans returning to Africa and died there himself, when he was the country's minister to Liberia. His speech remains a landmark in the history of abolitionism because of its eloquence, logic, and stirring tone.

Neither the Phelpses nor their pastor could have imagined a minister like Henry Garnet, who urged black men to take up arms to end slavery. (Library of Congress)

From Henry Highland Garnet, "An Address to the Slaves of the United States" (1843)

Take courage! Be filled with hope and comfort! Your redemption draws nigh, for the Lord is mightily at work in your behalf. Is it not frequently the darkest before day-break? The word has gone forth that you shall be delivered from your chains, and it has not been spoken in vain.

Although you have many enemies, yet you have also many friends—warm, faithful, sympathizing, devoted friends—who will never abandon your cause; who are pledged to do all in their power to break your chains; who are laboring to effect your emancipation without delay, in a peaceable manner, without the shedding of blood; who regard you as brethren and countrymen, and fear not the frowns or threats of your masters. They call themselves abolitionists. They have already suffered much, in various parts of the country, for rebuking those who keep you in slavery—for demanding your immediate liberation—for revealing to the people the horrors of your situation—for boldly opposing a corrupt public sentiment, by which you are kept in the great southern prison-house of bondage. Some of them have been beaten with stripes; others have been stripped, and covered with tar and feathers; others have had their property taken from them, and burnt in the streets; others have had large rewards offered by your masters for their seizure; others have been cast into jails and penitentiaries; others have been mobbed and lynched with great violence; others have lost their reputation, and been ruined in their business; others have lost their lives. All these, and many other outrages of an equally grievous kind, they have suffered for your sakes, and because they are your friends. They cannot go to the South, to see and converse with you, face to face; for, so ferocious and bloody-minded are your taskmasters, they would be put to an ignominious death as soon as discovered. Besides, it is not yet necessary that they should incur this peril; for it is solely by the aid of the people of the North, that you are held in bondage, and, therefore, they find enough to do at home, to make the people here your friends, and to break up all connexion with the slave system. They have proved themselves to be truly courageous, insensible to danger, superior to adversity, strong in principle, invincible in argument, animated by the spirit of impartial benevolence, unwearied in devising ways and means for your deliverance, the best friends of the whole country, the noblest champions of the human race. Ten years ago, they were so few and feeble as only to excite universal contempt; now they number in their ranks, hundreds of thousands of the people.—Then, they had scarcely a single anti-slavery society in operation; now they have thousands. Then, they had only one or two presses to plead your cause; now they have multitudes. They are scattering all over the land their newspapers, books, pamphlets, tracts, and other publications, to hold up to infamy the conduct of your oppressors, and to awaken sympathy in your behalf. They are continually holding anti-slavery meetings in all parts of the free States, to tell the people the story of your wrongs. Wonderful has been the change effected in public feeling, under God, through their instrumentality. Do not fear that they will grow weary in your service. They are confident of success, in the end. They know that the Lord Almighty is with them—that truth, justice, right, are with them—that you are with them. They know, too, that your masters are cowardly and weak, through conscious wrong doing, and already begin to falter in their course. Lift up your heads, 0 ye despairing slaves! Yet a little while, and your chains shall snap asunder, and you shall be tortured and plundered no more! Then, fathers and mothers, your children shall be yours, to bring them up in the nurture and admonition of the Lord. Then, husbands and wives, now torn from each other's arms, you shall be reunited in the flesh, and man shall no longer dare to put asunder those whom God has joined together. Then, brothers and sisters, you shall be sold to the remorseless slave speculator no more, but dwell together in unity. "God hasten that joyful day!" is now the daily prayer of millions.

The weapons with which the abolitionists seek to effect your deliverance are not bowie knives, pistols, swords, guns, or any other deadly implements. They consist of appeals, warnings, rebukes, arguments and facts, addressed to the understandings, consciences and hearts of the people. Many of your friends believe that not even those who are oppressed, whether their skins are white or black, can shed the blood of their oppressors in accordance with the will of God; while many others believe that it is right for the oppressed to rise and take their liberty by violence, if they can secure it in no other manner; but they, in common with all your friends, believe that every attempt at insurrection would be attended with disaster and defeat, on your part, because you are not strong enough to contend with the military power of the nation; consequently, their advice to you is, to be patient, long-suffering, and sub-missive, yet awhile longer—trusting that, by the blessing of the Most High on their labors, you will yet be emancipated without shedding a drop of your masters' blood, or losing a drop of your own.

The abolitionists of the North are the only true and unyielding friends on whom you can rely. They will never deceive nor betray you. They have made your cause their own, and they mean to be true to themselves and to you, whatever may be the consequence. They are continually increasing in number, in influence, in enterprise and determination; and, judging from the success which has already attended their measures, they anticipate that, in a comparatively short period, the entire North will receive you with open arms, and give you shelter and protection, as fast as you escape from the South. We, who now address you, are united with them in spirit and design. We glory in the name of abolitionists, for it signifies friendship for all who are pining in servitude. We advise you to seize every opportunity to escape from your masters, and, fixing your eyes on the North Star, travel on until you reach a land of liberty. You are not the property of your masters. God never made one human being to be owned by another. Your right to be free, at any moment, is undeniable; and it is your duty, whenever you can, peaceably to escape from the plantations on which you are confined, and assert your manhood.

Source: Garnet, Henry Highland. "An Address to the Slaves of the United States." *The Liberator,* June 2, 1843, 89.

Discussion Questions

1. How much should it matter in estimating the value of an historical figure that he many have been a talker more than a practical agent of change?
2. How would you characterize Garrison's handling of the English language? Are you surprised that he could mesmerize audiences?
3. Is it possible that Garrison was in love with his own way with words more than anything else? Can such verbal gifts be put to evil uses? Name recent or contemporary examples.
4. Do you admire Henry Highland Garnet more or less than Garrison? Why?

5. Are his suggestions for changing the world more down to earth and practical than Garrison's?

6. Do you think Garnet was wise to accept support for the abolition of slavery from "all religious" and "all parties"? Why or why not?

7. Why do you think Garnet and so many other abolitionists, including Douglass and Stowe, reject the idea of gradual abolition?

8. What is so bold in Garnet referring to Nat Turner as "patriotic"?

9. Why does Garnet keep reminding the slaves that there are four million of them?

10. Why does he tell the slaves that it is sinful of them to remain slaves?

11. If Twain's Jim had been in Garnet's audience, do you think he would have heeded his call to violent resistance? Why or why not?

12. Why does Garnet tell his audience that if the situation had been reversed and blacks had owned whites, the latter would have violently resisted the former?

13. Why does he challenge enslaved men to think about their manhood when they learn of white sexual exploitation of black women?

Suggested Readings

Budd, Louis J. 1983. *Our Mark Twain: The Making of His Public Personality.* Philadelphia: University of Pennsylvania Press.

Coulombe, Joseph L. 2003. *Mark Twain and the American West.* Columbia: University of Missouri Press.

Cummings, Sherwood. 1989. *Mark Twain and Science: Adventures of a Mind.* Baton Rouge: Louisiana State University Press.

De Voto, Bernard. 1932. *Mark Twain's America.* Lincoln: University of Nebraska Press.

Doyno, Victor. 1991. *Writing "Huck Finn": Mark Twain's Creative Process.* Philadelphia: University of Pennsylvania Press.

Emerson, Everett. 1984. *The Authentic Mark Twain: A Literary Biography of Samuel L. Clemens.* Philadelphia: University of Pennsylvania Press.

Ferguson, De Lancey. 1943. *Mark Twain: Man and Legend.* Court Lodge, England: Russell and Russell.

Fishkin, Shelley Fisher. 1996. *Lighting Out for the Territory: Reflections on Mark Twain and American Culture.* Oxford: Oxford University Press.

Gillman, Susan. 1991. *Dark Twins: Imposture and Identity in Mark Twain's America.* Chicago: University of Chicago Press.

Johnson, James L. 1982. *Mark Twain and the Limits of Power: Emerson's God in Ruins.* Knoxville: University of Tennessee Press.

Kaplan, Justin. 1966. *Mr. Clemens and Mark Twain, a Biography.* New York: Simon & Schuster.

Kaplan, Mark. 2005. *The Singular Mark Twain: A Biography.* Harpswell, ME: Anchor Publishing.

Mandia, Patricia M. 1991. *Comedic Pathos: Black Humor in Twain's Fiction.* Jefferson, NC: McFarland.

Marotti, Maria Ornella. 1990. *The Duplicating Imagination: Twain and the Twain Papers.* University Park: Pennsylvania State University Press.

Michelson, Bruce. 1995. *Mark Twain on the Loose: A Comic Writer and the American Self.* Amherst: University of Massachusetts Press.

Paine, Albert Bigelow. 1912. *Mark Twain, a Biography.* Ann Arbor: University of Michigan Library.

Powers, Ron. 2001. *Dangerous Water: A Biography of the Boy Who Became Mark Twain.* Cambridge, MA: Da Capo Press.

Powers, Ron. 2005. *Mark Twain: A Life.* New York: Free Press.

Skandera-Trombley, Laura. 1994. *Mark Twain in the Company of Women.* Philadelphia: University of Pennsylvania Press.

Smith, Henry Nash. 1962. *Mark Twain: The Development of a Writer.* Cambridge, MA: Belknap Press.

Steinbrink, Jeffrey. 1991. *Getting to Be Mark Twain.* Berkeley: University of California Press.

Stoneley, Peter. 1992. *Mark Twain and the Feminine Aesthetic.* Cambridge: Cambridge University Press.

Wieck, Carl F. 2000. *Refiguring Huckleberry Finn.* Athens: University of Georgia Press.

HISTORICAL EXPLORATIONS

Slavery and Christianity

As Douglass bitterly indicates at the end of *Narrative of the Life of Frederick Douglass* (1845), institutionalized Christianity in the South had little trouble accommodating another institution, slavery. Like Douglass, Twain in *Huckleberry Finn* repeatedly indicates his disgust for an institution that preaches about brotherly love and the Golden Rule but acts otherwise. He thought that if Christ were on earth, he would not be a Christian. On the other hand, Christianity gave African American slaves the one institution they had a measure of control over, the black church, which produced not only a center for many black communities but also a training ground for black leaders. Christianity also gave the slaves a language and theology that could be racialized to suit their particular spiritual and secular needs. Thus, a term that would signify an Egyptian leader to white ears, "pharaoh", could mean "the white man" to black ones. Or, a theological concept like the Second Coming could mean the return of Christ to earth in a white church but the end of slavery in a black one.

Nevertheless, from Twain's perspective, the juxtaposition of slavery and Christianity in the United States resulted in appalling hypocrisy. How could so many Americans claim to belief in Christianity and practice slavery? Easily, was his answer, because Christianity, in Twain's view, had no chance of victory when it fought greed and self-interest on the battlefield of history. Colonel Grangerford and Silas Phelps go to church every Sunday morning but practice slavery all the time. The two Christian defenders of slavery in this section use specious arguments, sloppy logic, appeals to authority, anything but legitimate arguments to justify owning human beings. As the latter do not exist, what other options did they have?

Introduction to James Henley Thornwell, "A Southern Christian View of Slavery" (1861)

James Henley Thornwell (1812–1862) was a Presbyterian minister who became president of what is now the University of South Carolina. He supported the break between the Presbyterian Church in the South and the one in the North because the Southern branch supported slavery, whereas the Northern branch did not. Very learned and the author of numerous works on theology, Thornwell argued that because slavery was legal in the South, it did not come into the sphere of the Presbyterian Church, which dealt with spiritual matters. This facile distinction resulted in Thornwell's great popularity with slaveholders, who did not want to acknowledge the contradiction between their professed Christian beliefs and their behavior; Thornwell also thought masters were obligated to take proper care of their slaves, which some failed to do but did not necessarily admit. Like the Phelpses in *Huckleberry Finn,* Thornwell was very comfortable with slavery.

From James Henley Thornwell, "A Southern Christian View of Slavery" (1861)

THE ANTAGONISM of Northern and Southern sentiment on the subject of slavery lies at the root of all the difficulties which have resulted in the dismemberment of the federal Union, and involved us in the horrors of an unnatural war.

The Presbyterian Church in the United States has been enabled by the Divine Grace to pursue, for the most part, an eminently conservative, because a thoroughly scriptural, policy in relation to this delicate question. It has planted itself upon the word of God and utterly refused to make slaveholding a sin or nonslave holding a term of communion. But though both sections are agreed as to this general principle, it is not to be disguised that the North exercises a deep and settled antipathy to slavery itself, while the South is equally zealous in its defense. Recent events can have no other effect than to confirm the antipathy on the one hand and strengthen the attachment on the other.

The Northern section of the church stands in the awkward predicament of maintaining, in one breath, that slavery is an evil which ought to be abolished and of asserting, in the next, that it is not a sin to be visited by exclusion from communion of the saints. The consequence is that it plays partly into the hands of Abolitionists and partly into the hands of slaveholders and weakens its influence with both. It occupies the position of a prevaricating witness whom neither party will trust. It would be better, therefore, for the moral power of the Northern section of the church to get entirely quit of the subject.

At the same time, it is intuitively obvious that the Southern section of the church, while even partially under the control of those who are hostile to slavery, can never have free and unimpeded access to the slave population. Its ministers and elders will always be liable to some degree of suspicion. In the present circumstances, Northern alliance would be absolutely fatal. It would utterly preclude the church from a wide and commanding field of usefulness.

This is too dear a price to be paid for a nominal union. We cannot afford to give up these millions of souls and consign them, so far as our efforts are concerned, to hopeless perdition for the sake of preserving an outward unity which, after all, is an empty shadow. If we would gird ourselves heartily and in earnest for the work which God has set before us, we must have the control of our ecclesiastical affairs and declare ourselves separate and independent.

And here we may venture to lay before the Christian world our views as a church upon the subject of slavery. We beg a candid hearing.

In the first place, we would have it distinctly understood that, in our ecclesiastical capacity, we are neither friends nor the foes of slavery, that is to say, we have no commission either to propagate or abolish it. The policy of its existence or nonexistence is a question which exclusively belongs to the state. We have no right, as a church, to enjoin it as a duty or to condemn it as a sin. Our business is with the duties which spring from the relation; the duties of the masters, on the one hand, and of the slaves, on the other. These duties we are to proclaim and to enforce with spiritual sanctions. The social, civil, political problems connected with this great subject transcend our sphere, as God had not entrusted His church with the organization of society, the construction of governments, nor the allotment of individuals to their various stations. The church has as much right to preach to the monarchies of Europe and the despotism of Asia the doctrines of republican equality as to preach to the governments of the South the extirpation of slavery. This position is impregnable unless it can be shown that slavery is a sin. Upon every other hypothesis, it is so clearly a question for the state that the proposition would never for a moment have been doubted had there not been a foregone conclusion in relation to its moral character. Is slavery, then, a sin?

In answering this question, as a church, let it be distinctly borne in mind that the only rule of judgment is the written word of God. The church knows nothing of the intuitions of reason or the deductions of philosophy, except those reproduced in the Sacred Canon. She has a positive constitution in the Holy Scriptures and has no right to utter a single syllable upon any subject except as the Lord puts words in her mouth. She is founded, in other words, upon express revelation.

Her creed is an authoritative testimony of God and not a speculation, and what she proclaims, she must proclaim with the infallible certitude of faith and not with the hesitating assent of an opinion. The question, then, is brought within a narrow compass: Do the Scriptures directly or indirectly condemn slavery as a sin? If they do not, the dispute is ended, for the church, without forfeiting her character, dares not go beyond them.

Now, we venture to assert that if men had drawn their conclusions upon this subject only from the Bible, it would no more have entered into any human head to denounce slavery as a sin than to denounce monarchy, aristocracy, or poverty. The truth is, men have listened to what they falsely considered as primitive intuitions, or as necessary deductions from primitive cognitions, and then have gone to the Bible to confirm their crotchets of their vain philosophy. They have gone there determined to find a particular result, and the consequence is that they leave with having made, instead of having interpreted, Scripture. Slavery is no new thing. It has not only existed for ages in the world but it has existed, under every dispensation of the covenant of grace, in the Church of God.

Indeed, the first organization of the church as a visible society, separate and distinct from the unbelieving world, was inaugurated in the family of a slaveholder. Among the very first persons to whom the seal of circumcision was affixed were the slaves of the father of the faithful, some born in his house and others bought with his money. Slavery again reappears under the Law. God sanctions it in the first table of the Decalogue, and Moses treats it as an institution to be regulated, not abolished; legitimated and not condemned. We come down to the age of the New Testament, and we find it again in the churches founded by the apostles under the plenary inspiration of the Holy Ghost. These facts are utterly amazing, if slavery is the enormous sin which its enemies represent it to be. It will not do to say that the Scriptures have treated it only in a general, incidental way, without any clear implication as to its moral character. Moses surely made it the subject of express and positive legislation, and the apostles are equally explicit in inculcating the duties which spring from both sides of the relation. They treat slaves as bound to obey and inculcate obedience as an office of religion, a thing wholly self-contradictory if the authority exercised over them were unlawful and iniquitous.

But what puts this subject in a still clearer light is the manner in which it is sought to extort from the Scriptures a contrary testimony. The notion of direct and explicit condemnation is given up. The attempt is to show that the genius and spirit of Christianity are so opposed to it that its great cardinal principles of virtue are utterly against it. Much stress is laid upon the Golden Rule and upon the general denunciations of tyranny and oppression. To all this we reply that no principle is clearer than that a case positively excepted cannot be included under a general rule.

Let us concede, for a moment, that the law of love, and the condemnation of tyranny and oppression seem logically to involve, as a result, the condemnation of slavery; yet, if slavery is afterwards expressly mentioned and treated as a lawful relation, it obviously follows, unless Scripture is to be interpreted as inconsistent with itself, that slavery is, by necessary implication, excepted. The Jewish law forbad, as a general rule, the marriage of a man with his brother's wife. The same law expressly enjoined the same marriage in a given case. The given case was, therefore, an exception, and not be treated as a violation of the general rule. The law of love has always been the law of God. It was enunciated by Moses almost as clearly as it was enunciated by Jesus Christ. Yet, notwithstanding this law, Moses and the apostles alike sanctioned the relation of slavery.

The conclusion is inevitable, either that the law is not opposed to it or that slavery is an excepted case. To say that the prohibition of tyranny and oppression include slavery is to beg the whole question. Tyranny and oppression involve either the unjust usurpation or the unlawful exercise of power. It is the unlawfulness, either in its principle or measure, which constitutes the core of the sin. Slavery must, therefore, be proved to be unlawful before it can be referred to any such category. The master may, indeed, abuse his power, but he oppresses, not simply as a master but as a wicked master.

But apart from all this, the law of love is simply the inculcation of universal equity. It implies nothing as to the existence of various ranks and graduations in society. The interpretation which makes it repudiate slavery would make it equally repudiate all social, civil, and political inequalities. Its meaning is not that we should conform ourselves to the arbitrary expectations of others but that we should render unto them precisely the same measure which, if we were in their circumstance, it would be reasonable and just in us to demand at their hands. It condemns slavery, therefore, only upon the supposition that slavery is a sinful relation that is, he who extracts the prohibition of slavery from the Golden-Rule begs the very point in dispute.

We cannot prosecute the argument in detail, but we have said enough, we think, to vindicate the position of the Southern church. We have assumed no new attitude. We stand exactly where the Church of God has always stood from Abraham to Moses, from Moses to Christ, from Christ to the reformers, and from the reformers to ourselves. We stand upon the foundation of the prophets and apostles. Jesus Christ himself being the chief cornerstone. Shall we be excluded from the fellowship of our brethren in other lands because we dare not depart from the charter of our faith? Shall we be branded with the stigma of reproach because we cannot consent to corrupt the word of God to suit the intentions of an infidel philosophy? Shall our names be cast out as evil and the finger of scorn pointed at us because we utterly refuse to break our communion with Abraham, Isaac and Jacob, with Moses, David and Isaiah, with apostles, prophets, and martyrs, with all who have gone to glory from slaveholding countries and from a slaveholding church, without ever having dreamed that they were living in mortal sin by conniving at slavery in the midst of them? If so, we shall take consolation in the cheering consciousness that the Master has accepted us.

We may be denounced, despised, and cast out of the synagogues of our brethren. But while they are wrangling about the distinctions of men according to the flesh, we shall go forward in our divine work and confidently anticipate that, in the great day, as the consequence of our humble labors, we shall meet millions of glorified spirits who have come up from the bondage of earth to a nobler freedom than human philosophy ever dreamed of. Others, if they please, may spend their time in declaiming on the tyranny of earthly masters; it will be our aim to resist the real tyrants which oppress the soul-sin and Satan. These are the foes against whom we shall find it employment enough to wage a successful war. And to this holy war is the purpose of our church to devote itself with redoubled energy. We feel that the souls of our slaves are a solemn trust, and we shall strive to present them faultless and complete before the presence of God.

Indeed, as we contemplate their condition in the Southern states, and contrast it with that of their fathers before them and that of their brethren in the present day in their native land, we cannot but accept it as a gracious providence that they have been brought in such numbers to our shores and redeemed from the bondage of barbarism and sin. Slavery to them has certainly been overruled for the greatest good. It has been a link in the wondrous chain of providence, through which many sons and daughters have been made heirs of the heavenly inheritance. The providential result is, of course, no justification if the thing is intrinsically wrong; but it is certainly a matter of devout thanksgiving, and no obscure intimation of the will and purpose of God and of the consequent duty of the church. We cannot forbear to say, however, that the general operation of the system is kindly and benevolent; it is a real and effective discipline, and, without it, we are profoundly persuaded that the African race in the midst of us can never be elevated in the scale of being. As long as that race, in its comparative degradation, coexists, side by side with the white, bondage is its normal condition.

As to the endless declamation about human rights, we have only to say that human rights are not a fixed but fluctuating quantity. Their sum is not the same in any two nations on the globe. The rights of Englishmen are one thing, the rights of Frenchmen, another. There is a minimum without which a man cannot be responsible; there is a maximum which expresses the highest degree of civilization and of Christian culture. The education of the species consists in its ascent along this line. As you go up, the number of rights increases, but the number of individuals who possess them diminishes. As you come down the line, rights are diminished, but the individuals are multiplied. It is just the opposite of the predicamental scale of the logicians. There, comprehension diminishes as you ascend and extension increases, and comprehension increases as you descend and extension diminishes.

Now, when it is said that slavery is inconsistent with human rights, we crave to understand what point in this line is the slave conceived to occupy. There are, no doubt, many rights which belong to other men-to Englishmen, to Frenchmen, to his masters, for example-which are denied to him. But is he fit to possess them? Has God qualified him to meet the responsibilities which their possession necessarily implies? His place in the scale is determined by his competency to fulfill its duties. There are other rights which he certainly possesses, without which he could neither be human nor accountable. Before slavery can be charged with doing him injustice, it must be shown that the minimum which falls to his lot at the bottom of the line is out of proportion to his capacity and culture, a thing which can never be done by abstract speculation.

The truth is, the education of the human race for liberty and virtue is a vast providential scheme, and God assigns to every man, by a wise and holy degree, the precise place he is to occupy in the great moral school of humanity. The scholars are distributed into classes according to their competency and progress. For God is in history.

To avoid suspicion of a conscious weakness of our cause, when contemplated from the side of pure speculation, we may advert for a moment to those pretended intuitions which stamp the reprobation of humanity upon this ancient and hoary institution. We admit that there are primitive principles in morals which lie at the root of human consciousness. But the question is, how are we to distinguish them? The subjective feeling of certainty is no adequate criterion, as that is equally felt in reference to crotches and hereditary prejudices. The very point is to know when this certainty indicates a primitive cognition and when it does not. There must, therefore, be some eternal test, and whatever cannot abide that test has no authority as a primary truth. That test is an inward necessity of thought, which in all minds at the proper stage of maturity is absolutely universal.

Whatever is universal is natural. We are willing that slavery should be tried by this standard. We are willing to abide by the testimony of the race, and if man, as man, has everywhere condemned it, if all human laws have prohibited it as crime if it stands in the same category with malice, murder, and theft, then we are willing, in the name of humanity, to renounce it, and to renounce it forever. But what if the overwhelming majority of mankind have approved it? What if philosophers and statesmen have justified it, and the laws of all nations acknowledged it; what then becomes of these luminous institutions? They are an ignis fatuus, mistaken for a star.

We have now, brethren, in a brief compass, for the nature of this address admits only of an outline, opened to you our whole hearts upon this delicate and vexed subject. We have concealed nothing. We have sought to conciliate no sympathy by appeals to your charity. We have tried our cause by the word of God; and though protesting against its authority to judge in a question concerning the duty of the church, we have not refused to appear at the tribunal of reason.

Are we not right, in view of all the preceding considerations, in remitting the social, civil, and political problems connected with slavery to the state? It is not a subject, save in the moral duties which spring from it, which lies beyond the province of the church? Have we any right to make it an element in judging of Christian character? Are we not treading in the footsteps of the flock? Are we not acting as Christ and His apostles have acted before us? Is it not enough for us to pray and labor, in our lot, that all men may be saved without meddling as a church with the technical distinction of their civil life?

We leave the matter with you. We offer you the right hand of fellowship. It is for you to accept it or reject it. We have done our duty. We can do no more. Truth is more precious than union, and if you cast us out as sinners, the breach of charity is not with us as long as we walk according to the light of the written word.

Source: Thornwell, James Henley. "Exposition of the Views of Slavery." *Minutes of the General Assembly of the Presbyterian Church in the Confederate States of America,* Volume 1, Augusta, GA, 1861, Appendix, pp. 55–59.

Introduction to Richard Furman, "Exposition of the Views of the Baptists Relative to the Coloured [*sic*] Population of the United States" (1822)

Although Richard Furman (1755–1825) is remembered today mainly because Furman University is named for him, during his adulthood he was recognized as an important leader in the Baptist Church in South Carolina and as the author of "Exposition of the Views of the Baptists . . .," in which he tried to justify slavery, much as the Phelpses would have if offered the opportunity. Opposed to slavery when he was young, Furman as an adult has no doubts that it has divine sanction in his exposition. Besides using specious arguments regarding slaves from the Bible, he also uses false analogies in his defense of slavery, arguing for instance that because a father expects his son's obedience, the son should not expect his father to be obedient to him. The Phelpses would also have endorsed Furman's con-descending attitude toward black people and his contention that whites are bound to meet the material needs of their racial "inferiors." He even goes so far as to say that "in present circumstances" the emancipation of the slaves would not result in their happiness. The Phelpses would certainly endorse this position in regard to Jim and their own slaves. Their willing-ness to pray with Jim would have received Furman's blessing.

From Richard Furman, "Exposition of the Views of the Baptists Relative to the Coloured [*sic*] Population of the United States" (1822)

DEAR SIR,

SEVERAL of your fellow-citizens who have perused the Rev. Dr. FURMAN'S communication, submitting the propriety of your recommending a Day of Thanksgiving and Humiliation, think the dissemination of it might be beneficial, and ask your sanction to have it published.

With regard, your's,
B. ELLIOTT.

His Excellency Gov. WILSON.
MY DEAR SIR,

THE request made by you, in behalf of yourself and several of your fellow-citizens, is most readily granted. There can be no doubt that such doctrines, from such a source, will produce the best of consequences in our mixed population, and tend to make our servants not only more contented with their lot, but more use-ful to their owners. The great piety and learning of Doctor FUR-MAN, his long established character with the religious of every denomination throughout our State, will at once command the re-spectful attention of every reader.

   Receive the assurances of my respect and regard.

JOHN L. WILSON.
BENJAMIN ELLIOT, Esq.
Charleston

Charleston, 24th December, 1822.

SIR,

WHEN I had, lately, the honour of delivering to your Excellency an Address, from the Baptist Convention in this State, requesting that a Day of Public Humiliation and Thanksgiving might be appointed by you, as our Chief Magistrate, to be observed by the Citizens of the State at large, in reference to two important recent events, in which the interposition of Divine Providence has been conspicuous, and in which the interests and feelings of our Citizens have been greatly concerned,—viz: The protection afforded them from the horrors of an intended Insurrection; and the affliction they have suffered from the ravages of a dreadful Hurricane— I took the liberty to suggest, that I had a further communication to make on behalf of the Convention, in which their sentiments would be disclosed respecting the policy of the measure proposed; and on the lawfulness of holding slaves—the subject being considered in a moral and religious point of view.

You were pleased, sir, to signify, that it would be agreeable to you to receive such a communication. And as it is incumbent on me, in faithfulness to the trust reposed in me, to make it, I now take the liberty of laying it before you.

The Political propriety of bringing the intended Insurrection into view by publicly acknowledging its prevention to be an instance of the Divine Goodness, manifested by a providential, gracious interposition, is a subject, which has employed the serious attention of the Convention; and, if they have erred in the judgment they have formed upon it, the error is, at least, not owing to a want of consideration, or of serious concern. They cannot view the subject but as one of great magnitude, and intimately connected with the interests of the whole State. The Divine Interposition has been conspicuous; and our obligations to be thankful are unspeakably great. And, as principles of the wisest and best policy leads nations, as well as individuals, to consider and acknowledge the government of the Deity, to feel their dependency on him and trust in him, to be thankful for his mercies, and to be humbled under his chastening rod; so, not only moral and religious duty, but also a regard to the best interests of the community appear to require of us, on the present occasion, that humiliation and thanksgiving, which are proposed by the Convention in their request. For a sense of the Divine Government has a meliorating influence on the minds of men, restraining them from crime, and disposing them to virtuous action. To those also, who are humbled before the Heavenly Majesty for their sins, and learn to be thankful for his mercies, the Divine Favour is manifested. From them judgments are averted, and on them blessings are bestowed.

The Convention are aware that very respectable Citizens have been averse to the proposal under consideration; the proposal for appointing a Day of Public Thanksgiving for our preservation from the intended Insurrection, on account of the influence it might be supposed to have on the Black Population—by giving publicity to the subject in their view, and by affording them excitements to attempt something further of the same nature. These objections, however, the Convention view as either not substantial, or over-balanced by higher considerations. As to publicity, perhaps no fact is more generally known by the persons referred to; for the knowledge of it has been communicated by almost every channel of information, public and private, even by documents under the stamp of Public Authority; and has extended to every part of the State. But with the knowledge of the conspiracy is united the knowledge of its frustration; and of that, which Devotion and Gratitude should set in a strong light, the merciful interposition of Providence, which produced that frustration. The more rational among that class of men, as well as others, know also, that our preservation from the evil intended by the conspirators, is a subject, which should induce us to render thanksgivings to the Almighty; and it is hoped and believed, that the truly enlightened and religiously disposed among them, of which there appear to be many, are ready to unite in those thanksgivings, from a regard to their own true interests: if therefore it is apprehended, that an undue importance would be given to the subject in their view, by making it the matter of public thanksgiving; that this would induce the designing and wicked to infer our fear and sense of weakness from the fact, and thus induce them to form some other scheme of mischief: Would not our silence, and the omission of an important religious duty, under these circumstances, undergo, at least, as unfavorable a construction, and with more reason?

But the Convention are persuaded, that publicity, rather than secrecy is the true policy to be pursued on this occasion; especially, when the subject is taken into view, in connexion with other truths, of high importance and certainty, which relate to it, and is placed in a just light; the evidence and force of which truths, thousands of this people, when informed, can clearly discern and estimate. It is proper, the Convention conceives, that the Negroes should know, that however numerous they are in some parts of these Southern States, they, yet, are not, even including all descriptions, bond and free, in the United States, but little more than one sixth part of the whole number of inhabitants, estimating that number which it probably now is, at Ten Millions; and the Black and Coloured Population, according to returns made at 1,786,000: That their destitution in respect to arms, and the knowledge of using them, with other disabilities, would render their physical force, were they all united in a common effort, less than a tenth part of that, with which they would have to contend. That there are multitudes of the best informed and truly religious among them, who, from principle, as well as from prudence, would not unite with them, nor fail to disclose their machinations, when it should be in their power to do it: That, however in some parts of our Union there are Citizens, who favour the idea of general emancipation; yet, were they to see slaves in our Country, in arms, wading through blood and carnage to effect their purpose, they would do what both their duty and interest would require; unite under the government with their fellow citizens at large to suppress the rebellion, and bring the authors of it to condign punishment: That it may be expected, in every attempt to raise an insurrection (should other attempts be made) as well as it was in that defeated here, that the prime movers in such a nefarious scheme, will so form their plan, that in case of exigency, they may flee with their plunder and leave their deluded followers to suffer the punishment, which law and justice may inflict: And that therefore, there is reason to conclude, on the most rational and just principles, that whatever partial success might at any time attend such a measure at the onset, yet, in this country, it must finally result in the discomfiture and ruin of the perpetrators; and in many instances pull down on the heads of the innocent as well as the guilty, an undistinguishing ruin.

On the lawfulness of holding slaves, considering it in a moral and religious view, the Convention think it their duty to exhibit their sentiments, on the present occasion, before your Excellency, because they consider their duty to God, the peace of the State, the satisfaction of scrupulous consciences, and the welfare of the slaves themselves, as intimately connected with a right view of the subject. The rather, because certain writers on politics, morals and religion, and some of them highly respectable, have advanced positions, and inculcated sentiments, very unfriendly to the principle and practice of holding slaves; and by some these sentiments have been advanced among us, tending in their nature, directly to disturb the domestic peace of the State, to produce insubordination and rebellion among the slaves, and to infringe the rights of our citizens; and indirectly, to deprive the slaves of religious privileges, by awakening in the minds of their masters a fear, that acquaintance with the Scriptures, and the enjoyment of these privileges would naturally produce the aforementioned effects; because the sentiments in opposition to the holding of slaves have been attributed, by their advocates, to the Holy Scriptures, and to the genius of Christianity. These sentiments, the Convention, on whose behalf I address your Excellency, cannot think just, or well-founded: for the right of holding slaves is clearly established by the Holy Scriptures, both by precept and example. In the Old Testament, the Isrealites were directed to purchase their bond-men and bond-maids of the Heathen nations; except they were of the Canaanites, for these were to be destroyed. And it is declared, that the persons purchased were to be their "bond-men forever;" and an "inheritance for them and their children." They were not to go out free in the year of jubilee, as the Hebrews, who had been purchased, were: the line being clearly drawn between them. [See Leviticus XXV. 44, 45, 46, &c.] In example, they are presented to our view as existing in the families of the Hebrews as servants, or slaves, born in the house, or bought with money: so that the children born of slaves are here considered slaves as well as their parents. And to this well known state of things, as to its reason and order, as well as to special privileges, St. Paul appears to refer, when he says, "But I was free born."

In the New-Testament, the Gospel History, or representation of facts, presents us a view correspondent with that, which is furnished by other authentic ancient histories of the state of the world at the commencement of Christianity. The powerful Romans had succeeded, in empire, the polished Greeks; and under both empires, the countries they possessed and governed were full of slaves. Many of these with their masters, were converted to the Christian Faith, and received, together with them into the Christian Church, while it was yet under the ministry of the inspired Apostles. In things purely spiritual, they appear to have enjoyed equal privileges; but their relationship, as masters and slaves, was not dissolved. Their respective duties are strictly enjoined. The masters are not required to emancipate their slaves; but to give them the things that are just and equal, forbearing threatening; and to remember, they also have a master in Heaven. The "servants under the yoke" [upo zugon Douloi: bond-servants, or slaves. Doulos, is the proper term for slaves; it is here in the plural and rendered more expressive by being connected with yoke—UNDER THE YOKE.] (bond-servants or slaves) mentioned by Paul to Timothy, as having "believing masters," are not authorized by him to demand of them emancipation, or to employ violent means to obtain it; but are directed to "account their masters worthy of all honour," and "not to despise them, because they were brethren" in religion; "but the rather to do them service, because they were faithful and beloved partakers of the Christian benefit." Similar directions are given by him in other places, and by other Apostles. And it gives great weight to the argument, that in this place, Paul follows his directions concerning servants with a charge to Timothy, as an Evangelist, to teach and exhort men to observe this doctrine.

Had the holding of slaves been a moral evil, it cannot be supposed, that the inspired Apostles, who feared not the faces of men, and were ready to lay down their lives in the cause of their God, would have tolerated it, for a moment, in the Christian Church. If they had done so on a principle of accommodation, in cases where the masters remained heathen, to avoid offences and civil commotion; yet, surely, where both master and servant were Christian, as in the case before us, they would have enforced the law of Christ, and required, that the master should liberate his slave in the first instance. But, instead of this, they let the relationship remain untouched, as being lawful and right, and insist on the relative duties.

In proving this subject justifiable by Scriptural authority, its morality is also proved; for the Divine Law never sanctions immoral actions.

The Christian golden rule, of doing to others, as we would they should do to us, has been urged as an unanswerable argument against holding slaves. But surely this rule is never to be urged against that order of things, which the Divine government has established; nor do our desires become a standard to us, under this rule, unless they have a due regard to justice, propriety and the general good.

A father may very naturally desire, that his son should be obedient to his orders: Is he, therefore, to obey the orders of his son? A man might be pleased to be exonerated from his debts by the generosity of his creditors; or that his rich neighbour should equally divide his property with him; and in certain circumstances might desire these to be done: Would the mere existence of this desire, oblige him to exonerate his debtors, and to make such a division of his property? Consistency and generosity, indeed, might require it of him, if he were in circumstances which would justify the act of generosity; but, otherwise, either action might be considered as the effect of folly and extravagance.

If the holding of slaves is lawful, or according to the Scriptures; then this Scriptural rule can be considered as requiring no more of the master, in respect of justice (whatever it may do in point of generosity) than what he, if a slave, could consistently, wish to be done to himself, while the relationship between master and servant should still be continued.

In this argument, the advocates for emancipation blend the ideas of injustice and cruelty with those, which respect the existence of slavery, and consider them as inseparable. But, surely, they may be separated. A bond-servant may be treated with justice and humanity as a servant; and a master may, in an important sense, be the guardian and even father of his slaves.

They become a part of his family, (the whole, forming under him a little community) and the care of ordering it and providing for its welfare, devolves on him. The children, the aged, the sick,

the disabled, and the unruly, as well as those, who are capable
of service and orderly, are the objects of his care: The labour of
these, is applied to the benefit of those, and to their own support,
as well as that of the master. Thus, what is effected, and often at
a great public expense, in a free community, by taxes, benevolent
institutions, bettering houses, and penitentiaries, lies here on the
master, to be performed by him, whatever contingencies may happen; and often occasions much expense, care and trouble, from
which the servants are free. Cruelty, is, certainly, inadmissible;
but servitude may be consistent with such degrees of happiness as
men usually attain in this imperfect state of things.

Some difficulties arise with respect to bringing a man, or class
of men, into a state of bondage. For crime, it is generally agreed, a
man may be deprived of his liberty. But, may he not be divested of
it by his own consent, directly, or indirectly given: And, especially,
when this assent, though indirect, is connected with an attempt to
take away the liberty, if not the lives of others? The Jewish law
favours the former idea: And if the inquiry on the latter be taken
in the affirmative, which appears to be reasonable, it will establish a principle, by which it will appear, that the Africans brought
to America were, slaves, by their own consent, before they came
from their own country, or fell into the hands of white men. Their
law of nations, or general usage, having, by common consent the
force of law, justified them, while carrying on their petty wars, in
killing their prisoners or reducing them to slavery; consequently,
in selling them, and these ends they appear to have proposed to
themselves; the nation, therefore, or individual, which was overcome, reduced to slavery, and sold would have done the same by
the enemy, had victory declared on their, or his side. Consequently,
the man made slave in this manner, might be said to be made so by
his own consent, and by the indulgence of barbarous principles.

That Christian nations have not done all they might, or should
have done, on a principle of Christian benevolence, for the civilization and conversion of the Africans: that much cruelty has
been practised in the slave trade, as the benevolent Wilberforce,
and others have shown; that much tyranny has been exercised by
individuals, as masters over their slaves, and that the religious
interests of the latter have been too much neglected by many

cannot, will not be denied. But the fullest proof of these facts, will not also prove, that the holding men in subjection, as slaves, is a moral evil, and inconsistent with Christianity. Magistrates, husbands, and fathers, have proved tyrants. This does not prove, that magistracy, the husband's right to govern, and parental authority, are unlawful and wicked. The individual who abuses his authority, and acts with cruelty, must answer for it at the Divine tribunal; and civil authority should interpose to prevent or punish it; but neither civil nor ecclesiastical authority can consistently interfere with the possession and legitimate exercise of a right given by the Divine Law.

If the above representation of the Scriptural doctrine, and the manner of obtaining slaves from Africa is just; and if also purchasing them has been the means of saving human life, which there is great reason to believe it has; then, however the slave trade, in present circumstances, is justly censurable, yet might motives of humanity and even piety have been originally brought into operation in the purchase of slaves, when sold in the circumstances we have described. If, also, by their own confession, which has been made in manifold instances, their condition, when they have come into the hands of humane masters here, has been greatly bettered by the change; if it is, ordinarily, really better, as many assert, than that of thousands of the poorer classes in countries reputed civilized and free; and, if, in addition to all other considerations, the translation from their native country to this has been the means of their mental and religious improvement, and so of obtaining salvation, as many of themselves have joyfully and thankfully confessed—then may the just and humane master, who rules his slaves and provides for them, according to Christian principles, rest satisfied, that he is not, in holding them, chargeable with moral evil, nor with acting, in this respect, contrary to the genius of Christianity.—It appears to be equally clear, that those, who by reasoning on abstract principles, are induced to favour the scheme of general emancipation, and who ascribe their sentiments to Christianity, should be particularly careful, however benevolent their intentions may be, that they do not by a perversion of the Scriptural doctrine, through their wrong views of it, not only invade the domestic and religious peace and rights of our

Citizens, on this subject; but, also by an intemperate zeal, prevent indirectly, the religious improvement of the people they design, professedly, to benefit; and, perhaps, become, evidently, the means of producing in our country, scenes of anarchy and blood; and all this in a vain attempt to bring about a state of things, which, if arrived at, would not probably better the state of that people; which is thought, by men of observation, to be generally true of the Negroes in the Northern states, who have been liberated.

To pious minds it has given pain to hear men, respectable for intelligence and morals, sometimes say, that holding slaves is indeed indefensible, but that to us it is necessary, and must be supported. On this principle, mere politicians, unmindful of morals, may act. But surely, in a moral and religious view of the subject, this principle is inadmissible. It cannot be said, that theft, falsehood, adultery and murder, are become necessary and must be supported. Yet there is reason to believe, that some of honest and pious intentions have found their minds embarrassed if not perverted on this subject, by this plausible but unsound argument. From such embarrassment the view exhibited above affords relief.

The Convention, Sir, are far from thinking that Christianity fails to inspire the minds of its subjects with benevolent and generous sentiments; or that liberty rightly understood, or enjoyed, is a blessing of little moment. The contrary of these positions they maintain. But they also consider benevolence as consulting the truest and best interests of its objects; and view the happiness of liberty as well as of religion, as consisting not in the name or form, but in the reality. While men remain in the chains of ignorance and error, and under the domination of tyrant lusts and passions, they cannot be free. And the more freedom of action they have in this state, they are but the more qualified by it to do injury, both to themselves and others. It is, therefore, firmly believed, that general emancipation to the Negroes in this country, would not, in present circumstances, be for their own happiness, as a body; while it would be extremely injurious to the community at large in various ways: And, if so, then it is not required even by benevolence. But acts of benevolence and generosity must be free and voluntary; no man has a right to compel another to the performance of them. This is a concern, which lies between a man and his God. If a man has obtained slaves by purchase, or inheritance, and the holding of them as such is justifiable by the law of God; why should he be required to liberate them, because it would be a generous action, rather than another on the same principle, to release his debtors, or sell his lands and houses, and distribute the proceeds among the poor? These also would be generous actions: Are they, therefore, obligatory? Or, if obligatory, in certain circumstances, as personal, voluntary acts of piety and benevolence, has any man or body of men, civil or ecclesiastic, a right to require them? Surely those, who are advocates for compulsory, or strenuous measures to bring about emancipation, should duly weigh this consideration.

Should, however, a time arrive, when the Africans in our country might be found qualified to enjoy freedom; and, when they might obtain it in a manner consistent with the interest and peace of the community at large, the Convention would be happy in seeing them free: And so they would, in seeing the state of the poor, the ignorant and the oppressed of every description, and of every country meliorated; so that the reputed free might be free indeed, and happy. But there seems to be just reason to conclude that a considerable part of the human race, whether they bear openly the character of slaves or are reputed freemen, will continue in such circumstances, with mere shades of variation, while the world continues. It is evident, that men are sinful creatures, subject to affliction and to death, as the consequences of their nature's pollution and guilt: That they are now in a state of probation; and that God as a Righteous, All-wise Sovereign, not only disposes of them as he pleases, and bestows upon them many unmerited blessings and comforts, but subjects them also to privations, afflictions and trials, with the merciful intention of making all their afflictions, as well as their blessings, work finally for their good; if they embrace his salvation, humble themselves before him, learn righteousness, and submit to his holy will. To have them brought to this happy state is the great object of Christian benevolence, and of Christian piety; for this state is not only connected with the truest happiness, which can be enjoyed at any time, but is introductory to eternal life and blessedness in the future world: And the salvation of men is intimately connected with the glory of their God and Redeemer.

And here I am brought to a part of the general subject, which, I confess to your Excellency, the Convention, from a sense of their duty, as a body of men, to whom important concerns of Religion are confided, have particularly at heart, and wish it may be seriously considered by all our Citizens: This is the religious interests of the Negroes. For though they are slaves, they are also men; and are with ourselves accountable creatures; having immortal souls, and being destined to future eternal reward. Their religious interests claim a regard from their masters of the most serious nature; and it is indispensible. Nor can the community at large, in a right estimate of their duty and happiness, be indifferent on this subject. To the truly benevolent it must be pleasing to know, that a number of masters, as well as ministers and pious individuals, of various Christian denominations among us, do conscientiously regard this duty; but there is a great reason to believe, that it is neglected and disregarded by many.

The Convention are particularly unhappy in considering, that an idea of the Bible's teaching the doctrine of emancipation as necessary, and tending to make servants insubordinate to proper authority, has obtained access to any mind; both on account of its direct influence on those, who admit it; and the fear it excites in others, producing the effects before noticed. But it is hoped, it has been evinced, that the idea is an erroneous one; and, that it will be seen, that the influence of a right acquaintance with that Holy Book tends directly and powerfully, by promoting the fear and love of God, together with just and peaceful sentiments toward men, to produce one of the best securities to the public, for the internal and domestic peace of the State.

It is also a pleasing consideration, tending to confirm these sentiments, that in the late projected scheme for producing an insurrection among us, there were very few of those who were, as members attached to regular Churches, (even within the sphere of its operations) who appear to have taken a part in the wicked plot, or indeed to whom it was made known; of some Churches it does not appear, that there were any. It is true, that a considerable number of those who were found guilty and executed, laid claim to a religious character; yet several of these were grossly immoral, and, in general, they were members of an irregular body, which called itself the African Church, and had intimate connection and intercourse with a similar body of men in a Northern City, among whom the supposed right to emancipation is strenuously advocated.

The result of this inquiry and reasoning, on the subject of slavery, brings us, sir, if I mistake not, very regularly to the following conclusions:—That the holding of slaves is justifiable by the doctrine and example contained in Holy writ; and is; therefore consistent with Christian uprightness, both in sentiment and conduct. That all things considered, the Citizens of America have in general obtained the African slaves, which they possess, on principles, which can be justified; though much cruelty has indeed been exercised towards them by many, who have been concerned in the slave-trade, and by others who have held them here, as slaves in their service; for which the authors of this cruelty are accountable. That slavery, when tempered with humanity and justice, is a state of tolerable happiness; equal, if not superior, to that which many poor enjoy in countries reputed free. That a master has a scriptural right to govern his slaves so as to keep it in subjection; to demand and receive from them a reasonable service; and to correct them for the neglect of duty, for their vices and transgressions; but that to impose on them unreasonable, rigorous services, or to inflict on them cruel punishment, he has neither a scriptural nor a moral right. At the same time it must be remembered, that, while he is receiving from them their uniform and best services, he is required by the Divine Law, to afford them protection, and such necessaries and conveniences of life as are proper to their condition as servants; so far as he is enabled by their services to afford them these comforts, on just and rational principles. That it is the positive duty of servants to reverence their master, to be obedient, industrious, faithful to him, and careful of his interests; and without being so, they can neither be the faithful servants of God, nor be held as regular members of the Christian Church. That as claims to freedom as a right, when that right is forfeited, or has been lost, in such a manner as has been represented, would be unjust; and as all attempts to obtain it by violence and fraud would be wicked; so all representations made to them by others, on such censurable principles, or in a manner tending to make them discontented; and finally, to produce such unhappy effects and consequences, as been before noticed, cannot be friendly to them (as they certainly are not to the community at large,) nor consistent with righteousness: Nor can the conduct be justified, however in some it may be palliated by pleading benevolence in intention, as the motive. That masters having the disposal of the persons, time and labour of their servants, and being the heads of families, are bound, on principles of moral and religious duty, to give these servants religious instruction; or at least, to afford them opportunities, under proper regulations to obtain it: And to grant religious privileges to those, who desire them, and furnish proper evidence of their sincerity and uprightness: Due care being at the same time taken, that they receive their instructions from right sources, and from their connexions, where they will not be in danger of having their minds corrupted by sentiments unfriendly to the domestic and civil peace of the community. That, where life, comfort, safety and religious interest of so large a number of human beings, as this class of persons is among us, are concerned; and, where they must necessarily, as slaves, be so much at the disposal of their masters; it appears to be a just and necessary concern of the Government, not only to provide laws to prevent or punish insurrections, and other violent and villainous conduct among them (which are indeed necessary) but, on the other hand, laws, also, to prevent their being oppressed and injured by unreasonable, cruel masters, and others; and to afford them, in respect of morality and religion, such privileges as may comport with the peace and safety of the State, and with those relative duties existing between masters and servants, which the word of God enjoins. It is, also, believed to be a just conclusion, that the interest and security of the State would be promoted, by allowing, under proper regulations, considerable religious privileges, to such of this class, as know how to estimate them aright, and have given suitable evidence of their own good principles, uprightness and fidelity; by attaching them, from principles of gratitude and love, to the interests of their masters and the State; and thus rendering their fidelity firm and constant. While on the other hand, to lay them under an interdict, as some have supposed necessary, in a case where reason, conscience, the genius of Christianity and salvation are concerned, on account of the bad conduct of others, would be felt as oppressive, tend to sour and alienate their minds from their masters and the public, and to make them vulnerable to temptation. All which is, with deference, submitted to the consideration of your Excellency.

With high respect, I remain, personally, and on behalf of the Convention,

Sir, your very obedient and humble servant,
RICHARD FURMAN.
President of the Baptist State Convention.
His Excellency GOVERNOR WILSON.

Source: Dr. Richard Furman's Exposition of the Views of the Baptists, Relative to the Coloured Population in the United States in a Communication to the Governor of South-Carolina. 2nd ed. Charleston: A. E. Miller, May 28, 1823.

Discussion Questions

1. Explain Thornwell's utterly smug, self-confident tone that Christianity has nothing to say about slavery because it is strictly a worldly matter.
2. Why were the masters so pleased with his view of slavery?
3. What is wrong with his argument that slavery must be an exception to the law of love because otherwise Christianity would be self-contradicted?
4. What is his unintended irony when he says "we shall take consolation in the cheering consciousness that the Master has accepted us"?
5. Why does Thornwell think slavery was so beneficial to Africans?
6. The insurrection Furman refers to was led by Denmark Vesey: why do you think Furman is so vague about it, as if it had no particular bearing on people like him and Governor Wilson, to whom Furman's letter is addressed?
7. Why does Furman go on at such length to reassure the governor of South Carolina that a black rebellion in that state would without doubt be defeated?

8. Why does Furman think that because the ancient Israelites owned slaves, it is acceptable for nineteenth-century South Carolinians to own them? Do you agree with him?

9. How is Furman able to brush aside the Golden Rule, as applied to slavery, so easily?

10. If slavery is as wonderful as Furman suggests, why do you think he did not become a slave?

11. How does Furman claim to know that emancipation would not be for the happiness of black people?

12. Why is Furman so ready to agree to emancipation when black people are ready for it? When would they be ready for it? Has "tomorrow" meant "never" for black Americans?

13. Do you think most people are like Furman in that they assume virtue and self-interest are indistinguishable?

Suggested Readings

Branch, Edgar M. 1950. *The Literary Apprenticeship of Mark Twain.* Whitefish, MT: Literary Licensing.

Brooks, Van Wyck. 1920. *The Ordeal of Mark Twain.* Boston: E. P. Dutton; Philadelphia: University of Pennsylvania Press.

Camfield, Gregg. 1994. *Sentimental Twain: Samuel Clemens in the Maze of Moral Philosophy.* Philadelphia: University of Pennsylvania Press.

Cardwell, Guy. 1991. *The Man Who Was Mark Twain: Images and Ideologies.* New Haven, CT: Yale University Press.

Cox, James M. 1966. *The Fate of Humor.* Columbia: University of Missouri Press.

Dempsey, Terrell. 2003. *Searching for Jim: Slavery in Sam Clemens's World.* Columbia: University of Missouri Press.

Dolmetsch, Carl. 1992. *Our Famous Guest: Mark Twain in Vienna.* Athens: University of Georgia Press.

Emerson, Everett. 2000. *Mark Twain: A Literary Life.* Philadelphia: University of Pennsylvania Press.

Fishkin, Shelley Fisher. 1993. *Was Huck Black?: Mark Twain and African-American Voices.* Oxford: Oxford University Press.

Florence, Don. 1995. *Persona and Humor in Mark Twain's Early Writings.* Columbia: University of Missouri Press.

Gibson, William M. 1976. *The Art of Mark Twain.* Oxford: Oxford University Press.

Hoffman, Donald. 2006. *Mark Twain in Paradise.* Columbia: University of Missouri Press.

Horn, Jason Gary. 1999. *Mark Twain: A Descriptive Guide to Biographical Sources.* New York: Scarecrow Press.

Knoper, Randall. 1995. *Acting Naturally: Mark Twain in the Culture of Performance.* Berkeley: University of California Press.

Krauth, Leland. 2003. *Mark Twain and Company: Six Literary Relations.* Athens: University of Georgia Press.

Lystra, Karen. 2006. *Dangerous Intimacy: The Untold Story of Mark Twain's Final Years.* Berkeley: University of California Press.

Mensh, Elaine and Mensh, Harry. 2000. *Black, White, and Huckleberry Finn: Reimagining the American Dream.* Tuscaloosa: University of Alabama Press.

Obenzinger, Hilton. 1999. *American Palestine: Melville, Twain, and the Holy Land Mania.* Princeton: Princeton University Press.

Railton, Stephen. 2003. *Mark Twain: A Short Introduction.* Hoboken, NJ: Wiley-Blackwell.

Rasmussen, R. Kent. 1996. *Mark Twain A-Z: The Essential Reference to His Life and Writings.* New York: Oxford University Press.

Sewell, David R. 1987. *Mark Twain's Languages: Discourse, Dialogue, and Linguistic Variety.* Berkeley: University of California Press.

Skandera-Trombley, Laura. 2010. *Mark Twain's Other Woman: The Hidden Story of His Final Years.* New York: Vintage.

Sloane, David E. E. 1979. *Mark Twain as a Literary Comedian.* Baton Rouge: Lousiana State University Press.

Stahl, J. D. 1993. *Mark Twain, Culture and Gender: Envisioning America Through Europe.* Athens: University of Georgia Press.

Stone, Albert. 1961. *The Innocent Eye: Childhood in Mark Twain's Imagination.* New Haven, CT: Yale University Press.

Willis, Resa. 1992. *Mark and Livy: The Love Story of Mark Twain and the Woman Who Almost Tamed Him.* London: Routledge.

Areas for Research

A particularly fruitful area of research is the question of how historically accurate Twain's depiction of Jim is. For example, are the superstitions associated with him of African or European origin? Is his version of English accurate or filtered through an ear that mishears the way an African

American in the 1830s or 1840s would have spoken English? And is his real-life model black, as has been argued in Shelley Fisher Fishkin's *Was Huck Black* (1994)?

Also intriguing is the subject of fathers and sons in *Huckleberry Finn.* Huck and his father, Pap, are on very bad terms, and some readers see Jim and Huck as in some sense father and son, but there are numerous other examples, including the fathers and sons associated with the Shepherdsons, the Grangefords, and the Phelpses. Keeping in mind that Twain and his father shook hands before bedtime, readers of *Huckleberry Finn* may want to research what Twain is suggesting about how nineteenth-century sons and fathers were disposed toward each other.

Twain has a lot of fun in *Huckleberry Finn* satirizing "genteel literature," that is, literature written to maintain certain nineteenth-century notions of decorum and respectability, such as Emmeline Grangerford's "Ode to Stephen Dowling Bots, Dec'd [deceased]." After noting that Stephen Dowling Bots "fell down a well and was drownded [*sic*]" (Chapter XVII), Huck quotes the poem and then observes that if "Emmeline Grangerford could make poetry like that before she was fourteen, there ain't no telling what she could a done by-and-by. Buck [her brother] said she could rattle off poetry like nothing. She didn't even have to stop to think" (Chapter XVII). Research into this area will reveal the context for Twain's satire here, because such sentimental poetry was very popular when Twain was writing his most famous novel. The once popular Julia A. Moore (1847–1930), for instance, wrote poems similar to Emmeline Grangerford's.

Black men and voting rights is also a topic that will repay research. Huck's father is outraged that a black man can vote: in an attack on government in general, Pap narrows his focus to a black college professor who "could talk all kinds of languages, and knowed [*sic*] every thing. And that ain't the wust [*sic*]. They [people in general] said he could vote, when he was at home. Well, that let me out. Thinks I, what is the country a-coming [*sic*] to?" (Chapter VI). Because skin color is the only basis for Pap's self-esteem, he is threatened by the very idea, let alone the fact, of a black man having the franchise. If the professor had been a black woman who was allowed to vote, Pap would have been even more upset.

Also worth looking into is the fact that many, but by no means all, white people in nineteenth-century United States saw nothing wrong with slavery (Lincoln thought if a person does not think slavery is wrong, nothing is). Silas Phelps is a good example: "He was the innocentest [*sic*], best old soul I ever see. But it warn't [*sic*] surprising; because he warn't [*sic*] only just a farmer, he was a preacher, too, and had a little one-horse log church down back of the plantation, which he built it himself at his own expense" (Chapter XXXIII). But he owns other people, which Huck does not see as a problem any more than Silas Phelps does. Later Huck says, "Jim told him [Tom Sawyer] Uncle Silas [Phelps] come in every day or two to pray with him, and Aunt Sally comes in to see if he was comfortable and had plenty to eat, and both of them was kind as they could be" (Chapter XXXVI). The Phelpses and Huck do not understand slavery is wrong. Research will explain this phenomenon in American society.

Finally, genealogy in *Huckleberry Finn* deserves examination through research because Twain suggests it, too, is an illegitimate source of social privilege. Huck mentions a warming pan that Silas Phelps valued "because it belonged to one of his ancestors with a long wooden handle that come over from England with William the Conqueror in the May-flower or one of them early ships" (Chapter XXXVIII). The Phelpses' aristocratic pretensions are based on the who-has-been-here-the-longest argument, as if that has anything to do with human decency. The Shepherdsons and the Grangerfords have been in the United States for generations, spending much of that time killing each other, although by the time of the setting for *Huckleberry Finn,* the 1830s or 1840s, they do not know the original cause of their feud, let alone that murdering each other is wrong.

WHY WE READ *ADVENTURES OF HUCKLEBERRY FINN* TODAY

Of the multiple reasons *Adventures of Huckleberry Finn* is still read, Twain's deft handling of the English language is prominent. Unforgettable phrases and sentences appear throughout the book: "I don't take no stock in dead people" (Chapter I), "Then she [Miss Watson] told me all about the bad place [hell], and I said I wished I was there" (I), "The men took their guns along [to church]" (XVII), "What you want, above all things, on a raft, is for everybody to be satisfied, and feel right and kind towards the others" (XIX), "It was enough to make a body ashamed of the human race" (XXIV), "soul-butter and hog wash" (XXV), "All right, then, I'll go to hell" (XXXI), "Human beings can be awful cruel to one another" (XXXIII), "but I reckon I got to light out for the territory ahead of the rest, because Aunt Sally she's going to adopt me and sivilize [*sic*] me and I can't stand it. I been there before" (Chapter the Last). Huck's words have an authentic ring to many readers' ears and a visual and down-to-earth quality that is extremely engaging, as is Huck himself: (for many readers) Huck is the way he talks.

A second explanation of the novel's continuing popularity is the undeniable power of its satire on American society. Huck's naive respect for Colonel Grangerford, because he puts on the whitest of white shirts every day, is countered by the fact that he owns people and supports murdering the children of the family he feuds with, the Shepherdsons. Twain's attack on the cruelty of small town life in the Mississippi Valley twenty or thirty years before the Civil War is particularly striking in the episode involving the murder of the town drunk, Old Boggs, by Colonel Sherburn: the townspeople laugh at Old Boggs's empty threats, aimed at Colonel Sherburn, but Boggs ends up dying from gunshot wounds inflicted by the colonel. The townspeople place one Bible under his head, another on his chest, as he breathes his last: Twain was especially scornful of institutionalized religion. The chapters concerning the Phelpses also provide devastating satire; Huck admires them because they are kind to him, but they see nothing wrong in keeping Jim tied up in one of their slave cabins, and when Sally Phelps asks Huck if anyone was hurt when the steamboat he pretends to have been on supposedly blew a cylinder head, Huck replies, "No'm, killed a nigger." To this she responds, "Well, it's lucky; because sometimes people do get hurt" (Chapter XXXII).

Another source of the book's appeal is its nostalgic depiction, to a degree, of an innocent, idyllic pre–Civil War United States, when life was recalled as simpler as and less hectic than it supposedly was after the Civil War. Huck and Jim enjoy, at times, floating down the Mississippi, fishing and talking, and not worrying about civilization. This is a boy's world, at least as Twain remembered it, before the onset of adult responsibilities and complexities.

Perhaps the key reason *Adventures of Huckleberry Finn* endures is Huck himself, by far Twain's most imaginative and memorable character. Resourceful, funny, unusually sensitive to others' feelings, and a master of colloquial English, Huck, next to Jim, is the most decent person in the novel, and yet, along with Jim, he is regarded as social trash. To Twain, that is a reliable indicator of how corrupt society is, that it would, for example, cause Huck to think he is going to hell because he is helping the runaway slave Jim escape from slavery. For many readers, Huck is what the United States is supposed to be.

Index

About the Author

Robert Felgar, PhD, is professor of English and department head at Jacksonville State University, Jacksonville, Alabama. His published works include *Richard Wright, Understanding Richard Wright's* Black Boy, and *Student Companion to Richard Wright.* Felgar holds a doctorate in English from Duke University.